THE RIMBAUD OF LEEDS

THE RIMBAUD OF LEEDS

The Political Character of Tony Harrison's Poetry

Christine Regan

CAMBRIA
PRESS

Amherst, New York

For my mother and father

TABLE OF CONTENTS

List of Tables

ACKNOWLEDGEMENTS

I am indebted to the learning and generosity of Ian Higgins, who introduced me to the work of Harrison and Rimbaud, and whose books have provided an inspiration and model for me.

My thanks to the librarians at Special Collections at the Brotherton Library in Leeds, particularly the late Chris Sheppard, and the Robinson Library and The Literary and Philosophical Society in Newcastle-upon-Tyne for permission to consult Tony Harrison's manuscripts and correspondence, and to librarians at other British and Australian libraries. I gratefully acknowledge the support provided by the School of Humanities at the Australian National University, including travel grants which made possible periods of study in British libraries.

My thanks also to Cambria Press, particularly Paul Richardson, for all their work in publishing the book. I am grateful to the literary agent Gordon Dickerson and M.D., respectively for enabling me to meet the poet to discuss aspects of his work, and to gain permission to quote from the poetry, letters, and manuscripts.

Most of all, I would like to thank Tony Harrison for his poems, which have been a wonderful voyage.

ABBREVIATED TERMS

Unless otherwise indicated all quotations are from Tony Harrison, *The Loiners*. London: London Magazine Editions, 1970 (abbreviated as *Loiners*).

Unless otherwise indicated all other quotations are from Tony Harrison, *Collected Poems*. London: Viking, 2007 (abbreviated as *CP*).

The major critical anthology on the poet: Neil Astley, ed., *Bloodaxe Critical Anthologies 1: Tony* Harrison. Newcastle-upon-Tyne: Bloodaxe Books, 1991 (abbreviated as *Bloodaxe 1*).

All quotations from the Bible are taken from *The Bible: Authorized King James Version*, ed. with an introduction and notes by Robert Carroll and Stephen Prickett. Oxford and New York: Oxford University Press, 1997.

The *MHRA Style Guide* is followed for all footnotes and bibliographic entries.

Table 1. Abbreviations

"Conversation"	"Tony Harrison in conversation with Richard Hoggart" (1986), in *Bloodaxe 1*, 36–45.
"Inkwell"	"The Inkwell of Dr Agrippa", in *Corgi Modern Poets in Focus: 4*, ed. Jeremy Robson. London: Corgi, 1971.Reprinted in *Bloodaxe 1*, 32–35. Quotations are from *Bloodaxe 1*.
"Interview"	"Tony Harrison in interview with John Haffenden" (1983),in *Bloodaxe 1*, 227–246.
Letter to Alan Ross	Letters to Alan Ross (28 January 1967–8 December 1973), included in items in *THP*, Special Collections, Brotherton Library, University of Leeds. Letters to Alan Ross (7 Mar 1972–14 Dec 1980), the Alan Ross Collection, in BC MS 20c *London Magazine*, Special Collections, Brotherton Library, University of Leeds.
Letter to Jon Silkin	23 letters to Jon Silkin/*Stand* editors (4 December 1962–8 August 1980), in BC MS 20c *Stand*/3/HAR–11, Special Collections, Brotherton Library, University of Leeds. 1 letter to Jon Silkin (29 September 1980), in BC MS 20c Silkin/8/HAR–4, Special Collections, Brotherton Library, University of Leeds.

Table 2. Abbreviations (Cont.)

School of Eloquence	Tony Harrison's major ongoing sonnet sequence *The School of Eloquence* which has progressively appeared in a variety of publications. This thesis examines the two most important publications of the sonnet sequence to date, *From "The School of Eloquence" and Other Poems*. London: Rex Collings, 1978; and *Continuous: Fifty Sonnets from "The School of Eloquence."* London: Rex Collings, 1981; and also discusses later sonnets from the sequence. Collections also in *CP*. Quotations from those sonnets are from *CP*.
"Shango"	"Shango the Shaky Fairy", *London Magazine*, new series, vol. 10, no. 6 (April 1970), reprinted in *Bloodaxe 1*, 88–103. Quotations are from *Bloodaxe 1*.
THP	Tony Harrison papers relating to *Loiners*, London Magazine Editions, 73 uncatalogued and unnumbered items, Special Collections, Brotherton Library, University of Leeds.
v.	*v.*. Newcastle-upon-Tyne: Bloodaxe Books, 1985. Quotations from the poem *v.* are from *CP*.

Table 3. Abbreviations (Cont.)

H, v. & O	Sandie Byrne, *H, v., & O: The Poetry of Tony Harrison*. Manchester: Manchester University Press, 1998.
Permanently Bard	Carol Rutter, ed., *Permanently Bard: Selected Poetry*, ed., Newcastle-upon-Tyne: Bloodaxe Books, 1995.
TH Holocaust	Antony Rowland, *Tony Harrison and the Holocaust*. Liverpool: Liverpool University Press, 2001.
TH: Loiner	Sandie Byrne, ed., *Tony Harrison:Loiner*. Oxford: Clarendon Press,1997.
RCWSL	Arthur Rimbaud, *Rimbaud: Complete Works, Selected Letters*, trans. with an introduction and notes by Wallace Fowlie, rev. and with a foreword by Seth Whidden, bilingual edition (Chicago: University of Chicago Press, 2005 [1966]). All quotations from Rimbaud's poems and letters are from *RCWSL* unless otherwise indicated.

THE RIMBAUD OF LEEDS

CHAPTER 1

OUT OF THE NORTH

This is a contextual study of the politics of Tony Harrison's (1937–) imaginative works. It offers a reassessment of the poet's political character, identifying a radical republicanism and humanism which encompasses an anti-colonial poetic. It shows that an identification with John Milton (1608–1674) lies at the heart of Harrison's republicanism, and it illuminates the haunting presence of Arthur Rimbaud (1854–1891) in his poetry. The book is based primarily on an examination of Harrison's major original poetry that appears in *The Loiners* (1970), the ongoing sonnet sequence *The School of Eloquence* (1978–), and the separately published *v.* (1985), while seeing this work within the context of his complete oeuvre. Reference is made to other poems and dramatic works where germane, and to Harrison's account of his work in interviews and prefaces. The book draws upon newly available manuscripts and archival material. The study largely excludes his "imitations" of Palladas and Martial and his dramatic poetry as these deserve separate study. The new level of attention accorded to Harrison's life in Africa in the 1960s, drawing upon his letters home for the first time, and to *Loiners*, substantially the poetic product of these years, enables a new understanding of what are enduring definitive features of Harrison's work.

Harrison's radical republican and humanist poetic engages with inter-related issues of class and colonialism, from Leeds to Africa. The colonial predicament of Harrison's North and the Celtic fringe addressed in the poetry is prescient, as it anticipates resurgent devolution debates and movements in the United Kingdom today. Introducing his poems at a reading in 1984, Harrison drew attention to the "complicated social and historical reasons" for his poetry.[1] The critical importance of history for understanding the poetry and its politics is emphasized in this study. Political and literary histories enrich the poetry, and the poet's view of these histories is disclosed by attending to the dense allusive fields of many of these poems. This approach has not been taken in Harrison scholarship to date.[2] Colonialism is a critically under-appreciated preoc-cupation of the poetry,[3] while the nature of Harrison's republicanism and its importance for the poems has been neglected. Harrison's humanism tends to be seen as at odds with his politics,[4] yet it will be argued that it finds radical expression in the way the poet gives the dispossessed a voice in his poetry. The book contends that Harrison's political principles and loyalties have remained fundamentally consistent and his stances on local and global histories essentially unchanged throughout his life as a poet. Harrison's *oeuvre* discloses a coherent radical republican and humanist politics.

The presence in Harrison's political poetry of the poets John Milton and Arthur Rimbaud is accorded close attention in this study. Milton figures prominently in Harrison's work. For Harrison he is a great republican poet, and he is a key figure in Harrison's identification with republican literary lineages and political traditions. The life and work of the nineteenth-century French poet and explorer Rimbaud is of the first importance for Harrison's idea of himself as a poet. Rimbaud's significance for Harrison's identity and poetic and his presence in Harrison's poetry have not been recognized in previous scholarship. I seek to illuminate Harrison's elective affinity with Rimbaud, as a regional poet with the wrong accent, as a "hoodlum poet," as a white "*nègre*," as a poet who fell silent and became an explorer and fortune-seeker in Africa. For Harrison,

Rimbaud is the great outsider now fêted as a high cultural poet and Rimbaud is a haunting presence in the poetry.

The meanings of the poems are recovered in this study through exploration of their allusive fields. It also recognizes the distinction the French Marxist structuralist critic Pierre Macherey made in *A Theory of Literary Production* (1966) between "what can be said of a work" and "what the work itself is saying." This can be true not only in the sense Macherey intended, of reading the work against the grain in order to reveal its unconscious ideology in its gaps and silences, but by disclosing Harrison's conscious topical historical allusions. The political character of the poetry is my principal focus, and the poems selected for examination are exemplars of Harrison's artistic engagement with the politics and history of England and Africa in particular. The poet's politics are examined primarily in the sense of consistent ideological commitments, but his politics of governance are also addressed. The shared preoccupations of the poetry as well as concerns specific to individual works will be discussed.

The book is organized by chronology and genre, and divided into eight chapters and a coda. This first chapter considers the biography and situates my readings of the poetry in relation to the main accounts of the work, with received interpretations also addressed in the chapters that follow. In each subsequent chapter a poem or a sequence of poems is given detailed exegesis in relation to some new or neglected contexts, and contextual information necessary for understanding political, historical, and literary references in the poems is provided. Harrison is a poet of place and the book is also partially organized by geography. The chapters focus upon the poems about the North of England, the African poems, and discuss poems and prose about both places and about colonial themes in the Americas. The book draws upon new and familiar biographical information that elucidates political arguments latent in the poetry. Many of the poems examined are deeply personal and also highly political. The book attempts to tie the poems more to his biography and the historical circumstances in which the poems were produced.

Chapter 2 explains the conception and controversial reception of *Loiners*, its republican vision of the North as an internal colony, and its introduction of key ideological and stylistic features of Harrison's poems about his native Leeds. Harrison employs a bastard high style and incorporates working-class Leeds content and idiom into formal verse. Chapter 3 shows how Harrison's African years are vital for understanding his political biography and poetry, particularly *Loiners* and *The School of Eloquence*. Chapter 4 explores the deep engagement with colonial history in the African poems, and the satirical mode of attack upon economic and sexual colonization. This chapter examines the political implications of the poems in their topical polemical circumstances and registers the correspondences between their rhetorical dimensions and republican ideals and anti-colonial movements. Chapter 5 interprets "Ghosts: Some Words before Breakfast" by making visible the haunting of Harrison by Rimbaud, and draws on Harrison's and Rimbaud's letters to discover one of the great unrecognized literary friendships between the dead and the living. Chapter 6 traces the significance of Rimbaud's African years for Harrison's African poems and argues that his elegiac vision is influenced by Rimbaud's "illuminations." Chapter 7 interrogates the importance of Milton and English republican literary and political traditions for Harrison's poetry. The chapter considers the creation of a republican political mythology for the Northern working class in *The School of Eloquence* and the radicalism of the political sonnets. Other sonnets discussed here reflect the poetry's concern with linguistic and political disempowerment in the regions. Chapter 8 is concerned with the contested critical question of the political character of *v.*, and it draws upon Harrison's working notebook for *v.* and draft versions of the poem for the first time in the scholarship. It also examines the aesthetic and political importance of *v.*'s literary model, Thomas Gray's *Elegy Written in a Country Churchyard* (1751), which has not hitherto been fully understood. It offers too an account of *v.* emphasizing the importance for

Harrison of Rimbaud in the period of what might be called his classical vandalism.[5] *v.* ends with the poet's epitaph. This book ends with a coda that reflects upon the epitaph of a steadfast poet who will be buried on Leeds ground.

THE MAN AND HIS WORK

Harrison is one of Britain's greatest political poets, elegists, and verse dramatists of the twentieth and twenty-first centuries. His biography has been made familiar to his readers through the non-dramatic poetry and his interviews, prose pieces, and prefaces. "Tony Harrison" is the main dramatic persona in the poetry, which also features his parents and uncles, and other family members. Other persons mentioned in the poems are often based upon people from his old neighborhood and school, and from his marriages, travels, and other experiences. However, the lyric, sonnets, elegies, dramatic monologues, and long poems examined in this study are not confined to the concerns of an individual but have ambitious scope in their politics and history and statements about the state of nations. The poems present an intimate relationship between the biographical and the historical, and see his relationship to his family and background as related to the historical struggle between the classes.[6] He has likened himself as poet to a pirate, and his daring adventure is "to colonize the high style" and "present it back as a gift to those people you were brought up with."[7] Harrison's parents did not regard poetry as a real and respectable job,[8] but it was his life with them and his understanding of the mistreatment of the Northern working class that is at the heart of a poetry engaged in a political battle of ideas.

Harrison was born in Leeds in 1937, to Florence, a housewife, and Harold, a laborer in a bakery. They lived in "a respectable working-class street" in Leeds, and at different times his uncles Jo and Harry and other relatives lived with them.[9] At the age of eleven Harrison won a scholarship to Leeds Grammar School, an event that would change the course of his life. In 1960 he married Rosemarie Crossfield, with whom he had a daughter Jane and son Max, who also figure in several poems. In 1962 he was writing a PhD in Classics, on verse translations of Virgil's *Aeneid* at the University of Leeds, when he took up a lectureship in Nigeria and stayed for four years. *Earthworks*, a pamphlet of his early poems, was published in 1964, while *Aikin Mata*, an adaptation of Aristophanes *Lysistrata*, appeared in 1966. He moved from Nigeria to Prague, lecturing from 1966–1967 and immersing himself in Czech theatre. Two essays from his dissertation were published in 1967 and 1969, under the name T.W. Harrison.[10] However, he wrote in letter that "I don't really like being an academic":[11] "I've had to work inhumanly hard on very uncongenial tasks...Needless to say the writing has suffered."[12]

When he returned to England in 1967, Harrison was determined "to make poetry a real job, and that's a question of hazarding the whole of your life on what you do."[13] He "made a defiant decision" to abandon the doctorate,[14] but without an academic position financial insecurity undermined his health and concentration.[15] He settled in Newcastle-upon-Tyne and was awarded the first Northern Arts Fellowship in Poetry in 1967–1968, when he wrote *Newcastle is Peru* (1969), his first important poem, which was published as a pamphlet. 1970 was the year his doctorate was regarded as formally lapsed,[16] and also the year his first major collection of poems, *Loiners*, was published.

Loiners included the previously published "Newcastle is Peru," in which Harrison celebrates seeing the North anew through the lenses of exotic lands he has travelled to, using a poetic conceit attributed to the metaphysical poet John Cleveland.[17] A cosmopolitan Leeds poet, Harrison's many travels in Europe, the Americas, and Africa have been an ongoing aspect of his life that is important for many of his poems. The poetry features literary geography, local histories and place names, and is peppered with languages like modern and ancient Greek, Hausa, Yoruba, Swahili, French, German, Czech, as well as "dead" languages like Cornish, Welsh, and Latin. In 1969, for example, he returned to Africa, to Senegal and Gambia, and also travelled to Cuba and Brazil as part of a UNESCO Fellowship,[18] and in 1971 spent four months in Mozambique. He lived in Wales in 1973–1974, as part of a Gregynog Arts Fellowship, and again held the Northern Arts Fellowship in 1976–1977. He regards Fellowships as special preserves for that endangered species, the poet, and wanted to make an independent living from poetry. On the strength of *Loiners* he was asked by the National Theatre in London to translate Molière's *The Misanthrope* (1973).[19] It was the beginning of what is to date four decades of dramatic verse and international theatre work, and also verse for film and television. The arduous gamble was rewarded and Harrison has made his living as a poet.

Harrison has always written both dramatic and non-dramatic verse. He began writing his major continuing sonnet sequence *The School of Eloquence* in 1971. His mother and father died in 1976 and 1980 respectively, and the elegiac filial sonnets appeared in *Continuous* (1981). His version of Smetana's Czech libretto for *The Bartered Bride* was performed in 1978 at the Metropolitan Opera in New York, where he met the Greek-Canadian soprano Teresa Stratas, who became his second wife. Through the 1980s he divided his time mainly between Newcastle-upon-Tyne, New York, and Florida. His life with Stratas in rural Florida is a subject of "the American poems," a dozen poems first published individually from 1979–1985, the most well known of which is *A Kumquat for John Keats* (1981). The American poems often bring metaphysical meditations to their dominant subjects of sexual love, nature, and death, and represent a self-conscious hiatus in Harrison's political engagement with England.

The autobiographically based long poem "Facing North" (1983) charts Harrison's movement between Northern England and the class political commitments of *The School of Eloquence*, and different territory in the American poems, and it divides the American poems from *The School of Eloquence* in the *Selected Poems* (1984 and 1987).[20] The title "Facing North" evokes a geographical and mental map, the idea of the poet-as-traveller, and signals the importance of the North for Harrison's poetry, and its literary geography. The poem is set in his study, "the dark one facing North,"[21] and ends with the poet's temporary departure for his wife's home in America. The "old pain" refers to his first marriage and "new hope" to Stratas (from whom he is now divorced). Hope, love, and regeneration depend on risk and illusion, on "memory shutting out half what it knows." The poem's nautical imagery subtly presents the poet-as-voyager navigating his way with a "telescope," only to become "lost" on a circular course, "the two cold poles all places are between."[22] He has felt that "I was on a ship about to sink." The tone of the poem is contemplative and it meditates upon the fraught journey of life and of poetic composition.

The epigraph to "Facing North" is "The North begins inside." It evokes a psychological landscape born of an intimate relationship to the place of origin, and the meanings we inscribe on that place and on our past. The North becomes a metaphor for the internal world of the man, and "The North wind" carries the memories that substantially make up who he is. An implicit analogy is drawn between the wind rattling his home and flaying his garden, and the memories and anxieties that assail him. When the North wind is high his house shakes, and the paper lantern and "flooded orchestra" of light in which he creates swing alarmingly and cause "fright":

> I have to hold on when I think such things
>
> and weather out these feelings so that when
>
> the wind drops and the light no longer swings
>
> I can focus on an Earth that still has men,[23]

An end line rhyme on "hate" / "procrastinate" suggests the difficulty of writing and its dependence upon an internal equilibrium.[24] The "struggle" to "concentrate" and to weather out anxieties are distinctive features of this poetic self-portrait of the poet and man. The images of the poet in his wind-besieged study struggling for "some inkling of an inner peace" intimates that ultimately he finds a home in his writing,[25] a possibility refuted by Theodor Adorno,[26] but poetry is a complex refuge in which he engages with biographical and historical strife.

The epigraph to "Facing North" signals that Harrison's withdrawal from the political in the American poems is an interlude by alluding to a holiday taken by the poets W.H. Auden (1907–1973) and Louis MacNeice (1907–1963). Their names raise the ghost of the literary image of the 1930s, of politics and poetry. In the 1930s Auden was at the centre of a group of politicized British poets with whom MacNeice, also left-leaning but skeptical of politically motivated writing, was associated. The epigraph to "Facing North" is taken from MacNeice's "Epilogue," a poem about his Icelandic holiday with Auden in 1936, for their travel book *Letters From Iceland* (1937). In "Epilogue" the Auden figure describes such sojourns as "Breathers from the Latin fire" of classical scholarship and elite learning.[27] MacNeice's and Auden's excursion to Iceland, like Harrison's time in Florida, is a respite from the ascetism of the writer's life and, as with MacNeice, from "the litany of doubt" after the breakdown of their first marriages.[28] "Epilogue" refers to the rise of Nazism and the fall of Seville to Franco's fascist forces, but the Spanish civil war erupted while the friends "rode and joked and smoked."[29] Both poets believed in the Spanish republican cause and each went separately to Spain during the war, and Auden's "Spain" (1937) is one of his best-known political verses. *Letters From Iceland*, a playful and innovative mixture of poetry and prose, conveys the happiness of MacNeice's and Auden's trip together but also their awareness "of a threatening horizon to their picnic."[30]

Harrison's holiday too is "sandwiched in a graver show" of destructive historical forces,[31] another signification of the powerful winds that threaten his home and the private sphere, and of the darkness that descends at the poem's close. The implicit anxiety about dark historical times in "Facing North" recalls the mood of the literati in the 1930s, as does the subject and metaphor of travel.[32] In *Modern Poetry* (1938)

MacNeice makes an anti-modernist "plea for *impure* poetry, that is, for poetry conditioned by the poet's life and the world around him."[33] MacNeice and Auden were, like Harrison, classically-trained scholars and formalist poets writing metrical, stanzaic, and rhyming poetry, and using a colloquial voice to speak lucidly about a wide range of private and public subjects. Harrison's poetry is also impure, speaking about his life and "open," like the study window in "Facing North," to the world outside.[34] The poem's epigraph signals that Harrison's retreat from the North and its politics in the American poems is temporary because, as MacNeice and Auden also realized, poets live in history.[35]

Harrison's poems, especially those about the North in *Loiners*, *The School of Eloquence*, and *v.*, are the fruits of his realization that "the North begins inside."[36] His poetic voice issues from a sensibility whose deepest stratum is Northern. A lifelong relationship to the North that is important to the poetry is part of why Harrison alludes to MacNeice and Auden in the epigraph to "Facing North." In Harrison's poetry the North is firstly the cities of Leeds and Newcastle-upon-Tyne and for MacNeice it is Northern Ireland. For Auden the North is a complex of places from Yorkshire to Iceland.[37] The location of "the North" varies geographically and imaginatively for different writers, though it is usually in a binary relation to "the South."[38] In "Epilogue" MacNeice discerns that the landscape of the North educed the Icelandic saga style. The North also elicits the poetry of Harrison and, less pervasively, that of MacNeice and Auden. For these three poets the North is a place, its peoples, its histories, and the literatures, and mythologies which emanate from it. Harrison's poetry, like MacNeice's, expresses an ambivalent relationship to the North, a painful sense of being between worlds, and contains a strong dialectic between a symbolic North and South, between past and present, dark and light, the sensual and the sense that "all our games" are "funeral games."[39] Both poets were outsiders in the North, Harrison by education, MacNeice firstly by religion. MacNeice writes in "Carrickfergus" that "I was born in Belfast" but, as the son of an Anglican rector, was "Banned for ever from the candles of the Irish poor."[40] However, MacNeice, like

Harrison, knows that the North is ineradicably constitutive of who he is: "But I cannot deny my past to which my self is wed, / The woven figure cannot undo its thread."[41]

The perception that "The North begins inside" is attributed to Auden in "Epilogue," which is also dedicated to Auden. In "Letter to Lord Byron," from *Letters to Iceland,* Auden writes that the coalfields and industrial decay of Northern England have since childhood been "my ideal scenery."[42] The 1930s' poets were an intellectual elite often based in universities, and their new concern with a troubled North was, by some accounts, another fashionable polemical posture,[43] but Auden's preoccupation with Northern England endured. Many of Harrison's poems also refer to the iconography of Yorkshire's industrial landscape, its pollution, decay, coal-mines, and unemployment, scenery also often found in "the Northern novel." Other elements of Northern English life familiar in literary representations that are also found in Harrison's poetry include the flat cap, "sentimental" portraits of mam and dad, "inarticulacy, and a warm, feeling, unbookish life," a world of men rarely graced by women except the mother, a world that particularly recalls Richard Hoggart's memoirs,[44] and the tribal rivalries of football.

In "Facing North" the Northern landscape referred to is not industrial but natural. The fierce "North wind" and "the winter's chill" recall many artistic representations of the inhospitable Northern climes. The poem's analogy for being possessed by "huge passion," the "wild" North wind, registers the parallel between "the power of the North wind" that assails the dwelling Wuthering Heights and the wild love,[45] and the historical circumstances of injustice and exile in which it exists, that visibly destroys Heathcliff and Cathy in Emily Brontë's Yorkshire novel. "Facing North" alludes to the literary history of representations of the North, a literary history of which this poem, and Harrison's oeuvre, is a part.

The cartographic image of "facing North" also points to the political map of the historic North-South divide, an important historical context for understanding this partisan political poet out of the North. In "Facing

North" Harrison speaks through Auden's "Letter to Lord Byron" to raise the politics and history of the North-South divide in England. In his letter-poem Auden explains to Byron that the promised riches of modernity have benefited the affluent South, "But in the North it simply isn't true."[46] Auden refers to Wigan in the same year George Orwell's grim account of the North-South divide, in *The Road to Wigan Pier* (1937), was published. The working class impoverished during the Industrial Revolution is still poor, and the "scars of struggle" between North and South on "the old historic battlefield" remain unhealed.[47] As Katie Wales observes, in the historically embedded binary of North and South in Britain, the North is synonymous with the working class, poverty, and industry, while the South, specifically London, Oxfordshire, Cambridgeshire, and other Home Counties are places of privilege. London is "the centre of power, of government, monarchy and cultural prestige located in the South,"[48] and the cultural, political, and economic marginalization of the North is a "postcolonial" phenomenon.[49] In its artistic engagement with history, Harrison's poetry explores ambiguities and contradictions and shades of grey, but it also presents the political view that "in literature as in so much else, the relationship of 'North' and 'South' is one of unequal power."[50]

In "Facing North" he poses a rhetorical question: "God knows why of all rooms I'd to choose / the dark one facing North for me to write."[51] The north-facing study symbolizes the poetry's multilayered articulation of Northern perspectives that seek to redress the "unequal and uneven forces of cultural representation involved in the contest for political and social authority,"[52] within the geopolitical division of North and South in Britain. As Philip Dodd comments, "artistic work on 'the North' is made by acquiescing in or struggling with available representations."[53] Harrison is a leading figure in the post-war decentralization of poetic authority in Britain, and of Northern writers gaining a voice in a discourse about the North traditionally dominated by the South. "Facing North" does not represent the poet's permanent shift of focus from the historical and political realities of the North and nor does it suggest a primarily existentialist notion of North, as a critic contends.[54] In an interview (with

John Haffenden in 1983) the year "Facing North" was published, Harrison
comments that in *The Misanthrope* Alceste's retreat to the country
speaks to the crisis of political disengagement amongst contemporary
intellectuals too. He observes that "it is not political involvement to run
off and live in the country."[55] In *v.* (1985) Harrison is no longer in a shack
on a Florida swamp writing the American poems. In *v.* he is back in
Leeds and poetically engaged with "*this class war*,"[56] and what he sees as
a neo-colonial war between the Thatcher government in the South and
the mining communities and other dispossessed people of the North.

Adorno writes that "for a man who no longer has a homeland, writing
becomes a place to live."[57] Harrison's exile of the imaginary is evoked by
the image of the poet "facing North" towards an absent home. But whereas
Adorno concludes that "in the end, the writer is not even allowed to live
in his writing," and that good writing depends on letting go of the familiar
and comfortable "to counter any slackening of intellectual tension," for
Harrison poetry provides both a home and a journey. The relationship
between home and foreign lands, the local and the cosmopolitan, is the
epiphany articulated in "Newcastle is Peru." This marriage of the familiar
and the new, in the work of the poet-as-traveller, is found in many of
his poems and is prominent in "Newcastle is Peru" and "Facing North."
Harrison's poetry is constituted by the familiar and compelling dramatic
persona "Tony Harrison," his recognizable colloquial speaking voice in
formal meter, the intimate layering of the biographical and the historical,
and a clear subject and narrative. It is a richly allusive and learned poetry
that explores many different literary and historical contexts.

HARRISON'S EDUCATION

A classical education and poetry were "not reconcilable" with a working-
class background "in the kind of class system we have in England."[58]
Harrison was a product of the Butler Education Act of 1944, which
introduced a scholarship system to place the brightest working-class
children into the grammar schools.[59] The ensuing experience of class

transition and cultural dislocation, and the politics of language are major preoccupations particularly of *The School of Eloquence* and *v.*. Dismissed as a "barbarian" by his schoolmaster, his thick Leeds accent was deemed inferior to Received Pronunciation,[60] the "everyday speech in families of Southern English persons" who have been educated in public schools.[61] The "elaborate" code of language used in the schools was "*not* the English that I speak at home."[62] But his continued belonging to his community of origin fundamentally depended upon speaking his mother tongue, a dilemma whose colonial dimensions are dramatized in the poems.

Harrison would "like to be the poet my father reads!"[63] The lack of serious education and high culture is regarded in the poetry as a deep injustice visited on the spirit, and with real political consequences. He responds to this injustice by writing poems about his family and their class, mainly in Standard English but using the Leeds demotic and Northern cultural references. The poetry's clarity of language and subject and direct address to the heart offers itself especially to people like his dad, "people with no time like you in Leeds."[64] The poetry is for "uz," the Northern pronoun of "inclusion, solidarity, and family feeling."[65] He works to make the most beautiful and elite art and scholarship as accessible as possible, and the same scholarly and aesthetic sophistication of the poetry also "gives maximum gratification" to "Them," "a composite dramatic figure" of bourgeois authority and privilege.[66] Harrison intends to make the "*hypocrite lecteur, mon semblable, mon frère*" pay for "that literary frisson...in the consciousness of social gaps and divisions."[67] Placing non-aesthetic content, like working-class speech, in and alongside high cultural forms and content, the quotation from Baudelaire's "To the Reader" conveys that the assumed bourgeois reader is one of the poetry's cultural targets.[68]

Harrison values his education in Latin and Greek. But he is hostile to a system that removes bright working-class pupils from their culture and forces them to choose between their backgrounds and cultural participation. A political and aesthetic victory in the poetry is "the deft and opportunistic annexation of classical authority by a poet not born to it."[69] Harrison wants Greek and Latin to be taught in the schools and was President of the Classical Association in 1987–1988,[70] and of the Virgil Society in 2000.[71] A secular humanist, he believes that progressive dimensions of humanity lie in education and the high cultural traditions of European culture. The generosity of spirit towards humanity associated with strands of humanism finds radical expression in the inclusion of the voices of the inarticulate and dispossessed in the classical forms of Harrison's poetry.

READING THE METER

"A Yorkshire poet who came to read the metre,"[72] this punning poet-as-tradesman writes in strict formal, rhyming poetic meters. He bends the iambic pentameter, the archetypal meter of English poetry usually regarded as privileging Received Pronunciation,[73] to accommodate the Leeds demotic, a voice not normally found in inherited meters. He frequently uses elision, breaks words across lines, and greatly varies the number of syllables in a line. A wide range of verse forms are used, including elegiac and heroic couplets, sonnets, lyric stanzas, epodic stanzas, and terza rima. The genres and modes of the verse include lyric, epic, elegy, epigram, ode, tragedy, comedy, and satire. Widely diverse linguistic registers are integrated into the poetry, including popular and learned, religious and obscene. The smooth surface of received poetic forms is visually ruffled by the unusually varied typography: upper and lower case, italics, roman type, phonetic alphabet, gothic, bold, brackets, parentheses, asterixes, footnotes, and pronounced spacing between lines.

An iconoclast bringing subaltern voices into received poetic forms, the poet is the high cultural vandal we meet in *v.*. The strained meter and syntax of the poetry embodies his point that eloquence is struggled for by the laboring class his poetry comes from.[74] Rudyard Kipling also put working-class voices into poetry and valorized the working class who built the British Empire. Harrison has read Kipling's poetry and uses Kiplingesque rhythms in the African poems. Kipling is a writer of whom the Left would not approve. Harrison is not so unique in his use of demotic in poetry as is often suggested. Harrison's use of classical forms is conservative in its sustaining of a tradition, but he also re-energizes those forms by bringing new voices and subjects into them.

Harrison's poetics of occupation is also a humanist poetics of inclusion. His appropriation of the traditional forms of the British literary tradition is presented as a people's occupation in "Them & [uz], II": "So right, yer buggers, then! We'll occupy / your lousy leasehold Poetry."[75] In "On Not Being Milton" the bourgeoisie's ownership of cultural capital is paralleled to Capital's ownership of the means of production.[76] In the sonnet the poet's struggle is, to continue the metaphor, to nationalize Poetry and make cultural wealth the inheritance of the common people. He regards himself as an artisan, a wordsmith akin to a blacksmith, skillfully wielding a sledge-hammer on "owned language."[77] Harrison's job "had to be hard work," as his father's sweated labor in a bakery was.[78] This is a working-class poet who rose into the leisured class only to bring with him "the whole weight of the Protestant Ethic in its death agonies, a monstrous North of England millstone grit."

POETRY TO DATE

A poet of the page, stage, and screen, the scope and diversity of Harrison's work is formidable and, like Milton, age does not weary him. Britain's principal theatre poet, his dramatic verse includes *The Misanthrope* (1973), *Phaedra Britannica* (1975), *Bow Down* (1977), *The Bartered Bride* (1978), *The Oresteia* (1981), *The Mysteries* (1985), *Medea: A Sex-War Opera* (1985), and *Fram* (2008). The plays have been performed internationally from Russia to Greece in metropolitan and regional theatres. The verse for film and television includes *The Big H* (1984), *v.* (1987), *The Blasphemer's Banquet* (1989), and *Loving Memory* (1992). *Prometheus*, his feature film, was screened on Channel 4 and in small cinemas in 1998. Harrison also translated versions from the Greek of Palladae of Alexandria in *Palladas:*

Poems (1975), and the Latin poet Martial into New York vernacular in *U.S. Martial* (1981). The dramatic and non-dramatic verse has also been translated into many languages, including his French version of *The Misanthrope* being translated back into English. It was not until the publication of the *Selected Poems* in 1984 (second edition 1987) that Harrison began to gain recognition as a lyric poet approaching the acclaim he had received as a theatre poet. The *Collected Poems* were published in 2007.

Harrison's publishing history reflects his increasing cultural capital. His first poems *Earthworks* and then *Newcastle is Peru* were published by small Northern imprints. *Loiners* was published with the small metropolitan publishing house London Magazine. Rex Collings, a relatively small London imprint, published the dramatic and non-dramatic verse in the 1970s and also *Continuous* and *The Oresteia* in 1981. From the 1980s onwards his books have been published by Newcastle-upon-Tyne publishing house Bloodaxe Books and the major publishing houses Faber and Faber and Penguin (which published his *Selected Poems* and *Collected Poems*). Harrison has also published poems individually in magazines throughout his career. The poetry was first published in student magazines and magazines like *Stand*, but increasingly appeared in major literary journals like *The Times Literary Supplement*.[79] In the sonnet "Them & [uz], II" he observes dryly how "My first mention in the *Times* / automatically made Tony Anthony!'[80] Harrison tends to publish major poems in the *London Review of Books*, including *v.* and later works such as "Piazza Sannazaro,"[81] "Cornet and Cartridge,"[82] and "Polygons."[83]

LAURELS

The most prestigious British and international awards have recognized the stature of Harrison's contribution to literature. In 1972 the Geoffrey Faber Memorial Prize was awarded for *Loiners*. *The Oresteia* won the European Poetry Translation Prize in 1983. *v.* won the Royal Television Society Award in 1987. The Whitbread Poetry Award for 1992 went to

The Gaze of the Gorgon (1992). In 1994 the Prix Italia was awarded for his film *Black Daisies for the Bride* (1993). *The Shadow of Hiroshima and Other Film-Poems* (1995) won the Heinemann Award in 1996. The Northern Rock Foundation Writer's Award went to Harrison in 2004.[84] He received the Wilfred Owen Poetry Award in 2007, and in 2009 the PEN Harold Pinter Literary Prize. The European Prize for Literature in 2010, and the David Cohen Prize in 2015, were awarded to Harrison for lifetime achievements in literature. In "Polygons" (2015), a meditation that weighs up the life and work in the context of the extinction of individuals and empires, he hopes for another decade that will be artistically his best, and he quotes the last words of "that great Irish spirit" Seamus Heaney (1939–2013): "*noli timere.*"

Harrison's poetry has attained canonical status, with major prizes awarded by his peers and the poetry taught in universities. His stance towards the canon is ambivalent. He is ambitious for his work to gain a lasting readership and to achieve fame in a traditional sense ("*exegi monumentum aere perennius*").[85] But his political intention is to subvert the use of the canon as a prop to the *status quo.*[86] He believes in a canon and in high culture as a distinct sphere but his art is also consonant with Raymond Williams's view that culture is ordinary, a way of life mutually inhering in the arts and learning.[87] By bringing the way of life and culture he grew up with into the canon, and working to be as accessible as possible, he "rescues" Art from "a closed order of appreciators."[88] The canonization of his poetry is a collective win for "uz."

LAUREATE OF THE REPUBLICAN LEFT

Classical republicanism is one of the major intellectual traditions that Harrison is shaped by, and he sees his role as similar to a classical republican orator or to the Milton of *Areopagitica*, his eloquence at the service of the people. In Ancient Greece, "the poets were central to the whole ability of a culture to understand itself,"[89] and Harrison identifies with the classical tradition of poetry as a public act. The work has commanded full houses in the theatre for decades and a mass audience through television and newspapers. He has published urgent polemical verse in newspapers, and not in the arts pages but in the news section. The commissioned poems about the Bosnian war, for example, were written in Bosnia while the war was raging and appeared on the front page of *The Guardian*. All the poetry is "part of the same quest for a public poetry."[90] But poetry is for the most part not a popular art and the skinhead in *v.* voices Harrison's doubts about its political efficacy when he cries "*it's not poetry we need in this class war.*"[91] Like Heaney, Harrison sees what poetry "does" as deeply personal, as a way to fortify the capacity for concentration and the inner life. But poetry is equally his way of expressing imaginative dissent against the "internal colonialism" of "the class system" that "I keep banging my head against."[92] Humanist Marxism, with its emphasis on experience, history, compassion, and agency is another formative intellectual tradition for Harrison.

RECEIVED VIEWS

There is a substantial corpus of criticism surrounding Harrison's life and work, and it includes distinguished commentary.[93] It is often observed in Harrison scholarship that the poetry is preoccupied with the relationship between class, language, and power, and by biographical, historical, political, and metaphysical divisions. The critical reception of the poetry is also characterized by division. The Marxist literary critic Terry Eagleton, for example, writes that we expect from Harrison "a radical rather than a liberal perspective, since we aren't likely to get it from ninety percent of his literary colleagues."[94] By contrast, Sandie Byrne's view is that much of the poetry does not offer a serious radical perspective on social injustice and that its political commitments are quite limited.[95] The largest problem in Harrison scholarship is a tendency to not engage fully with the political preoccupations of the poetry or to recognize the critical importance of history to understanding the poems. An explication of the poetry's detailed engagement with history discloses the richness of its political vision. There has been limited exploration of the poetry's engagement with colonial history, for example, but attention to colonial history is necessary for recognizing its strong anti-colonial poetic.

Harrison is generally understood as a singular presence in contemporary British poetry and his literary influences are usually seen to be classical and seventeenth century. Peter Forbes observes that Harrison could like William Blake "be a complete one-off" because he is not part of any school and has few followers.[96] However, leading Northern poets of a younger generation including Simon Armitage and Don Paterson express indebtedness to Harrison. Armitage comments that Harrison's establishing a written version of Yorkshire utterance "spared those of us from the same region the strife of having to write in another hand and read in another tongue."[97] In "Polygons," which considers the deaths of poets and the canon, Harrison links himself to two other Northerners of his generation, Ted Hughes (1930–1998) and Heaney. He has been compared with Heaney and the Scottish poet Douglas Dunn (1942–) as knowing "barbarians writing from outside the traditional cultural centre."[98] Dunn's "The Come On,"[99] and "Gardeners,"[100] and Heaney "walking, by God, all over the fine / Lawns of elocution,"[101] resonate with Harrison's humanist poetics of occupation and inclusion.[102]

The investigation of some new or neglected contexts in which Harrison's poems can be read discloses new dimensions of meaning in them. While his class political analysis is central to much of the discussion of his poetry, his concern with colonialism has generated relatively little commentary, a neglect which I attempt to rectify here. This book emphasizes the radical inclusiveness of his humanism and the importance of republican literary and political traditions for the poetry, offering the first fully detailed contextual account of these remarkable poems and their politics.

Notes

1. *Tony Harrison: Poets and People*, a Freeway Films Production for Channel 4 (1984).
2. The partial exception is an essay by Colin Nicholson, see Colin Nicholson, "'Reciprocal Recognitions': Race, Class, and Subjectivity in Tony Harrison's *The Loiners*," *Race & Class*, vol. 51, no. 4 (2010), 59–78.
3. The exceptions to the neglect is an earlier essay by Bruce Woodcock, see Bruce Woodcock, "'Internal Colonialism': Is Tony Harrison a Post-Colonial Poet?," *New Literatures Review*, no. 35, (1998), 76–94.
4. See for example Sean O'Brien, "Tony Harrison: Showing the Working," in *The Deregulated Muse: Essays on Contemporary British and Irish Poetry* (Newcastle-upon-Tyne: Bloodaxe Books, 1998), 51–64, 63.
5. I have adopted Bruce Woodcock's description of Harrison's poetry as "classical vandalism," as it appears in the title of his article, and I have extended the phrase to Rimbaud's poetry. See Bruce Woodcock, "Classical Vandalism: Tony Harrison's Invective," *Critical Quarterly*, vol. 32, no. 2 (Summer 1990), 50–65.
6. "Interview," 230.
7. "Interview with Bailey," Radio 3.
8. *Them & [uz]: A Portrait of Tony Harrison*, Arena, BBC (15 April 1985).
9. *Them & [uz]: A Portrait*, BBC.
10. T.W. Harrison, "English Virgil: *The Aeneid* in the XVIII Century," *Philologica Pragensia*, X (1967), 1–11, 80–91; and T.W. Harrison, "Dryden's *Aeneid*," in *Dryden's Mind and Art*, ed. Bruce King (Edinburgh: Oliver and Boyd, 1969), 143–67.
11. Letter to Ross (5 April 1968).
12. Letter to Silkin (8 November 1964).
13. "Interview," 246.
14. "The Poetic Gaze," *The Guardian* (24 October, 2009).
15. Letter to Ross (7 October, 1970).
16. PhD acceptance document, *THP*.
17. See "Introduction," *Newcastle is Peru*, second ed. (Newcastle-upon-Tyne: Northern House, 1974), unnumbered; and "Inkwell," 35. See also John Cleveland, "News from Newcastle: Upon the Coal-Pits about Newcastle-upon-Tyne," in *Minor Poets of the Caroline Period*, vol. 3, ed. George Saintsbury (Oxford: Oxford University Press, 1921), 88.

18. "Shango," 88.
19. "Interview," 20.
20. In *CP* "Listening to Sirens" precedes "Facing North" as the first poem following *The School of Eloquence* and preceding the American poems. "Listening to Sirens" is a very different poem but it also makes reference to the dialectic between an actual and symbolic North and South.
21. "Facing North," *CP*, 218.
22. *CP*, 219.
23. *CP*, 219.
24. *CP*, 218.
25. *CP*, 219.
26. Theodor Adorno, *Minima Moralia: Reflections from Damaged Life*, trans. E.F.N. Jephcott (London: New Left Books, 1974 [1951]), 87.
27. Louis MacNeice, "Epilogue," *Letters From Iceland* (London: Faber and Faber, 1967 [1937]), 251.
28. MacNeice, "Epilogue," 253.
29. MacNeice, "Epilogue," 252. See also W.H. Auden, "Foreword," in *Letters From Iceland* (London: Faber and Faber, 1967 [1937]), 7–9, 8.
30. Auden, "Foreword," 8.
31. MacNeice, "Epilogue," 251.
32. Samuel Hynes, *The Auden Generation: Literature and Politics in England in the 1930s* (London: Bodley Head, 1976), 229. Another of Auden's works that has themes of travel and the North is the verse text he wrote for the collaborative documentary film *Night Mail* (1936), which follows the journey of the Royal mail train delivery service from London to Glasgow. Harrison's film-poem *Crossings* (2002) refers to *Night Mail.* See *Crossings*, *CP*, 399–414, 404.
33. Louis MacNeice, "Preface," *Modern Poetry: A Personal Essay*, with an Introduction by Walter Allen (Oxford: Clarendon Press, 1968 [1938]), xxi.
34. *CP*, 218.
35. Hynes, *The Auden Generation*, 291.
36. "Facing North," *CP*, 218.
37. Peter Davidson, *The Idea of North* (London: Reaktion Books, 2005), 85.
38. Katie Wales, "North and South: An English Linguistic Divide?," *English Today* 61, vol. 16, no. 1 (January 2000), 4–15, 4.
39. Louis MacNeice, "Sports Page," *Selected Poems*, ed. Michael Longley (London: Faber and Faber, 1988), 155.
40. Louis MacNeice, "Carrickfergus," *Selected Poems*, ed. Michael Longley (London: Faber and Faber, 1988), 24.

41. Louis MacNeice, "Valediction," *Selected Poems*, ed. Michael Longley (London: Faber and Faber, 1988), 13.
42. W.H. Auden, "Letter to Lord Byron," *Letters From Iceland* (London: Faber and Faber, 1967 [1937]), 49.
43. George Orwell, *The Road to Wigan Pier*, foreword by Victor Gollancz (London: Victor Gollancz, 1937), 147.
44. Philip Dodd, "Lowryscapes: Recent Writings About the North," *Critical Quarterly*, vol. 32, no. 2 (Summer 1990), 17–28, 21.
45. Emily Bronte, *Wuthering Heights*, an authoritative text, with essays in criticism, ed. William M. Sale, Jr. (New York: Norton, 1972 [1963], 14.
46. Auden, "Letter to Lord Byron," 48.
47. Auden, "Letter to Lord Byron," 48.
48. Wales, "North and South," 5–6.
49. Katie Wales, *Northern English: A Social and Cultural History* (Cambridge: Cambridge University Press, 2006), 4.
50. Dodd, "Lowryscapes," 18.
51. *CP*, 218.
52. Homi K. Bhabha, "The Postcolonial and the Postmodern: The Question of Agency," in *The Location of Culture* (London and New York: Routledge, 2005 [1994]), 245–282, 245.
53. Dodd, "Lowryscapes," 17.
54. *TH Holocaust*, 123.
55. "Interview," 239.
56. *v.*, *CP*, 273.
57. Adorno, *Minima Moralia*, 87.
58. "Interview," 246.
59. See for example Ken Worpole, "Scholarship Boy: The Poetry of Tony Harrison," in *Bloodaxe 1*, 61–74.
60. "Them & [uz], I," *CP*, 133; and "Harrison in Interview with John Tusa," BBC Radio 3 (March 2008).
61. Daniel Jones, *The Cambridge English Pronouncing Dictionary*, rev. ed., ed. Peter Roach, James Hartman and Jane Setter (Cambridge: Cambridge University Press, 2006 [1909]), v.
62. Basil Bernstein, *Class, Codes, and Control: Theoretical Studies Towards a Sociology of Language* (London and New York: Routledge, 2003 [1971]), 150–1; and "Classics Society," *CP*, 130.
63. "Rhubarbarians, II," *CP*, 124.
64. "A Good Read," *CP*, 152.
65. "Interview," 233, and "Them & [uz], II," *CP*, 134.

66. Richard Hoggart, *The Uses of Literacy: Aspects of Working-Class Life, with Special Reference to Publications and Entertainments* (London: Chatto & Windus, 1957), 62.

67. "Interview," 232.

68. "Tony Harrison in interview with Clive Wilmer," "Poet of the Month," BBC Radio 3 (February 1991), transcript published in *Poets Talking: The "Poet of the Month" Interviews from BBC Radio 3*, ed. Clive Wilmer (Manchester: Carcanet, 1994), 97–103, 99.

69. Patrick Deane, *At Home in Time: Forms of Neo-Augustanism in Modern English Poetry* (London: McGill-Queen's University Press, 1994), 30.

70. "Facing Up to the Muses," Presidential Address to the Classical Association (12 April 1988), first published in *Proceedings of the Classical Association*, 85 (1988), reproduced in *Bloodaxe 1*, 429–454.

71. "The Tears and the Trumpets," Presidential Address to the Virgil Society (3 June 2000), in *Arion*, vol. 9, no. 2 (2001), 1–22.

72. "Preface," *The Mysteries* (London: Faber and Faber, 1985), 6.

73. Antony Easthope, *Poetry as Discourse* (London: Methuen, 1983), 68.

74. Blake Morrison, "The Filial Art," in *Bloodaxe 1*, 54–60, 57.

75. "Them & [uz], II," *CP*, 134.

76. "On Not Being Milton," *CP*, 122.

77. "On Not Being Milton," *CP*, 122.

78. "Inkwell," 33. See also for example "Currants, I, II," *CP*, 164–65 and "Marked with D," *CP*, 168.

79. For a fuller account of Harrison's publishing history see Sandie Byrne, "Tony Harrison's Public Poetry," in *TH: Loiner*, 1–27.

80. "Them & [uz], II," *CP*, 134.

81. "Piazza Sannazaro," *London Review of Books*, vol. 32, no. 20 (21 October 2010), 27.

82. "Cornet and Cartridge," *London Review of Books*, vol. 33, no. 4 (17 February 2011), 19.

83. "Polygons," *London Review of Books*, vol. 37, no. 4 (19 February 2015), 16–17.

84. Tony Harrison quoted in Maya Jaggi, "Beats of the Heart," *The Guardian* (25 March 2004).

85. "Interview," 233 and 235.

86. "Interview," 245. In this interview Harrison's comments about the Classics "as a prop to the *status quo*" are suggestive of his view of the wider canon.

87. Raymond Williams, "Culture is Ordinary," in *Resources of Hope: Culture, Democracy, Socialism*, ed. Robin Gale (London: Verso, 1989), 3–19, 3–16.

88. "Interview with Wilmer," 102.

89. "Tony Harrison in Interview with Melvyn Bragg," *The Southbank Show*, London Weekend Television (28 March 1999).

90. "Author's Statement," 9.

91. *v., CP*, 273.

92. "Interview," 231, 236.

93. See my bibliography.

94. Terry Eagleton, "Metre v. Madness," *Poetry Review*, vol. 82, no. 4 (Winter 1992/3), 53–4, 54.

95. *H, v. & O*, 162.

96. Peter Forbes, "In the Canon's Mouth: Tony Harrison and Twentieth-Century Poetry," in *TH: Loiner*, 189–199, 198.

97. Simon Armitage, "Tony Harrison is Sixty," *New Statesman*, vol.126, no. 4331 (1997), 45. See also Don Paterson, quoted in Christina Pattison, "Don Paterson: Playing the Beautiful Game," *The Independent* (9 January 2004).

98. Simon Armitage and Robert Crawford, "Introduction: The Democratic Voice," in *The Penguin Book of Poetry from Britain and Ireland Since 1945*, ed. Simon Armitage and Robert Crawford (London: Viking, 1998), xix–xxvii, xxi. See also Robert Crawford, *Devolving English Literature* (Edinburgh: Edinburgh University Press, 2000 [1992]), 282–4.

99. Douglas Dunn, "The Come-On," *Selected Poems 1964–1983* (London: Faber and Faber, 1986), 99–100.

100. Douglas Dunn, "Gardeners," *Selected Poems, 1964–1983* (London: Faber and Faber, 1986), 105–6.

101. Seamus Heaney, "The Ministry of Fear," *New Selected Poems 1966–1987* (London: Faber and Faber, 1990), 82–3.

102. "Them & [uz], II," *CP*, 134.

Chapter 2

Harrison's *Loiners*

"Loiners" is local argot for the citizens of Leeds, in Yorkshire,[1] and *The Loiners* was Harrison's first professional collection of poetry. It received mixed reviews when it was published in 1970, and the poet from working-class Leeds was angered not by criticisms but by the condescension of some reviewers.[2] But he kept a copy of a review by the English poet David Tipton who described *Loiners* "as one of the most entertaining and serious books I've read for some time," and observed its iconoclastic wit and combination of colloquial and cosmopolitan language.[3] In a letter to Alan Ross, the editor of London Magazine Editions which published *Loiners*, Harrison also quoted the Irish poet Derek Mahon's review of the volume "as among the liveliest and most exciting to be published in Britain for some time."[4] Tipton had concluded that *Loiners* was such an outstanding first volume "it would be hazardous to predict the directions the author may take." Harrison went on to become recognised as the leading English poet of his generation, but his brilliant and highly referential first volume remains largely neglected in the critical and academic commentary to date.

The concerns of these poems include "loins in a general sense."[5] Harrison wondered whether *Loiners* might be "too *dirty* for them, or not good enough" to win any prizes,[6] but in 1972 it was awarded the prestigious Geoffrey Faber Memorial Prize. Mrs Harrison saw the headline in the local Leeds newspaper announcing her son's award: '4-LETTER WORD POEMS WIN TONY £250 PRIZE."[7] Harrison had avoided showing *Loiners* to his "mam,"[8] and in "Bringing Up" recalls that it was only because she had the library copy that his mother refrained from burning *Loiners* in the lounge room fire. The scene in the sonnet, and the conflict between the poet's artistic freedom and his mother's Christianity, resonates with Baudelaire's "Benediction," from *Flowers of Evil* which Harrison has read, in which the Catholic mother has darker longings to throw not just the book but her poet son "into the flames."[9]

The hanging line of "Bringing Up" is a direct quotation of his distraught mother's assessment, in memorable iambic pentameter, of *Loiners*:

> But I still see you weeping, your hurt looks:
>
> *You weren't brought up to write such mucky books!*[10]

Harrison animatedly agrees: "And I wasn't, I wasn't brought up to write such mucky books" but "the lack of discussion about such topics as sex was one of the things I wanted to become a part of what I articulated when I cultivated the powers of the poet."[11]

In the original book description for *Loiners*, held in manuscript form in the Alan Ross Collection, Harrison explained that it is concerned with "sex and history," with "the realization that the nightmare of history is not only outside but inside under the bed, and enacted in the very forms our sexuality chooses to express itself."[12] His perception that history is manifest in the forms our sexuality takes also suggests that conversely history can be read through sex. *Loiners* offers an historical contextualization of sexuality that yields an account of the human experience and the ideology of that history. Different poems examine sex in different historical contexts but the focus on loins is most sustained and explicit in the African poems in Part Two of the volume.

In the original publication Harrison divided *Loiners* into five related parts, and attention was drawn to this division on the contents page, the title pages that preceded each part, and in Harrison's own unpublished account of *Loiners*.[13] The division of the volume is an important aspect of its form and meaning though it was dropped from *Collected Poems* (2007), perhaps for ease in preparations for publication. The division is based upon the different places in which the poem's protagonists are located and the distinct histories and cultures that these poems of place explore. Part One contains five poems set in Leeds during WWII and the post-war period, and it is these poems which are the main focus of this first chapter about *Loiners*. Harrison had intended to give these poems the general title "The Leeds Quatrains" although only the first poem,[14] "Thomas Campey and the Copernican System," is in the strict quatrain form of four line stanzas with alternate rhymes. The poems mix learned and popular registers and dictions, use aggressive slang liberally, and have various formal rhyme schemes but the meter is usually varied iambic pentameter. *Loiner is* written in what might be called Harrison's "bastard high style."

The different parts of *Loiners* are linked by the travels of a Loiner, a peripatetic protagonist broadly linked to the dramatic persona "Tony Harrison" and to aspects of different characters in the poems. The shifting locations in different parts of the book mirror Harrison's wide-ranging travels in the 1960s from Leeds to Africa, Eastern Europe, South America, and concluding with his return to the Northern city of Newcastle-upon-Tyne. Part Two of *Loiners* contains four poems set in Africa mainly in the 1960s but also in earlier centuries. The seven poems in Part Three are set in Eastern Europe, England, Cuba, and Brazil in the twentieth century, and in sixteenth-century Spain. Part Four, "Newcastle is Peru," and Part Five, "Ghosts: Some Words before Breakfast," are set in Newcastle-upon-Tyne in the 1960s. *Loiners* consists of eighteen poems but one of the African poems, "The White Queen," also contains further sequences of poems. Romana Huk comments that criticism of *Loiners* as "uneven" because of its varied locations, voices, and rhythms misrecognizes the complex polycentrism of the sequence,[15] and that this misrecognition is part of why *Loiners* has been less praised and less discussed than the more accessible *School of Eloquence*. Harrison explained to Alan Ross that "The book moves obsessively in a circle from the North of England out into the world and back again."[16]

The transnational scope of *Loiners* provides the world stage upon which Harrison shows the poetic worthiness of his native city and begins his artistic reclamation of the people and place he came from, which had not seemed "to be the stuff that literature could be made of."[17] A photo of "the author in native dress" appeared on the dust jacket of *Loiners*,[18] and is a paratextual framing device that conveys the cultural and class specificity of the poet and the poems inside the cover. Harrison's "native dress" in the photo is working-class denim and he is smoking, a sign of working-class identity and solidarity that he will employ again in his film poem *Prometheus* (1998). The photo, which Harrison provided to his publisher during preparations for publication of *Loiners*,[19] shows him leaning against a street corner lamp-post with a disaffected expression, and is a classic portrait of an angry young working-class man. His choice of photo and identification of his "native dress" intends to convey that the poet and his poetry are culturally Northern and working-class. He has said that his ambition was to "make things that were classically formed, but in my own voice,"[20] and his poetry is defiantly Northern working-class in its content and idioms while using high literary forms.

The Leeds poems in *Loiners* were also inspired by James Joyce's *Dubliners*, and Harrison was determined to bring the life of the city and Joycean and dramatic influences to bear on his poetry about the North. [21] He "began writing stories about Leeds; they were a little like imitations of Joyce's *Dubliners*," which he was "very impressed with."[22] Like *Dubliners*, the Leeds poems tell stories about the ordinary people of the city and illuminate the underlying meanings of unremarkable experiences. The political topography in *Loiners* presents Leeds and also Newcastle-upon-Tyne as colonial cities presided over by weathered statues of the "Empress, Queen" Victoria, symbols of an unwelcome, lingering imperial presence in the North, and resonating with Joyce's vision of Dublin as a colonial city. Harrison's egalitarian republicanism is also signaled by his definition of Loiners as "citizens of Leeds, *citizens* who bear their loins alone through the terrors of life, 'loners.'"[23] A bleak existential sense of human aloneness co-exists with the shared right and responsibility of the common people to have a political "role as a citizen of Leeds and the world."[24]

The first edition of *Loiners* had two epigraphs which together signified that the poet has been ambivalently nurtured by the culture of Leeds, and that the North has been produced by the military history of empire:

> There was a young man of Leeds
>
> Who swallowed a packet of seeds.
>
> A pure white rose grew out of his nose
>
> And his arse was covered with weeds.
>
> Traditional
>
> inventa Britannia et subacta
>
> Tacitus, Agricola[25]

The combined epigraphs signal the relationship between poetry and history, and the hybridity of popular and learned culture in the poems. The first epigraph, an anonymous quatrain about Leeds, is a traditional limerick wherein the pure rose of poetry blooms incongruously from a man whose "arse was covered with weeds." The organic metaphor shows Harrison's poetry growing from Leeds soil, and his native roots are reaffirmed in *v.* where, back in Leeds again, he tells us that his poetry grows from "SHIT."[26]

The white rose has a number of associations that Harrison activates. Formerly a royal dynastic emblem of the House of York and the House of Stuart, it is the floral emblem of Yorkshire. Harrison transplants the emblem in his poetry. He remembers playing cricket "with white roses cut from flour-sacks on our caps' in v..[27] The white rose is used in the logo of Leeds United Football Club, whose fans desecrate the graveyard in v.. His dad places roses on the family grave in v..[28] The white rose is emphatically a symbol of Harrison's native culture, and from *Loiners* to v. it becomes a sign of the poet's native cultural nationalism. The royal rose is now associated with indigenous Northern culture and grafted onto Harrison's republican poetics. It is the flower of Loiners.

The second epigraph to *Loiners* recalls the subjugation of the native peoples of Britain by the Roman Empire. The Latin epigraph is taken from the Roman historian Tacitus's eponymous biography of Agricola, a Governor of Roman Britain who expanded the Empire to the furthest Northern point of the known world. The epigraph, "*inventa Britannia et subacta*" ["We have both discovered and subdued Britain"], is from Agricola's address to his soldiers before battle with the Caledonians (the Scots).[29] He recalls victories against Rome's enemies, most appositely here the Brigantes, a Celtic tribe who had controlled most of Northern England. The Roman battle against the "Brigantes, the British / guerrillas,"[30] is also imagined in "The Excursion," whose immediate setting is Newcastle-upon-Tyne. The poem's reference to Hadrian's Wall and modern day British soldiers moving, like the Romans, from Northern England to Scotland, recalls that boundaries laid by Rome are still reflected in the political topography of Britain. Military and other forms of dominance continue to characterize the ancient divide between North and South, and the North is still part of the "empire we can't get away from."[31] A prophecy of revolution in Seneca's *Medea*, in which Thule, the North, overcomes its marginalization in the empire is alluded to in an epigraph to "Newcastle is Peru." The epigraph from Seneca's *Medea*, the classical allusion in "The Excursion," and the epigraph from *Agricola* at the start of *Loiners* signpost its vision of Northern England as a defeated colonial region.

Harrison's conception of Britain as an empire whose unity, he believes, still derives from the cultural and economic oppression of the regions by London is first signaled by the epigraph from *Agricola*. It reminds us that Britain began with Rome's military imposition of one nation and language on culturally diverse tribes. The Roman's view of the natives as barbarians, as well as the Ancient Greek's definition of non-Greek speakers as barbarians in a different sense, is a source for the complex and subversive identification of contemporary Northerners as barbarians in *The School of Eloquence* sonnets.[32] The epigraph from *Agricola* is also significant for the African poems in *Loiners* because it hints at a parallel between the history of native Britons being subjugated by Rome and the colonization, centuries later, of African countries by the British Empire. The independence from the British Empire achieved by many African countries in the 1960s is implicitly contrasted, in the collection as a whole, to the continuing subjugation of the North by the British state. In a variation upon Edward Said's defining colonialism as "a dominating metropolitan centre ruling a distant territory," the Leeds poems suggest that the Northern city was subject to colonial rule by the relatively close Southern metropolitan centre of government, monarchy, and cultural and economic power.

The concern with internal colonialism and its complex interrelations with issues of class in Harrison's poetry about Leeds in *Loiners, The School of Eloquence, v.,* and other works begins with "Thomas Campey and the Copernican System." Campey was a Loiner, a figure from Harrison's childhood who survived by scavenging and selling books.[33] Harrison has a personal bookplate of Campey,[34] which he has drawn attention to by giving permission for it to be reproduced in the *Bloodaxe Critical Anthologies 1: Tony Harrison*, and by discussing its significance in interview:

> While the reader is enjoying the sentiment of the achieved literary poem he should be reminded, at the very same moment, that there is a cost to pay, and that it is probably someone other than the reader who has paid that cost. The first poem in *The Loiners* is about a man named Thomas Campey, who—without partaking

of this culture—dragged books to market with his bad back, and enabled me to equip myself with a "gentleman's" library. In all my books I now have a bookplate with a drawing of this man— Thomas Campey, with his "warped spine," this man from whom I bought my books—and that's exactly the kind of reminder that is in my poetry.[35]

The long dead Campey is a specter the poem materializes.

Harrison thought Campey carried the weight of English culture on his back,[36] and above the sketch of Campey the bookplate also has a line of verse from the poem: "And every pound of this dead weight is pain / to Thomas Campey (Books)...." Campey, illiterate and ill, bears the weight of the literary inheritance he delivers for the benefit of the educated. Harrison's sense of indebtedness to Campey, of the way his education and art are made possible by Campey's toil and similarly, in the *School* sonnets "Currants, I, II," by his father's labor in a bakery,[37] recalls Walter Benjamin's view that the cultural heritage "owes its existence not only to the toil of the great geniuses, who created it, but also to the nameless drudgery of its contemporaries."[38] The German-Jewish critic's now famous observation that "there has never been a document of culture, which is not simultaneously one of barbarism" has resonance with Harrison's poetic sense that the production and transmission of culture is implicated in the divisions between the privileged and the oppressed. Campey prefigures the succession of "worn out" working-class men in *The School of Eloquence* sonnets, like the old busker in "Punchline" and the pensioners in "Painkillers," who are figured as a series of paternal ghosts.

Like Harrison's dad, Campey wears the flat cap, an icon of his class, generation, and region. In *The School of Eloquence* sonnet "Turns" the scholar son dons *"your dad's cap"*: "I thought it made me look more 'working class'."[39] He bitterly mocks himself for having "turned," treacherously, into a busker for "the class that broke him for the pence." Nonetheless, Harrison wore the flat cap in his portrait for the National

Portrait Gallery in London in 1999, a sartorial code expressing allegiance to his place and class of origin.[40] In the photographic portrait there is a pronounced gleam of light from the camera in Harrison's right eye. This mirrors, perhaps inadvertently, "the gleam, the light" in his father's "blind right eye" in one of two family photographs taken by Harrison and described in the *School* sonnet "Background Material."[41] The accidental light in the photo contains a minute reflection of the son photographing his father, while the photo of his mother has a shadow in which her son is reflected. Although the accidental light and shadows would "mar each shot" for a professional photographer, for the poet his reflection in photos of his parents becomes symbolic of their imprint upon his memory. In the official portrait the light in Harrison's eye may be an intentional "marring" by the photographer in order to invite interpretation of it through the lens of "Background Material," and to see the light in the poet's eye as reflecting the metaphorical ghost of his father.

The young Harrison used to talk to the real Thomas Campey, who said that he thought England had been a great nation but had gone into decline after WWI, and he kept books he could not read on the decline of empire,[42] as he does in the poem: Edward Gibbon's *The Decline and Fall of the Roman Empire*; Theodore Mommsen's *The History of Rome*; and Oswald Spengler's *The Decline of the West*. Campey's spine was bowed by dragging the books in his handcart and by *tabes dorsalis*, the Latin for syphilitic spinal sclerosis, and the poem begins the trope of syphilis for empire that runs through *Loiners*. It is only in death that Campey will find "leisure of the simplest kind,"[43] and the poem suggests that he was killed by hard labour, by the third world conditions experienced by an underclass in a first world economy, an intersecting system of class and colonial exploitation dramatized through the trope of syphilis.

The statue of "that Imperial Host" in "Thomas Campey and the Copernican System,"[44] and of the "Empress, Queen" in "Ghosts,"[45] symbolize the British class system Queen Victoria represents and the empire that doubled during her reign (1837–1901), while "Newcastle is Peru" refers

to the seventeenth-century Royalist domination of the North and repro-
duces the royalist motto that is still on the city's Coat of Arms.[46] Harrison
also humorously describes his encounter with a statue of Victoria when,
as a Leeds Grammar schoolboy, he escapes a physical education class:

> I ducked behind the pedestal of a huge Queen Victoria for a furtive
> drag. At her draped feet Africa and India did obeisance, the very stone
> kow-towed, and I, exhausted and bent double, was more or less slumped
> in a like posture of devotion.[47]

He laments the melting of statues of Victoria into *chapatti* pans upon
independence in India, when they could have been "sent back home to
congest our parks," and "felt only triumph as the Empire fell to pieces."[48]
The prose adds an explicit, humorous angle to the poem's far more
complex articulation of political anger at the imperial presence in the
North, symbolized by the statues of Victoria.

The highly allusive scatological last quatrain of "Thomas Campey and
the Copernican System" images the Empress "squat" upon her "thrones,"
as if defecating upon her Northern territories and subjects. Victoria's
"thrones" "literally base the city's wealth in its mills on colonialist
trade."[49] Her throne is "Swathed in luminous smokes like factories,"
and set against "a dark, Leeds sky."[50] The poem invites comparison of
Leeds with the "dark Satanic mills" of Blake's "Preface" to *Milton*.[51] The
modern industrial landscape of Leeds was once made up of cotton mills
and Leeds like Manchester was a major site of the textile industry. The
exploitation of the Northern industrial working class who worked in
the mills and the colonial trade are different dimensions of the same
empire. The history Harrison evokes in this poem and elsewhere, as in
The School of Eloquence sonnet "Working,"[52] points to the exploitation
of the domestic proletariat and the spread of syphilis and exposes the
hypocrisy of Victorian morality.

The elevated statue of Victoria "Most High" in the closing quatrains is
a site of homage to empire: "Leeds! Offer thanks to that Imperial Host."
Leeds's subservience to its long dead Empress is rendered with bitter

irony but it also symbolizes the continuing power of the system she represents. The poem suggests that "Britain" designates not a nation but the Southern-based ruling elite, for whom Victoria is also a figurehead. The Crown enriched itself, and the class that attends fee paying schools like Leeds Grammar, by plundering the North's resources.

An allusion to Milton's great republican damnation of monarchy occurs in the final quatrain of "Thomas Campey and the Copernican System." Queen Victoria is depicted squatting over the dark industrial landscape of Leeds:

> Leeds! Offer thanks to that Imperial Host,
>
> Squat on its thrones of Ormus and of Ind,
>
> For bringing Thomas from his world of dust
>
> To dust, and leisure of the simplest kind.[53]

The stanza clearly alludes to Milton's *Paradise Lost*, Book II, lines 1 6:

> High on a throne of royal state, which far
>
> Outshone the wealth of Ormus and of Ind,
>
> Or where the gorgeous East with richest hand
>
> Showers on her kings barbaric pearl and gold,
>
> Satan exalted sat, by merit raised
>
> To that bad eminence.[54]

The poem demonizes Victorian imperialism as satanic and Harrison associates his own hostility to the monarchy with England's great republican poet.

There is a further allusion to *Paradise Lost* in "Thomas Campey and the Copernican System" that evokes the merged power of state and capital.

The deified Crown is surrounded by armed angels swathed in factory smoke: "These angels serried in a dark, Leeds sky."[55] This line alludes to *Paradise Lost*, Book I, line 548, where Milton describes the warring angels with their "serried shields in thick array."[56] "Serried" is a military term and by using it Harrison evokes the might of the state, for which Victoria is a figurehead in the poem:

> And round Victoria Regina the Most High
>
> Swathed in luminous smokes like factories,
>
> These angels serried in a dark, Leeds sky
>
> Chanting *Angina –a, Angina Pectoris.*[57]

The poem's depiction of Victoria Regina replete with angels makes her, like Milton's Satan, a monarchical figure with god-like pretensions.

The poem which follows "Thomas Campey and the Copernican System" in *Loiners* is "Ginger's Friday." Joyce's *Dubliners* was an inspiration for *Loiners* and this collection about Leeds people and colonialism also contains a poem on an Irish Catholic. Ginger's birth name is John Kelly, a typically Irish name, and his nickname derives from the fair "ginger" coloured hair typical of the Irish. Ginger has taken Friday off school, and the title puns upon the Christian Good Friday, the anniversary of the crucifixion of Jesus Christ, and hints at the boy's victimization. The poem begins with Ginger's visit to the Catholic Church to make his confession to the priest: "Grateful, anonymous, he catalogued his sin," notably masturbating while secretly watching his neighbor "Mrs Daley, all-bare on her knees" fellating her husband.[58] The priest says: "*Remember me to Mrs Kelly, John.*" Ginger's confession has not been anonymous and the priest knows his mother. In the last lines of the poem it is clear that the priest has betrayed the sacrament of confession and told Ginger's parents his sins. The boy runs home shouting his prayers only to find his father and Mr Daley cracking their "broad, black belts." Ginger is imaged as if in "Hell."

The published poem centres on the depiction of Irish Catholic taboos, and its emphasis upon the treachery of the priest reflects Harrison's anti-clerical sentiment. A manuscript version of "Ginger's Friday" contains a dropped stanza which makes explicit the poem's concern with the divided Irish diaspora settled in Maude Place, in the working-class suburb of Beeston where Harrison grew up. The cut stanza depicts the continuation of religious conflict between Catholic and Protestant Irish, and also satirizes the local population's bigotries against outsiders from Jews to blacks to Irish, which co-exist with traditional working-class hostility to the Tories. Ginger is depicted as running a gauntlet of racial abuse. The Catholic Irish in Leeds are pariah figures identified with the Jews:

> The potato-famine Irish of Maude Place
>
> Kept up their church connections through their kids.
>
> Gangs yelled: *'ail Mary, wash yer mucky face!*
>
> Or, *Down wi' Catlicks! Down wi' Yids!*
>
> *Down wi' Conservatives* and *Down wi' Blacks!'*
>
> As Ginger ran the gauntlet down the street.
>
> They'd send the Jews to Dublin on your backs,
>
> Swimming with four wogs tied to your feet.[59]

The activity of the IRA and the Troubles as well as popular anti-Catholicism might explain why the Leeds mob wants Ginger as a sacrifice.

Harrison may have cut the stanza because in it the oppressors are the working-class of Leeds, who are anti-Catholic, anti-Semitic, and hate Blacks and Irish. Its depiction of the bigotries of the local population is at odds with the otherwise humorously sympathetic or compassionate portrayal of working-class Loiners in Part One. White working-class hatred for Jews and Blacks in the cut stanza does though anticipate the hatred for "Yids" and "Niggers" by the Leeds skinhead in *v.*.[60] The cut stanza, as Antony Rowland observes, clearly shows Harrison's intention to link "various victims of religious, racial and political ideologies."[61] The cut stanza does show the politics of the poem since it is particularly concerned with the working-class Irish diaspora's historical origins and fate—the continuing victimhood of those Catholic Irish who escaped the Great Hunger in "the coffin ships": "The potato-famine Irish of Maude Place."

Ginger, the Kelly family, and their brawling neighbors show the influence of Joyce. In "The Dead," the last story in *Dubliners*, and in *Ulysses* the potato-famine is a sign of British misrule. The potato-famine is also a sign of British misrule in "Ginger's Friday." In "The Dead" the feast held to celebrate Christmas continues "the tradition of genuine warm-hearted courteous Irish hospitality, which our forefather's have handed down to us."[62] An implicit irony of the story is that the Irish known for their hospitality starved to death in their millions in their own country during the Great Hunger. The Irish forefathers who fell during the Great Hunger are especially and implicitly figured among the "vast hosts of the dead" that fall like snow in the last lines of "The Dead."[63] In a less reverent tone than Joyce, "Ginger's Friday" also raises the memory of the "potato-famine Irish" through their descendants, now settled in Maude Place.

The allusion to the potato famine as a sign of British misrule in "Ginger's Friday" might also recall Joyce's *Ulysses*. In *Ulysses* the Citizen, based on the one-eyed Cyclops of Homer's *Ulysses*, is a stereotype of a myopic, bigoted nationalist. The Citizen says that the British Sassenach had a policy of mass starvation, continuing to export crops and livestock from Ireland during the famine.[64] Harrison follows a poem about Queen Victoria's satanic presence in the North with a poem referring to the Irish potato famine. His intertextual association of Victoria with the potato famine agrees with the Citizen's view, who at this point seems to be a mouthpiece for Joyce. Harrison presents the Great Hunger, as Joyce does, that is, as a horrific chapter in the history of the British Empire. The historian A.J.P. Taylor controversially compared the impact of the potato famine, in which nearly two million Irish died in five years, to the Jewish holocaust,[65] and "Ginger's Friday," along with "Allotments" and "The Pocket Wars of Peanuts Joe," are instances of Harrison's concern with the history of holocaust, as Rowland discusses.[66] The first two poems in *Loiners*, therefore, explicitly focus on a dark "satanic" empire. The first poem focuses on the consequences of the empire for Northern England and the second poem focuses on its consequences for one of the islands in the British archipelago. The vision of Victoria as Satan in "Thomas Campey and the Copernican System" casts the shadow of her empire over "the potato famine Irish" in "Ginger's Friday."

"The Pocket Wars of Peanuts Joe" and "Allotments" are the poems that follow "Ginger's Friday" and they are both very funny verses that depict the ways WWII and its genocides permeate the sexual imagination of Loiners. Like "Ginger's Friday," "The Pocket Wars of Peanuts Joe" and "Allotments" depict the general atmosphere of sexual repression in respectable working-class Leeds in the post-war period, and recall adolescent sexuality and religious taboos like "The vicar's bogey against wankers' doom."[67] All three poems also have rhymes that require pronunciation in the Leeds vernacular to be full rhymes, such as "doom" / "Home" in the first stanza of "The Pocket Wars of Peanuts Joe," or "epitaph" / "laugh" in the first stanza of "Allotments,"[68] early instances of the regional character of some of Harrison's rhymes. In "Allotments" the young narrator's sexual forays in former *Dig for Victory* plots are interrupted by a half-crazed Pole, who likens the "*murder*" at the nearby abattoir to what he witnessed at Auschwitz and Buchenwald. A deep association forms in the boy's imagination between the systematic killing of animals and humans, and of both these with sex: "and I cried / For the family still pent up in my balls, / For my corned beef sandwich, and for genocide."[69] The dialectic between Eros and Thanatos, and between the capacity for personal joy and the apprehension of historical horror will become familiar in Harrison's oeuvre.

The punning title of "The Pocket Wars of Peanuts Joe" refers to a harmless social misfit the local children dubbed "Peanuts Joe" because he is "peanuts" or crazy, and because of his indiscreet masturbation, and introduces the poem's association of masculinity with militarism. The first line of the poem tells us that the children call Jo "pea-nuts" as a code for the forbidden word "penis": "The -*nuts* bit really -*nis*." Lonely Jo masturbates while illicitly watching lovers, but his big mistake is to publicly salute "VD Day" celebrations with "the cock / That could gush Hiroshimas...." In Joe's mind his penis and semen are military hardware, and before his suicide he thoughtfully "Bequeathed his gonads to the Pentagon." The poem uses Jo's inadvertently theatrical sexual display to caricature the pervasive cultural inscription of militarism on the phallus.

The last of the five poems in Part One of the original edition of *Loiners* is "A Proper Caution," a title which idiomatically signifies "a bit of a lad" who is mildly badly behaved, while the poem draws its allusions from the famous Yorkshire and crypto-republican poet Andrew Marvell. This one stanza verse has a cartoon-like quality but lends dignity to the common man and to Harrison's Loiner, a "fat man."[70] "Red-conked and ludicrous, but still a man," he throws proper caution to the wind and runs along the English seashore with his lover. This Loiner responds to his mortality with *carpe diem* "seize the day" argument, and takes his lover with him. The poem alludes to Andrew Marvell's "To His Coy Mistress," where Marvell's narrator is urging his mistress to hasten to amorous sport. In the last line of "A Proper Caution" Harrison's Loiner, like Marvell's lover, urges active lovemaking. Marvell's lovers cannot make the sun stand still, "yet we will make him run."[71] The Loiner cannot stop death but does run after life. He "Shouts" "To death and darkness: *Stop!* to prove they ran."[72] A rhyme on "man" / "ran" emphasizes the urgent pursuit of private pleasures in response to the speed of "Time's winged chariot" and the nearness of death.[73] In Harrison's later poem "Deathwatch Danceathon" Marvell's seduction argument in "To His Coy Mistress" is summarized as "we're soon dead, / my sweetest darling, come to bed!"[74]

Harrison recognizes Marvell as a fellow Yorkshire poet and has observed the dark Yorkshire humor of "To His Coy Mistress," which is reportedly one of his favorite poems to recite at dinner parties.[75] Marvell alludes to his Yorkshire origins in the poem, whose speaker resides in Hull: "I by the tide / Of Humber would complain."[76] Marvell is also a significant model for Harrison's wider aesthetic of "using the forms of a genre to resist or subvert its traditional content."[77] "A Proper Caution" alludes to Marvell's poem as an amatory lyric and not as a political allegory, but it contains republican references which might recall the wit of "To His Coy Mistress," which "consists partly in transferring a recognizable political discourse to the erotic sphere."[78]

"A Proper Caution" is a cautionary republican tale about the absurdity of monarchies and how all men stand equal before larger forces and before each other. The Loiner by the sea-side on "his deck chair" is implicitly likened to "King Canute," the Danish King of England (994–1035) who had a seat placed by the sea and commanded the waves "not to flow over my land, nor presume to wet the feet and robe of your lord."[79] Canute's purpose, however, was to "Let all men know how empty and worthless is the power of kings," and he symbolically surrendered his crown to God.[80] The Loiner like Canute tries to command larger forces by shouting "To death" to "*Stop!*," but finally accepts "the ebbing sea." The allusion to Canute reflects Harrison's hostility to English monarchy and rejection of its original divine right justification, and he later exclaims "Good riddance, Divine Right!" in the anticipatory "A Celebratory Ode on the Abdication of King Charles III."[81] In the "Ode" Canute again appears as a king who saw "the tides of change" "lapping at his well-licked boot," while "later kings chose to ignore / the breakers crashing on the shore."[82] "A Proper Caution" uses poetic conceits to deliver a republican caution to kings who refuse to surrender their crowns.

Part One of *Loiners* introduces the republican character of Harrison's politics and poetry, and this is more fully developed in the poems examined in the next chapter. His preoccupation with WWII and historical atrocities against the Jews and Japanese, and in a nineteenth-century context against the Irish, are also reflected in these poems. Part One recreates the Leeds of Harrison's childhood but it is, like all the poems in *Loiners*, preoccupied with the penetration of the most intimate spaces of the human psyche by history. Harrison's vision of the history and legacy of the British Empire within the United Kingdom is particularly important to the first two poems of Part One of *Loiners*, and continues in Parts Four and Five, and in *The School of Eloquence*. Throughout *Loiners* there are also recurring allusions to revolutionary thought and action.[83] Firstly, the reference in "Thomas Campey and the Copernican System" to Copernicus' disproving of the Ptolemaic account of an earth and man-centred universe in *De Revolutionbus*, the book that began the scientific challenge to Papal authority, and also to the revolutionary republicanism of Milton. *Loiners* explores the dialectical interplay between class and colonial experiences and in Part Two, where its interest in Empire shifts to West Africa, it looks to the example of anti-colonial literary and political movements. The importance of Harrison's life in Africa in the 1960s for his anti-colonial poetic, particularly for poems from Part Two of *Loiners* and from *The School of Eloquence*, will now be considered.

NOTES

1. Letter to Alan Ross (5 April 1968).
2. Letter to Alan Ross (7 March 1972).
3. David Tipton, *Twentieth Century*, copy in *THP*, uncatalogued and unnumbered.
4. Derek Mahon in the *Dublin Fortnightly*, quoted in Letter to Alan Ross (8 September 1970). See also Peter Porter, "In the Bosom of Family," *London Magazine*, new series, vol. 10, no. 5 (1970), 72–8, 74–6.
5. Letter to Alan Ross (5 April 1968).
6. Letter to Alan Ross (7 March 1972).
7. Letter to Alan Ross (undated postcard).
8. "Interview with Bragg."
9. Charles Baudelaire, "Benediction," *Flowers of Evil*, trans. James McGowan (Oxford: Oxford University Press, 1993 [1857]), 11. See also "Interview," 232.
10. "Bringing Up," *CP*, 178.
11. *Them & [uz]: A Portrait*, BBC
12. *THP*, uncatalogued and unnumbered.
13. *THP*, uncatalogued and unnumbered.
14. Letter to Alan Ross (28 January 1967).
15. Romana Huk, "Tony Harrison, *The Loiners*, and the 'Leeds Renaissance'," in *Bloodaxe 1*, 75–83, 80. See also Alan Young, "Weeds and White Roses: The Poetry of Tony Harrison," in *Bloodaxe 1*, 167–173, 169.
16. *THP*, uncatalogued and unnumbered.
17. "Conversation," 39.
18. Letter to Alan Ross (30 December 1969).
19. Letter to Alan Ross (30 December 1969).
20. "Conversation," 40.
21. "Conversation," 40.
22. "Conversation," 40.
23. "Inkwell," 34.
24. *THP*, uncatalogued and unnumbered.
25. *Loiners*, 7.
26. *v.*, *CP*, 279.
27. *CP*, 276.
28. *CP*, 264.

29. Cornelius Tacitus, *Agricola*, in *Agricola, Germania, Dialogus*, trans. William Peterson and Maurice Hutton, rev. ed. (Cambridge, Massachusetts: Harvard University Press, 1970 [1914]), 87.
30. "The Excursion," *Loiners*, 72.
31. *Loiners*, 71.
32. "Them & [uz], I," *CP*, 133; "The Rhubarbarians, I," *CP*, 123; and "Classics Society," *CP*, 130.
33. Letter to Alan Ross (1 February 1970).
34. "Interview," 233.
35. "Interview," 233. In the Acknowledgements in *Bloodaxe 1* its editor Neil Astley writes that the frontispiece drawing of Thomas Campey is from Tony Harrison's own bookplate.
36. *Harrison: Poets and People*, Channel 4.
37. "Currants, I, II," *CP*, 164–65.
38. Walter Benjamin, "Theses on the Philosophy of History," in *Illuminations*, ed. Hannah Arendt, trans. Harry Zohn (New York: Schocken, 1969), 253–64, 256.
39. "Turns," *CP*, 162.
40. "Hats and head-attire," portrait of Tony Harrison by Mark Gerson ©, National Portrait Gallery, London.
41. "Background Material," *CP*, 185.
42. *Harrison: Poets and People*, Channel 4.
43. *Loiners*, 12.
44. *Loiners*, 12.
45. "Ghosts: Some Words before Breakfast," *Loiners*, 91.
46. "Newcastle is Peru," *Loiners*, 81.
47. Tony Harrison, "Black and White and Red All Over: The Fiction of Empire," *London Magazine*, new series, vol. 12, no. 3 (August/September 1972), 90–103, 93.
48. "Fiction of Empire," 94.
49. *Permanently Bard*, 126.
50. *Loiners*, 12.
51. William Blake, "Preface" to *Milton*, *The Complete Poetry and Prose of William Blake*, ed. David V. Erdman, rev. ed. (Berkley: University of California Press, 1982 [1965]), l. 8, 95.
52. 'Working," *CP*, 135.
53. *Loiners*, 12.

54. John Milton, *Paradise Lost, The Poems of John Milton*, ed. John Carey and Alastair Fowler (Harlow: Longman, 1968), Book II, ll. 1– 6, 508–09. See now also Nicholson, "'Reciprocal recognitions'," 62.

55. *Loiners*, 12.

56. Milton, *Paradise Lost*, Book I, l. 548, 494.

57. *Loiners*, 12.

58. "Ginger's Friday," *Loiners*, 13.

59. Northern Arts Ms. Collection Vol. 6, "Tony Harrison," Literary and Philosophical Society, Newcastle-upon-Tyne. Also quoted in *TH Holocaust*, 52.

60. *v., CP*, 269.

61. *TH Holocaust*, 52.

62. James Joyce, "The Dead," in *Dubliners: an illustrated edition with annotations*, ed. John Wyse Jackson and Bernard McGinley (New York: St. Martin's Press, 1995), 181.

63. Joyce, *Dubliners*, 198.

64. James Joyce, *Ulysses*, ed. Hans Walter Gabler with Wolfhard Steppe and Claus Melchior (New York: Garland, 1984), 709–11.

65. A.J.P. Taylor, "Genocide," in *Essays in English History* (London: Hamilton, 1976), 73–79, 73.

66. *TH Holocaust*, 45–53.

67. "The Pocket Wars of Peanuts Joe," *Loiners*, 14.

68. "Allotments," *Loiners*, 16.

69. "Allotments," *Loiners*, 17.

70. "A Proper Caution," *Loiners*, 18.

71. Andrew Marvell, "To His Coy Mistress," *The Poems of Andrew Marvell*, ed. Nigel Smith (Pearson: Longman, 2003), ll. 45–6, 84.

72. *Loiners*, 18.

73. Marvell, "To His Coy Mistress," l. 22, 82.

74. "Deathwatch Danceathon," *CP*, 327.

75. Desmond Graham, "The Best Poet of 1961," in *TH: Loiner*, 29–41, 32. Harrison also chose to read "To His Coy Mistress" for "Poets on Screen," *Literature Online*.

76. Marvell, "To His Coy Mistress," ll. 6–7, 81.

77. Sandie Byrne, "On Not Being Milton, Marvell, or Gray," in *TH: Loiner*, 57–83, 64.

78. David Norbrook, *Writing the English Republic: Poetry, Rhetoric and Politics 1627 –1660* (Cambridge: Cambridge University Press, 1999), 285.

79. Lord Raglan, "Canute and the Waves," *Man*, vol. 60 (1960), 7.

80. Raglan, "Canute and the Waves," 7.
81. "A Celebratory Ode on the Abdication of King Charles III," *CP*, 321.
82. *CP*, 322.
83. See also Huk, "The 'Leeds Renaissance'," 81.

CHAPTER 3

LOINER IN AFRICA

Harrison's political character and poetry were deeply influenced by the years he lived in Nigeria and "explored" Africa, but the importance of this period for him is rarely noticed or discussed, even though he has drawn attention to its significance.[1] The African years are, indeed, absolutely crucial for understanding his political biography and poetry, particularly *Loiners* and *The School of Eloquence.* Drawing upon Harrison's letters from Nigeria for the first time in the scholarship, this chapter offers a biographical account of his life there from 1962–1966, working as an academic and writing many of the poems that became *Loiners.*[2] What he experienced in Nigeria is of vital relevance to the African poems in *Loiners*, and to his conception of British education as a form of "internal colonialism," which he develops in "the poems of education and history" in *The School of Eloquence.* In Nigeria Harrison was also imbibing *négritude*, an African literary movement that influences his humanist and republican politics, which encompass his anti-colonialism.

Observing Africans' responses to British literature and pedagogy at the University and reading the *négritude* writers expanded Harrison's understanding of education and poetry as spheres of political struggle, translating it from contexts of class to empire. Terry Eagleton has observed that Harrison shows "how in a class-divided society language is cultural warfare and every nuance a political valuation."[3] But the cultural aggression of *Loiners* and "the poems of education and history" are also concerned to subvert colonial hegemony. Culture, in the sense of art but particularly of lived customs, traditions, education, and language, are what "constitutes a particular people as distinctive. And since these are primary targets of colonial power, they are inevitably arenas of political conflict."[4] The *négritude* poet Aimé Césaire in particular is a significant influence for Harrison's interest in bringing the native voice into dialogue with the cosmopolitan. Harrison's approach is very much to speak in one's own voice but also to learn other languages.

The poems discussed in this chapter are about colonial history, litera-ture, and education, and are exemplars of Harrison's humanist and repub-lican poetic. "*Travesties*, I, II, II" from *Loiners* are included, for example. These poems are linked by genre—they are Harrison's translations—and by content—they reflect his immersion in the colonial confronta-tion and cultural interpenetration between Europe and Africa. Several of "the poems of education and history" from *The School of Eloquence* are discussed here because they show Harrison's understanding of the internal colonialism of British education, and the dialectical interplay of class and race in his writing. Harrison (in the interview in 1983 with John Haffenden) called "On Not Being Milton" his "poem to Africans,"[5] and its African contexts and intricate concern with *négritude* are discussed in this chapter. "On Not Being Milton" is Harrison's most important political sonnet and can "be read as a gloss on all his poetry,"[6] and its English republican poetic is discussed in the chapter about the political sonnets in *The School of Eloquence*. In this chapter I also attend to several of Harrison's prose pieces germane to his republican and anti-colonial politics and literary interests which help to elucidate the poetry.

I

Harrison's fascination with Africa began as a boy when the greengrocer gave him *Livingstone's Travels*,[7] and the adventures that begin with Africa and provide the map for *Loiners'* shifting locations were nurtured by the internationalized environment at Leeds University when he was a student there in the 1950s.[8] Harrison was writing his PhD in Classics when he accepted a lectureship at Ahmadu Bello University in Northern Nigeria and, arriving there in 1962, found an "absolutely feudal" society.[9] He describes the ceremony installing the Emir, Sir Ahmadu Bello, as the University's first Chancellor as a staging of feudal power, "with feudal retinue keeping back the crowd with long hide whips, striking from rearing Arab stallions."[10]

Nigeria declared independence from Britain in 1960 and the establishment of the University was part of a fraught process of modernization associated with the culture of the former colonial power. Aware that the British literature courses set by a board in England were culturally alien to Africans,[11] Harrison introduced African, Afro-Cuban, and Afro-American Literature courses.[12] He also began a study of the literature of colonialism, part of which appeared in "Black and White and Red All Over: The Fiction of Empire," published in *London Magazine*. In the literature review he presents the high cultural and popular literature of colonialism, from E.M. Forster's *Passage to India* to G.A. Henty's novels, as popularizing the imaginative allure of the British Empire.[13] Harrison's study of the literature of colonialism drew on early work by scholars like Benita Parry and anticipated the postcolonial scholarship which was established in the universities in the 1980s. He also distributed to his students an English translation of Jean-Paul Sartre's *Black Orpheus*, which had appeared in *Stand*, the Leeds-based magazine Harrison briefly edited and contributed to.[14] *Black Orpheus* was an influential interpretation of *négritude*, which Sartre defined "as being *against* Europe and colonization."[15] Harrison's disruption of colonial education also displays sympathy with the politics of anti-colonial Black writers.

Harrison and the Irish poet James Simmons also translated and adapted Aristophanes ancient Greek comedy *Lysistrata* into a modern Nigerian setting in *Aikin Mata* ["Women's Work"], directing and staging it there in 1965. *Lysistrata* is a sex-comedy which proposes that women stage unarmed resistance to war by refusing their soldier-husbands sex. The hierarchy in *Lysistrata* between the Attic Greek of the Athenians and the despised Doric Greek of the Spartans is translated into Standard and Pidgin English, and assigned respectively to the dominant Muslim Fulani and the Christian Igbo minority in Northern Nigeria. In the "Preface" Harrison describes directing *Aikin Mata* in such a way as to encourage camaraderie between students from different tribal backgrounds, and refers to "latent or blatant tribal rivalries,"[16] which had escalated into mass killings in 1962, 1964, and 1966. *Aikin Mata* brings *Lysistrata*'s "'indecent' but deeply pacifist plea" for peace to Nigeria,[17] translating its laughter into a prescient warning against the approaching Nigerian-Biafran War (1967–70).[18]

Christianity began as a colonial import in Nigeria and Harrison was unimpressed by the paternalism of Christian staff at the University "who dare to talk about 'liberalising Islam'."[19] He taught students who had sometimes come straight from missionary schools, and observed that their education alienated Africans from their communities:

> Christians have done great harm here. They drag people from the bush and a limited but in many ways very fine society, and educate them. The educated then despise their origins and wear Christian principle like old maids in England.... I hope the harm done them is not irrevocable.[20]

Harrison's sensitivity to "the harm done" to missionary-educated Africans is also suggestive of his realization that his own estrangement from his origins was produced by the internal colonialism of British education.

Harrison came to a stark understanding of his own education through his teaching experience in Nigeria:

My education had already opened my mind to other cultures through learning other languages. What Africa did for me was literally to put in perspective my own education: it's one of the reasons why *The School of Eloquence* begins with a poem to Africans. I found the drama of my own education dramatically posed in black and white: people coming from illiterate backgrounds and reading about Wordworth's daffodils because it was set in their exam papers, when they didn't know what a fucking daffodil was. There was an almost surrealistic perversity about 'O' level questions, which were set by a board in England for African students. That kind of dichotomy made me think about my own education and dramatise it, and find some of the polarities through that dramatisation. Harold Acton talked about external and internal colonialism, and I found in the history of colonial Africa a very broad, dramatic portrayal of some of the things that had happened to me.[21]

In Africa he refused to acculturate Africans in Britishness by teaching them poems about, for example, British daffodils. As a teacher in Nigeria and as a poet of working-class Leeds, Harrison focuses on the alienness of the high cultural English canon to the "natives." Wordsworth's "Daffodils" is alien both to the Nigerians and to his own working-class Leeds, where Wordsworth was the local man who built church organs and daffodils are not symbols in the poetry of high culture, but simply flowers which his father puts on the grave.[22]

The Nigerian experience of English cultural hegemony Harrison found replicated in the imposition of that same Southern English ruling-class culture on the Northern English working class. His identification with Africans in the context of education directly leads to his understanding of the colonial character of his education in England, a realization given poetic expression over a decade later in "the poems of education and history" in *The School of Eloquence*.

II

In *The School of Eloquence* education is part of an internal colonialism. Interestingly, a very fine poem in *Loiners* presents the universities in England as part of the ideological apparatuses of the State, but does not apply the lens of colonialism. "Durham," like "Newcastle is Peru" and "Ghosts: Some Words before Breakfast," is a long poem in which the narrator, implicitly "Tony Harrison," presents his vision of a Northern city, of his predicament, social and political ills, and the human condition, whose motif is his own circular journey. "Durham" was therefore placed between "Newcastle is Peru" and "Ghosts" in the *Selected Poems* and *Collected Poems*.[23] "Durham" is comprised of ten rhyming eight line stanzas, and the meter and diction create the effect that the poet is speaking to a mute listener, the lover directly addressed in the poem and also the reader. The poet looks out over the city from the tower of its famous Gothic Cathedral and imagines "all the enemies there've ever been / of Church and State, including me" being guillotined by the choppers of prison helicopters.[24] "The enemies" of "Church and State" include "me," Harrison, as an anti-clerical poet interested in fundamental political transformations to the society he surveys from the church tower.

In "Durham" the University is linked to a grimly imagined nexus of power in the last line: "University, Cathedral, Gaol."[25] Harrison held a joint Fellowship at Durham and Newcastle Universities in 1968 and the poem reflects political disaffection with the Universities. "Durham" may also reflect Harrison's reading of *The Origin of the Family, Private Property and the State*, in which Frederic Engels argues that in a society of "irreconcilable anatagonisms" and conflicting class interests "it became necessary to have a power, seemingly standing above society, that would alleviate the conflict and keep it within the bounds of 'order'," and that power was the State.[26] Irreconcilable antagonisms are signaled in the poem by repeated references to "the enemies" of the "State," to communists, liberals, prisoners, rapists, thieves, escapees, and the lovers. The "Quiet" repressiveness of the Northern town and of England, where

"Threat / smokes off our lives like steam,"[27] is reflected in Durham's topography. The institutions and servants of the state are standing above society imposing order on it. The judges move "from courtrooms to the Castle,"[28] and in the poem the Castle is a towering architectural symbol of the *status quo*, to which the institutions of law and order are linked in "Durham." Harrison, as a University Fellow, is at one level a metonym for the University and he is also "standing above society," from his position in the Cathedral that also towers over the city. In "Durham" the University, the Church, and institutions of law and order are implicitly presented in Marxist terms as arms of the State whose persuasive and coercive function is to legitimize and enforce England's *status quo*.

Harrison is the hunchback of Durham. The solitary poet in the bell tower has "Quasimodo's bird's eye-view." He then addresses the lover: "I feel like the hunch- / back taking you for lunch." The literary allusion is of course to the hunchback Quasimodo in Victor Hugo's *Notre-Dame de Paris* (1831), a novel set in fifteenth-century Paris. Breaking "hunchback" across the line enables the rhyme on "hunch"/"lunch" and evokes the "enormous hump" on Quasimodo's back.[29] Hugo is attractive to Harrison as an anti-clerical writer and a republican writer.[30] In "Durham" he speaks through Hugo and *Notre-Dame de Paris* to express strong anti-clerical and republican sentiments. The poem also echoes Hugo's rejection of the cruelties and injustices perpetrated by institutions of law and order.

There are a number of explicit references and implicit allusions in the poem to *Notre-Dame de Paris*. A "bird's eye-view" of Durham from a tower of its Gothic Cathedral refers for example to part II of Book Three of Hugo's novel, "A Bird's Eye View of Paris," a reference to the view from the top of the towers of the Notre-Dame Cathedral.[31] In "Durham" the presentation of key features of the city's landscape, the "University, Cathedral, Gaol," mirrors the "three townships of City, University, and Town" in *Notre-Dame de Paris*.[32] The Cathedral and the city are central presences in both works and this is signalled by their titles. "Durham" also reflects Harrison's interest in Hugo's aesthetic and philosophical ideas about the history and role of architecture and its relationship to printing, subjects most expansively addressed in part II of Book V of *Notre-Dame de Paris*. For example, the poet in "Durham" likens himself, and the lover, to "medieval masons,"[33] an allusion to Hugo's idea that before the fifteenth century stones served as letters and that in the Middle Ages anyone born a poet became an architect.[34]

If Harrison is the reclusive and unlikely hero Quasimodo then the unnamed lover is the gypsy dancer La Esmeralda, Hugo's heroine. Unlike Quasimodo, the poet's passion is requited, but "Durham" extends the analogy with Quasimodo and Esmeralda by suggesting that the lovers are in the Church. It is "God's irritating carillon" that "brings you to me," and it is in the Church that the lover's make a shrine to their "liberty." They listen to the "church- / high" helicopters. The poem implicitly imagines that, like Quasimodo, Harrison tries to give "Esmeralda" refuge from the judicial authorities by keeping her in the church, whose sanctuary is threatened in the novel:

> All afternoon two church-
>
> high prison helicopters search
>
> for escapees down by the Wear
>
> and seem as though they're coming here.
>
> Listen! Their choppers guillotine
>
> all the enemies there've ever been
>
> of Church and State, including me
>
> for taking this small liberty.[35]

"Durham" presents sexual liberty as a refusal of the moral authority of the church, but the atheistic and libertine poet also appropriates the religious register of "beatitude" to describe the secular blessing of sexual love as a refuge from "the public mess."

The private realm is, however, overshadowed by historical forces and intimacy contaminated by ideologies in "Durham," as it is in other *Loiners* poems. Fascism and militarism are figured as sexual predators breathing "down small countries' necks." The lover complains that problems of "Power" "shouldn't interfere with sex," to which the poet replies "They *are* sex, love, we must include / all these in love's beatitude." The poem predominantly evokes the helplessness of individuals at the mercy of historical circumstances and the State, recalling Quasimodo's ultimate inability to save Esmeralda from execution in Hugo's novel. The rhyme on "include" / "beatitude" suggests Harrison's belief in a politics of inclusiveness, perhaps in which dignity and compassion are extended to all citizens, even the wretched poor like Hugo's Esmeralda and Quasimodo.

Harrison's atheism and belief in the French republican principle that "men are born and remain free and equal" is suggested by his refusal to "genuflect" before priests, judges, "bigwigs and their retinue."[36] He is one of those who "stay standing." The poem's allusion to "liberty" also recalls the ideals of the 1789 Revolution enshrined in the *Declaration of the Rights of Man and the Citizen*. The significance of French republican history for "Durham" is also signaled by its allusions to Hugo's work. In *Notre-Dame de Paris* the King is portrayed as greedy and cruel, and the method of execution for prisoners like Esmeralda is hanging. But in "Durham" the imagined execution method for enemies of the state is the guillotine, a reference to the guillotining of thousands of citizens during Robespierre's Reign of Terror. The Republican Revolution of 1789 and the July Revolution of 1830, which installed a constitutional monarchy, are alluded to in *Notre-Dame de Paris*, and the 1789 Revolution is also the backdrop to Hugo's *Les Misérables*. The historical memory of the Terror imposed by the Committee of Public Safety is part of why Harrison adds a libertine and anarchist inflection to his republicanism in "Durham."

"Liberty" is rhymed with "me," suggesting the anarchist emphasis on individual agency in opposition to representative governing bodies and institutions of authority like the Church, the Courts, and the University.

The first word of "Durham" is "ANARCHY" reproduced in the capitals used by the graffitists who have written it on "crumbling stone," and the poem contains two other references to anarchy. The significance of anarchy in "Durham" is ambiguous and might include a threat to the *status quo*. As Carol Rutter observes, anarchy stands opposite the institutions of social order in the poem, like the Gaol, Courts, and Church.[37] However, "ANARCHY" is written alongside "GROW YOUR OWN," suggesting that the "student smokers getting high" are probably the graffitists. The students' irreverent attitude towards authority, which recalls the students in Hugo's novel, and their claimed anarchism are implicitly youthful posturing. The absence of hope in the poem's grim vision of England is partly caused precisely by the absence of any challenge to "the power-driven mill" of the State, which would attempt to crush any serious opposition.[38] The underlying contrast between Durham's stoned students and the direct political action of students in Paris in 1968 is signaled by the anarchy and graffiti, which were prominent elements in May, 1968, whose events were unfolding in Paris while Harrison was at Durham University. In "Durham" the citizenry is comprised of the students, church choirs, tourists, and impotent prisoners who "circle and circle at their exercise," and whose incarceration is also a metaphor for the invisible hegemony controlling the free citizenry. The image of a dog chasing its tail in the second last line of the poem suggests that the citizens of Durham are creatures with no sense of the futility of their existence, and the misanthropic element of the poet's vision may be another reason he likens himself to Quasimodo.

"ANARCHY" painted on the wall in "Durham" importantly alludes to the Greek word 'ANAΓKH written on the wall in capital letters in *Notre-Dame de Paris* by the archdeacon Claude Frollo, and translated in the novel by the student Jehan as "fatality."[39] In the novel 'ANAΓKH signals that regimes, like human beings, are destined for a fatality and that all things must pass.[40] Hugo's view was that "one power was going to succeed another power" and that religion would pass away.[41] Like Hugo writing in the 1830s about fifteenth-century Paris, in "Durham" Harrison responds to Hugo with the benefit of historical hindsight. The presence of the atheist poet in the Church tower, and of tourists who come to admire the Cathedral seems to recall Hugo's view that in the future the architecturally magnificent Gothic Cathedrals will no longer belong to the priests but will be "invaded by the citizens."[42] However, in "Durham" the Church, the choirs, and the wider condition of the citizenry are among the signs that religion remains a powerful force, even though the Church no longer dominates society as it did in the Middle Ages.

In the last lines the poet is "glowering at Durham" as the train leaves the station:

> there, lighting up, is Durham, dog
>
> chasing its own cropped tail,
>
> University, Cathedral, Gaol.[43]

The "dog / chasing its own cropped tail" also alludes to part IV of Book Four of *Notre-Dame de Paris*, which is entitled "The Dog and his Master" and which explains Quasimodo's slavish devotion to archdeacon Frollo, who raised him: "In Quasimodo the archdeacon had the most submissive of slaves, the most docile of servants" because Quasimodo loves Frollo as much as he loves the Cathedral.[44] "Durham" alludes to Quasimodo's blind devotion to the archdeacon, who represents the Church, as an allegory for the psychological enslavement of religion. The poem suggests that the Church still casts its spell over the citizenry of Durham, just as fifteenth-century Parisians were blinded by the magic of priests. Hugo's view was that "Every civilization begins with theocracy and ends in democracy."[45] "The press will kill the church" because "human thought" will be "volatized by the printing press" and liberated from "its theological container."[46] In "Durham" religion has not been destroyed by printing and mass literacy, and education has not liberated human intelligence. Instead the poem implicitly aligns religion and education as hegemonic institutions which have impeded the liberation of the people in what Harrison suggests is the failure of meaningful democracy in contemporary English society. In the poet's vision the Church and the Universities have the free citizenry of "Quiet Durham" and of England ideologically entrapped as surely as the judges and the Gaols physically imprison the political enemies of the State.

The *Loiners* poem introduces a theme that is also central to *The School of Eloquence*. The *School* sonnet "Classics Society," for example, is an instructive poem for analysing Harrison's presentation of the colonial character of his classical education. The title "Classics Society" suggests that a classical education gives you access to an elite society, and its first line is a quotation from the preface to *The Grounde of Artes* by Robert Recorde:[47] "*The grace of Tullies eloquence doth excell / any Englishmans tongue...my barbarous stile....*"[48] Recorde expresses the historical view that Latin, the language of Marcus Tullius Cicero, was a superior language. The dedication to "Leeds Grammar School 1552–1952" signals the focus of the sonnet. The Grammar schools were founded in the sixteenth century to teach Latin in the belief that it was superior to the vernacular and because it was Britain's official language, the language of Church, law, government, and learning. The sonnet focuses on language teaching. It emphasizes the importance of the classical languages as a class marker, the tongue of the governing class's institutions. But the sonnet shows that it is the working-class Harrison who gets the As and puts the fact of class schism into Latin.

The sonnet is punning on translation. The working-class schoolboy Harrison is working "the hardest in his class at his translation" into the upper class. He is literally translating the Hansards, the official reports of the proceedings of Parliament written in what Harrison elsewhere calls Received Pronunciation or RP, "the educated pronunciation of the metropolis, of the court, of the pulpit, and of the bar,"[49] into the official language of the fallen Roman Empire, Latin: "We boys can take old Hansards and translate / the British Empire into SPQR." SPQR (*Senatus Populusque Romanus*, the Senate and People of Rome) is the Latin logo of the Roman Empire. "Classics Society" suggests that historically changing hierarchies of language reflect the rise and fall of empires, and also correspond to hierarchies of class, and shows that the idea of inferior languages applies within the English language itself. When Latin was the official language of England, English was denounced as "rude." Now Standard English and RP, the dialect and pronunciation generally used by the English ruling class, excludes the "vile" dialect of Harrison's family and class and wider colloquial language from public discourse.

Harrison's description at a poetry reading of the way his dialect was regarded as inferior at Leeds Grammar suggests that there is a general correlation between the dialect spoken and the political view expressed, and reflects his focus on language as the carrier of specifically political messages. Introducing "Classics Society" Harrison comments: "And there was I, speaking the wrong kind of English, and there was I, translating bits of Tory philosophy into Roman upper class Latin."[50] In the sonnet the schoolboy translates into Latin the conservative political theorist Edmund Burke lamenting "*a dreadful schism in the British nation,*" that is, he speaks against class division in Britain at the height of the French Revolution. The dialect of the ruling class is used to express views which protect the political and economic interests of that class and its empire. The sonnet's specific concern with the role of language in governance is also signaled by the references to Hansards and SPQR. Latin and Received Pronunciation are "the tongue our leaders use to cast their spell," but the sonnet exposes how linguistic hierarchies correspond to historical shifts in power, and justify the exclusion of languages or dialects in which the interests of subordinate classes or races are expressed. The preoccupation in "Classics Society" with the politics of language and the suppression of "native" working-class voices is very much representative of the *School* "poems of education and history." My second example from *The School of Eloquence* sonnets on this theme is "Them and [uz], I, II."

Harrison's native voice emerges from his assimilationist education and attacks that system, in "Them & [uz] I, II." The title signals the importance of the Northern vernacular and the worldview it carries for the sonnet and its politics. "[Uz]," the Northern pronoun of "inclusion, solidarity, and family feeling,"[51] signals that Harrison's politics extends the best values associated with Northern working-class families to their working-class communities. His politics of inclusion and solidarity also recalls other seeming influences such as the Marxian history of Raymond Williams. The title also refers to a Northern working-class conception of "Them," "a composite dramatic figure" of bourgeois authority and privilege.[52] The title uses an upper case "T" for "Them" and a lower case "u" for "[uz]," a typographical pun on upper and lower class. Square brackets are a phonetic convention and "[uz]" typographically suggests the insertion of the otherwise absent Northern vernacular into a high cultural sonnet. The phrase "them & uz" alludes to a chapter in Richard Hoggart's *The Uses of Literacy.* The sonnet's dedicatees are Harrison's fellow Leeds scholarship boys Professor Hoggart, and "Professor" Leon Cortez, a music hall comedian who "translated" Shakespeare into Cockney. Harrison identified the techniques of stand-up comedians like Cortez, whom he saw at the music halls as a child, as one of the two specifically cultural influences upon *The School of Eloquence,* the other influence being Milton's sonnets.[53] The dedication underlines the capacity of the working class to speak in learned and popular registers. The sonnet proceeds to give a virtuoso performance of the normally divided high and low registers of Them and uz.

"Them & [uz], II" launches a full frontal attack on the system represented by the schoolmaster, who really did call Harrison a "barbarian" because he did not speak RP:[54] "you barbarian, T.W.!".[55] The rejection of his "native" identity at Leeds Grammar is represented by the schoolmaster's replacing his name, the more working-class sounding

"Tony," with the pretentious "T.W.". Harrison continued to use "the initials I'd been harried as" as late as 1969,[56] in the second of two essays published from his PhD under the name T.W. Harrison, as was his earliest pamphlet of poems, *Earthworks* (1964), and *Aikin Mata* (1966). It is not until after living in Africa and the completion of *Loiners* that he reclaims "my *name* and own voice," and realizes he no longer has to choose between his education and his background.

"Them & [uz], II" names "dozing Daniel Jones" because Jones' *English Pronouncing Dictionary* (1917) established models for "received pronunciation" and "standard English" that were regarded as socially, intellectually, and aesthetically superior.[57] Because of his thick Leeds accent, the schoolboy is not allowed to read poetry. Harrison remembers, in comically forlorn tone, that "I played the Drunken Porter in *Macbeth*," a prose comic part in keeping with low social rank. He is not allowed to read other parts of the tragedy in blank verse because "Poetry's the speech of kings."[58] The sonnet shows that "[uz] can be loving as well as funny,"[59]capable of the dramatic as well as comic parts. Harrison's education gave him the cultural weaponry to intellectually master "dozing" Jones and the system he helped to establish. But the schoolboy does not yet know "All poetry (even Cockney Keats?) you see / 's been dubbed by [AS] into RP."[60] He learns that "Wordsworth's *matter / water* are full rhymes." The sonnet suggests elements of cultural piracy in British literature's canon formation. But the main point is that if "uz" keep their language then they can get pleasures out of high art that speakers of RP do not get. RP deprives the reader of the pleasures of rhyme.

By writing a canonical sonnet in "my *name* and own voice" Harrison discredits the exclusion of the "barbarians," those who traditionally are not meant to be the subjects of poetry and certainly not to be poets. "Them & [uz], II" dramatizes the cultural aggression of Harrison's politico-poetic project of occupying high cultural forms on behalf of uz, opening with a vernacular declaration of warfare: "So right, yer buggers, then! We'll occupy / your lousy leasehold Poetry." "Them & [uz], II" also implies an empowering identification between the Northern working class and other "barbaric" peoples, particularly the Africans he feels an affinity to. In the sonnet "barbarian" is also deployed in the Greek sense of one who is not a speaker of the master tongue but it also has the sense of "savage"—Harrison is seeing himself as a barbarian. He is on the side of the barbarians, the Africans, and Uz. The class his colonial education removed him from will benefit from his education through his poetry.

III

Harrison's recognition of the colonial character of his education and its ideological and affective impacts also importantly came through reading the *négritude* poet Aimé Césaire's account of his French education. He saw the essence of his experience in Césaire's:

> And I also remember in this poem Aimé Césaire, who was a poet from Martinique and went through a French colonial education system, became as French as possible, sat on a train with a black sailor and suddenly found himself feeling racial prejudice and said "what on earth has happened to me," what has my education done to me that I should feel this, and I felt something similar in the way my education and my commitment to poetry had uprooted me from my background, so I quote *Cahier d'un retour au pays natal*, Césaire's poem, in this one, "On Not Being Milton."[61]

In this interview from the BBC documentary *Them & [uz]: A Portrait of Tony Harrison* he points to the importance of Césaire and *négritude* for his major political sonnet "On Not Being Milton."

Harrison announces his *négritude*, "my *Cahier d'un retour au pays natal*, / my growing black enough to fit my boots," in "On Not Being Milton."[62] Césaire's *Cahier d'un retour au pays natal* [*Notebook of a return to the native land*] is a major poem of *négritude*, of anti-colonial empowerment through the development of a black aesthetic in which to express black experience and recover and reinvent black subjectivity, and it examines the deep psychological grip of the colonizer's culture upon the black subject.[63] The English contexts of "On Not Being Milton" are explained in the chapter on *The School of Eloquence* but here I am discussing its dedication and its relationship to *négritude* and this will explain why Harrison called "On Not Being Milton" his "poem to Africans."[64]

Harrison's identification with Césaire has an historical basis in some parallels between the embourgeoisement of the post-war British working-class academic elite and the acculturation of the African elite. The 1944 Butler Education Act placed bright working-class children like Harrison into the grammar school system, and "estranged them from their own families (and therefore from their own class) and disinherited them from their political and cultural traditions."[65] The political impact of the Butler Education Act was typically to direct the most able working-class children through the grammar school system and away from the Labor and socialist allegiances of their class, and recruit them to Toryism. Ken Worpole has compared this "pre-emptive attack on the possibility of a popular working-class socialist politics" in England to Herod of Judea's Massacre of the Innocents to protect his throne from potential rivals.[66] In the poetry Harrison's tries to "make connections where I can," of a cultural kind, with his family and class.[67] However, his education does not seem to have disrupted his allegiance to the political traditions of his class and he remained "quite bolshie in my attitude to the school, always."[68]

In the *School of Eloquence* sonnet "Me Tarzan," first published in 1972, Harrison's education at Leeds Grammar is presented as a process of ideological colonization, which implicitly threatens to remove the next generation of the working class' intelligentsia and artists. In the sonnet the scholarship boy ruefully rejects an invitation to go "*laikin', then to t'fish oil*" with the neighborhood boys.[69] Putting his head through the skylight of his study to address the boys on the street below, he resembles the Roman orator Cicero addressing the people:

He shoves the frosted attic skylight, shouts:

Ah bloody can't ah've gorra Latin prose.

His bodiless head that's poking out's

like patriarchal Cissy-bleeding-ro's.[70]

The image in the final couplet of the Ciceronian decapitation of his head, or intellect, suggests his classical education ruptures his relationship with the "body" of his family and community. The young classicist still speaks the Leeds vernacular but he reads Latin. Eventually, "the tongue that once I used to know / but can't bone up on now" will be "mi mam's." Losing his mother tongue means losing his native culture. However, the schoolboy Harrison's intuitive political stance is unequivocal. He resolves to oppose Rome as an archetype of imperial power and declares that "he's against / all pale-face Caesars, *for* Geronimo," the last Native American to lead military resistance to colonization, and the sonnet valorizes resistance.

Rick Rylance comments that in "On Not Being Milton" and elsewhere Harrison "invites analogies between the post-war educational enfran-chisement of his generation of the working-class, and the history of colonial and post-colonial independence movements."[71] It needs to be stressed that in the poems Harrison's generation of the working-class were not educationally enfranchised. "All the boys" are barely literate in "Me Tarzan" and thought the studious Harrison a "Cissy." "Me Tarzan" mocks the grunting ape-man version of masculinity that Tarzan is a popular cultural icon of. But it also laments the cultural betrayal of working-class boys and men by dominant cultural scripts, which encour-aged them to reject education. The machismo, bare literacy, and terminal unemployment of young Northern men will be the subjects of *v.*, "Divi-sions I, II," and 'Passer.' To be accepted as a Northern working-class man Harrison would have had to reject meaningful literacy: "down with polysyllables."[72] He is forced to choose between his education and his tribe. In "Me Tarzan" education is for cissies and for the ruling class.

In "On Not Being Milton" Harrison's "mute" class still "stammers" and is "tongue-tied."

In the poetry's vision of post-war Britain, and historically, it is only the academic elite of the working class who receive a rigorous classical education. The educational enfranchisement Rylance refers to would be the introduction of free secondary education for all in the post-war period, but under the tripartite system introduced by the Butler Education Act, working-class children were mainly channeled into the non-academic "practical" tiers. The academic education that the brightest children received was, in Harrison's poems, a rote education in the classic canon and official culture that excluded other voices and experiences.[73] African enfranchisement from colonialism, with all the limitations and complexities emphasized in the poetry, was not paralleled by working-class educational enfranchisement. Instead, Harrison's point of identification with Césaire and the African academic elite is that their education also directs them away from communities of origin that are in need of their loyalties.

In the poems Harrison's embourgeoisement is also presented as a process of acculturation that is strongly resonant with Sartre's description of the European "white washing" of the African elite:

> The European élite undertook to manufacture a native élite. They picked out promising adolescents; they branded them, as with a red-hot iron, with the principles of western culture, they stuffed their mouths full of high-sounding phrases, grand glutinous words that stuck to the teeth. After a short stay in the mother country they were sent home, whitewashed.[74]

He has almost certainly read Sartre's account of the "whitening" of the African elite, from his "Preface" to Wretched of the Earth by the French-educated, Martinican revolutionary Frantz Fanon, whom Harrison has also read.[75] "Growing black enough to fit my boots" in "On Not Being Milton" suggests Harrison will now undo his education's "white washing" of his working-class identity, which he links in the poems to a "black" identity and experience.

Harrison's sense of being "black" and "white," of being between antagonistic classes and languages, is a point of identification with Césaire's liminalist poetry. *Cahier d'un retour au pays natal* dramatizes the conflict between Césaire's Negro and French cultural inheritances. "The quarrel with ourselves" in *The School of Eloquence* often emanates from conflicts between the proletarian and bourgeois dimensions of Harrison's complex identity. The title "On Not Being Milton," in which Harrison defines himself by what he is not, also registers Césaire's defining his *négritude* by what it is not in *Cahier d'un retour au pays natal*:

> my *négritude* is not a stone, its deafness hurled against the clamor of the day
>
> my *négritude* is not a leukoma of dead liquid over the earth's dead eye.[76]

Cahier d'un retour au pays natal is a prose poem, written in Césaire's "black French," which uses French Surrealism's liberation of unconscious forces to release the black subject buried beneath French rhetoric and constrained by accepted poetic forms.[77] Inspired by Césaire, Harrison bends traditional poetic forms to give a high cultural poetic voice to working-class Leeds.

Harrison adapts the master language to speak through and against it, as Césaire does in *Cahier d'un retour au pays natal* and as Sartre advocated in *Black Orpheus*. The imposing of the colonizer's culture takes a specific and intensified form in the education of the "native" elite, as with Harrison and Césaire, but is also part of a wider process of colonization. Harrison's politics of language enables him to adapt *négritude* to his predicament and to the wider circumstances of his class. He has said (in the interview in 1983 with Haffenden) that "the language of the powerful ruling class always kills off the language of the class beneath it."[78] Harrison was referring to the extinction of languages of colonized races, but uses the word "class" instead of "race", suggesting his sense of the intersections in predicaments of class and race. His translation of *négritude*, on display in "On Not Being Milton," reveals the continuities in his analysis of colonialism and class, a vital feature of *Loiners* and *The School of Eloquence*.

As part of its meditation upon Harrison's return from Africa to the North, "On Not Being Milton" declares his reclamation of his native roots, after the cultural exile produced by his education. "Growing black enough to fit my boots," with an end line rhyme on "boots" / "roots," suggests he is growing black enough for his black roots. The defiant term *négritude* is derived from the racist "*négre*'" or "nigger," as "a violent affirmation" in a world where to be black was to be ashamed, and was coined by Césaire in *Cahier d'un retour au pays natal*.[79] Harrison's *négritude* affirms his pride in being of the Northern working class, just as *négritude* was most simply an affirmation of pride in being black. *Négritude*'s cultural empowerment of Negroes inspires Harrison to give a powerful poetic voice to his people in his poetry.

The translation of *négritude* and the motif of "blackness" in "On Not Being Milton" and other poems invites the reader to see historical parallels between the experience of the Africans and the industrial enslavement of the Northern working class. "Black" is the skin color of Africans and the color of coal, mines, slagheaps, pollution, and other features of the industrial landscape. As Rutter observes:

> Harrison's struggle politicises art and articulacy in order to discover an aesthetic of language and poetry that can accommodate a voice that emerges out of the working class of Leeds, a city that turned its native sons black with the grime of post-Industrial Revolution urban pollution.[80]

In "All Out" (1971), a review of an anthology of socialist verse, Harrison likened coal-mine owning Abolitionist's treatment of miners with the enslavement of blackamoors.[81] He describes the mines as "the classic battlefield between capital and labour in the nineteenth century."[82] In

"On Not Being Milton" "the stutter of the scold out of the branks / of condescension" refers to the iron bridles used to silence "scolds," or outspoken women, but similarly recalls the bridles used on black slaves. The allusion to the Norse "skold" or poet suggests the stuttering Northern poet's struggle to speak for himself and on behalf of his silenced people in the tradition of *négritude.*

"On Not Being Milton" is dedicated to the poets Sergio Vieira and Armando Guebuza, who in 1971, the year "On Not Being Milton" was written, were leading members of the anti-colonial liberation army *Frelimo,* which became the Marxist governing party of Mozambique. The allusion to *Frelimo* and Césaire, who as a politician was directly involved in the political process of the decolonization of Martinique, shows Harrison's construction of a small canon of poets who were also directly engaged in political or military struggle against colonialism, while the republican revolutionary John Milton fought a different form of tyranny. The allusions to *Frelimo* and Césaire also register conflicting perspectives on *négritude,* an aspect of the ambivalence expressed in the sonnet, as is characteristic of Harrison's poetry. *Frelimo* rejected *négritude* as "nothing more than the theories of the ruling classes of neo-colonialism, hence of imperialism."[83] Poetry though was central to *Frelimo's* cultural struggle for national liberation, as it was for the *négritudinists.* Accomplished poets like Vieira and Guebuza "used poetry as a new way of pamphleteering."[84] Poetry was no longer used for individual expression but in the struggle for national liberation. Poetry and mass literacy campaigns were very important to *Frelimo's* struggle to redefine Mozambique's culture and accompanied their military struggle against the colonial power Portugal.

Harrison met *Frelimo* members in Dar-es-Salaam in 1971:

> I had all night conversations, discussions, with *Frelimo,* the liber-
> ation army of Mozambique, who were writing poetry and were
> guerrilla soldiers. They were fighting a war then, a war of liberation
> and they were there at the conference, and we had long, all night

discussions on poetry and revolution, poetry and politics, and they had no doubt about what poetry should do, it should serve their struggle, and when I came back to England I wrote the first poem of *The School of Eloquence* series, "On Not Being Milton'," which is dedicated to those two *Frelimo* members, one I think ended up becoming Minister of Culture and the other a Minister of Finance, but then they were poets in khaki battle dress.[85]

The dedication of "On Not Being Milton" to members of *Frelimo* salutes their absolute commitment to the "poetry of combat,"[86] to the role of poetry and of education in their war of liberation.

Meeting *Frelimo* may have also influenced Harrison's decision to find a way to place his poetry and education at the service of his class in *The School of Eloquence*, implicitly expressed in "On Not Being Milton." There was considerable conflict in *Frelimo's* ranks about whether those privileged with elite education could honorably pursue individual ambitions abroad, or should come back to support their struggling communities. The dedication of the sonnet may also signal respect for *Frelimo's* Marxist commitment that a new native class of exploiters would not enable multinationals to continue extracting Mozambique's wealth after independence.[87] Harrison's witness of such corruption in Nigeria is a subject of the African poems discussed in the next chapter.

"*Dichtung und Wahrheit*" ["Poetry and Truth"] was also written in 1971 and is dedicated to "*Frelimo's* fluent propagandist," Marcelino Dos Santos, who "speaks / the cloven tongues of four colonial powers" through translation, education and poetry.[88] The sonnet expresses the hope that educational tools like translation and propaganda will always outweigh reliance on Kalashnikovs, *Frelimo's* main weapon in its successful war of independence, which took a million lives.[89] The dedications of "On Not Being Milton" and "*Dichtung und Wahrheit*" to *Frelimo* members suggest the radicalism of Harrison's politics, his supporting armed guerrilla struggle against colonialism. He has also written many poems that reflect an anti-militarist stance, including the "Sonnets for August 1945," "A Cold Coming," and "The Krieg Anthology." "On Not Being Milton" and

"*Dichtung und Wahrheit*" particularly reflect Harrison's enthusiasm for the cultural struggles waged through translation, education, and poetry by Frelimo and the *négritude* literary movement.

In 1962 Harrison was reading through back copies of *Présence Africaine*, a highly influential French speaking journal of Negro culture and the main voice of the *négritude* movement, whose debates were particularly prominent amongst francophone intellectuals in the 1950s.[90] Harrison had great regard for *Présence Africaine*,[91] which published creative writing and political essays, and appears to be where he first read *Cahier d'un retour au pays natal*, where it was republished in 1956, 1960, and later in 1971. *Présence Africaine* was founded by leading black diaspora intellectuals including Césaire and Léopold Senghor and had eminent French writers on its editorial board including Sartre and André Gide, all writers of particular interest to Harrison.

Harrison read the *négritude* manifestos and was inspired by the efforts of African intellectuals "to de-westernise humanism and culture in order not to Africanize it but to *universalize* it":

> The African or negro intellectual has a sharp picture of the severe limitations of Europe. The great thing, as yet only aspiration...the plea of a persecuted race not for themselves but for ALL men.[92]

Senghor explained the historical purpose of *Présence Africaine* as to be the forum for Africa's "great dialogue, so long awaited, with the West": "*Présence Africaine*, that, by way of the black man, has never ceased to defend Man."[93] The commitment to defend the universal "Man" through the historical and cultural specificity of the black man is, as Harrison observes, characteristic of the humanist politics of *négritude*.[94]

The *négritude* debates about Marxism contribute to Harrison's "awakening solidarity with the oppressed of the Empire together, 'the internal and external proletariat'."[95] Césaire argued that "the problem of the proletariat and the colonial problem" are produced by the barbarism of European capitalism.[96] Harrison also found an examination of the continuities between class and colonial servitude in Senghor's "Nationhood and the African Road to Socialism."[97] He observes that Senghor also "probes the fallacy of the solidarity between the European proletariat and the African colonized."[98] An example of the fallacy Senghor points to, and a source of Harrison's unspecified reservations about *Black Orpheus*, may include Sartre's calls for Africans to transcend *négritude* and join the universal proletariat.[99] *Négritude*'s insistence on the dialectic between cultural specificity and universality,[100] the cosmopolitan dialogue between cultures, and its anti-colonial humanism are significant areas of its influence upon the political philosophy woven into Harrison's poetic.

IV

The discussion will now address other poems in *Loiners* that illustrate Harrison's ambivalent use of *négritude*, and that reflects his interest in African-Spanish poetry. I will also discuss a prose piece which elucidates his interest in African cultural movements. Harrison holds onto the empowering aspects of *négritude* in "On Not being Milton," but "*Postcard, XVIII*" suggests that some European appropriations of *négritude* involved a lascivious fascination with sexualized African bodies. "From *The Zeg-Zeg Postcards*" is a sequence of short poems whose fictional author is the White Queen, a homosexual poet, professor, and Negrophile in Africa. In "*Postcard, XVIII*" his reflections upon the metrical possibilities of an African pronunciation of "buttocks" stimulates a pornographic wordplay, and leads to a rhyme on "buttocks" (pronounced "loo" "cocks") and "BUTOX":

Buttocks. Buttocks.

You pronounce it as though

the syllables rhymed: *loo*; *cocks*.

I murmur over and over:

buttocks...buttocks...BUTOX,

marketable essence of beef —

négritude—dilute to taste![101]

The White Queen's wordplay leads to what resembles an advertising jingle, and the reduction of *négritude* to an exotic marketing gimmick for "BUTOX" or reduced soup, and the poem's perspective is redolent of Frantz Fanon's anger at the use of racist caricatures of Africans to sell commercial products. Huk observes in "*Postcard* XVIII" "a single, isolated cartoon in words which packages in a familiar, memorable image the product of imperialism: reduced humanity."[102] "*Postcard*, XVIII" registers the skepticism about *négritude* expressed by commentators like Fanon and the Igbo Chinua Achebe. The Yoruba Wole Soyinka, whom Harrison knew through their shared time at Leeds University, regarded *négritude* as an exaggerated rhetorical claim by francophone intellectuals often living outside Africa, and not part of the authentic revolutionary traditions of Africa.[103]

Harrison also questions whether an African-Spanish parallel to *négritude, negrista*,[104] has been reduced to an "Africa in the head" in "Shango the Shaky Fairy."[105] This short prose piece was written when Harrison went to Cuba, as part of a UNESCO Fellowship in poetry, and his "search for that Africa I came to know and love" shifted to Cuba's African heritage. "Shango" is the thunder god of the Yoruba, who were shipped in their thousands to the Catholic Spanish colony as slaves. He did not find the rich cultural legacy of the Yoruba slaves in *negrista*, a subcultural movement at its height between 1930 and 1940.[106] Instead, he observes that "like many similar movements" "its verses chime with rumba dancers."[107] Harrison does translate from the Spanish two *negrista* poems with themes of interest to him in "*Travesties*, II, III." "*Travesties*, I, II, II" are his translations of poetry in *Loiners* and the title humorously disparages them as "travesties," debased imitations of serious literature.[108]

"Travesties" also refers in the etymological sense to dressing in the attire of the opposite sex or cross-dressing.[109] "*Travesties*, II, III" are homosexual variations of Afro-Spanish heterosexual poems, while "*Travesties*, I" is a translation of a Latin epic. "*Travesties*, II," "*The Ancestor*," is after "*Balada de los dos Abuelos*" ["Ballad of the Two Grandfathers"], a poem by "a Yoruba from Cuba," the mulatto Nicolás Guillén.[110] In his poem Guillén "calls together his white Spanish ancestor and his black slave ancestor and presents them in a synthesis of anguish and celebration."[111] In Harrison's "*Ancestor*" a Negro watches his white lover dancing and similarly discerns their shared ancestry.[112] "*Travesties*, III," "*Rumba*," is after the poem "*Rumba*" by the Cuban poet Emilio Ballagas.[113] Harrison changes Ballagas' dancing Negress to a black man whose navel is the still point in the hurricane of his dance and an eye "utterly transfixed, devoted utterly, / trained on Shango in his shrine."[114] "*Rumba*" drew Harrison's attention because references to Shango are rare in *negrista* poetry.

Harrison names himself "a son of Shango," and imagines Shango travelling in the slave ships with the captured Yoruba and invokes the thunder god's powers to avenge the wronged. It is "questions of punishment and love" that Harrison is "worried to the point of madness by."[115] Like the thunder god, the poet has "double axes to grind" on behalf of "the dead, the living, and the yet to be."[116]

"*Travesties*, I," "*Distant Ophir*," is a prophesy of retribution for the terrible destructions wrought by colonial conquests. The *terza rima* invokes the powers of Apollo, the Greek and Roman god of poetry and prophesy, to avenge Africa, Cuba, and Peru for the sufferings brought to their shores by "Westerners."[117] "*Travesties*, I" is Harrison's translation of a section of Book III of the sixteenth-century Latin epic *Syphilis* by Hieronymus Fracastorius. The passage translated from *Syphilis* depicts the first days of Columbus and his crew in Ophyre (Haiti), and the Spaniard's massacre of the island's parrots, who in the epic are the sacred birds of Apollo. In *Syphilis* a "feather'd Prophet" escaped the massacre and "with humane voice (O dire portent)" foretells that civil war and obscene disease will befall the murderous Spaniards: "Nor end your sufferings here, a strange Disease, / And most obscene shall on your Bodies seize".[118] In "*Travesties*, I" the prophetic poetic voice is figured in "the dark bird," one of "the flocks of Apollo": "your crimes abroad brought home as civil war. / And also *Syphilis*: sores, foul sores...."[119] In "*Travesties*, I," but not in *Syphilis*, the conquerors "rape" of the New World is punished because they will contract and carry the syphilis infection back to Europe. As Colin Nicholson observes, Fracastorius rejects "the notion that syphilis was brought to Europe from the New World by Columbus," but Harrison does not.[120] In "*Travesties*, I" the metaphor of syphilis as retribution for conquest has its historical origins in the late fifteenth century when, according to some accounts, Columbus's crews did set off a syphilis pandemic in Europe upon their return from the Americas.[121]

   "*Travesties*, I" and *Syphilis* are part of the literary history of syphilis and the wider literature of disease. The metaphor of syphilis for imperialism which links the different parts of *Loiners* is established in "*Travesties*, I," which begins the third of five parts in "The White Queen" poem sequence and can be regarded as its literal and thematic centerpiece. Harrison's translation of *Syphilis* encompasses Fracastorius' focus on the Spanish in Ophyre but widens its address to "Westerners" in Africa, Cuba, and Peru:

> You'll only find the Old World in the New,
>
> and you'll rue your *discubrimiento*, rue
>
> it, rue Africa, rue Cuba, rue Peru![122]

Unlike Fracastorius, Harrison refers not to "Ophyre," Haiti, but to "Ophir," fine gold, whose meaning is derived from the fabled land of Ophir, from which King Solomon took gold in the Old Testament:[123] "This land, where you are now, is that Ophir / your flashy maps show off like jewellery."[124] The pun on "Ophir" symbolizes the plundering of gold in foreign lands since Old Testament times, and parallels the timelessness of myth with the historical repetition of conquest.

In *Syphilis* Harrison has chosen to translate a poem which, unlike other Latin accounts of Columbus' voyage to the New World, does not attack the Indians or their religion.[125] It is the island's birds who are massacred by the Spanish, not its peoples, and it is for the massacre of Apollo's birds that the Spaniards will be reduced to a "Wretched" state. The passage from Fracastorius might be regarded as a parable for the Spanish massacres of the Indians and hope for divine retribution. There are only two lines in *Syphilis* in which Spain's foreseen subjugation of Ophyre is definitely addressed: "The Natives of long liberty deprive, / Found cities and a new Religion give."[126] By contrast, "*Travesties*, I" is an explicit dramatization of the conquerors "porphyry and rape" and "destructions greater than the siege of Troy." It is for their "crimes" against "quiet peoples, until now quite free" that the Spanish will be visited with "dreadful sufferings."[127]

Like *Syphilis*, "*Travesties*, I" registers Catholic Spain's notion of Christian conquest.[128] However, in *Syphilis* the Spanish "give" their religion to the Indians whereas in "*Travesties*, I" the Spanish "impose" "new sacraments" on "the strangers" they destroy. Fracastorius' purpose in writing a poem about Columbus' voyage to the new world is "to provide an historical setting for the myth of the origin of syphilis."[129] "*Travesties*, I" creates a mythology of retribution for conquest. Harrison has spoken of "the relativity of translation," the way it can be "used as a prop to the *status quo*."[130] In "*Travesties*, I" translation is instead a tool of poetic reckoning, and Fracastorius' more innocent representation of Columbus' voyage becomes a powerful damnation of all imperial conquest.

The epigraph to "*Travesties*" is a quotation from "A Defence of Poetry" by the nineteenth-century English Romantic and republican poet Percy Bysshe Shelley expressing "the vanity of translation."[131] In a more recent poem, "Piazza Sannazaro" (2010), Harrison also disparages his translation of *Syphilis* after "almost half a century's gone by."[132] "Piazza Sannazaro," a major poem, is the first time Harrison has used the *terza rima* since "Travesties": "I gave *terza rima* my first feeble try / translating

Fracastorius' *Syphilis*." Taking the epigraph for "*Travesties*" from Shelley's "Defence" allows Harrison to speak through Shelley and to locate himself in the English republican literary lineage of Shelley and Milton. In the "Defence" Milton's refusal to write poetry worshipping "the triumph of kingly power over liberty" is praised.[133]

   "*Travesties*, I" implicitly echoes Shelley's affirmation of poets in earlier epochs as secular prophets and as the people's "unacknowledged legislators."[134] The mythology of retribution visited on the conquerors in "*Travesties*, I" also unites the sufferings of a broader humanity and recalls the revolutionary Shelley of "The Mask of Anarchy," written on the occasion of the Peterloo massacre at Manchester, 1819. Harrison invokes Shelley's clarion call for the English working class and other oppressed peoples to "Rise, like lions after slumber."[135] The "Defence" mediates Harrison's own alignment of poetry with republican "national struggle for civil and religious liberty,"[136] from Africa to Cuba to Peru to Northern England.

   Parallel republican visions of the Spanish Empire's rape of foreign lands, and the exploitation of the internal colony of Newcastle-upon-Tyne by the British Empire are mediated by literary allusions in "*Travesties*, I." Its subtitle, "*Distant Ophir*," is a quotation from the nautical poem "Cargoes" by the English poet-laureate John Masefield. The allusions to "Cargoes" mediates Harrison's vision of Newcastle in the age of industrial capitalism. In three five-line stanzas Masefield consecutively depicts three ships of three different empires carrying home foreign treasures, romanticizing the Roman's quinquireme "rowing home" with exotic goods "from distant Ophir," and a Spanish galleon carrying jewels from distant Isthmus home to the Spanish monarchy. However, the third stanza of "Cargoes," as Luke Spencer notes, counters the romance of imperial trade found in Masefield's poem.[137] It presents an unromantic vision of a "dirty British coaster" carrying "a cargo of Tyne coal, /Road-rails, pig-lead" away from Newcastle.[138] Masefield accepts the despoliation of "dirty" Newcastle as the price of industrialization. Harrison, however, conveys that the British state and capitalist class shipping out the black Ophir of the internal colony of Newcastle is also imperial plundering.

The phrase from "*Travesties*, I," "the Old World in the New," is reversed in the title of "New Worlds for Old" (1970), Harrison's review of new English translations of Latin American poetry.[139] The reversed phrase reflects the shared preoccupation in review and poem with continuities between old and new empires in Latin America and Africa. In "New Worlds for Old" Harrison clearly suggests multinationals are the new conquistadors, in the lineage of Francisco Pizarro, destroyer of Peru: "From Pizarro to United Fruit there has been the naming of parts, the signing of papers."[140] Pizarro is a key historical figure in the poetic rendering of the Spanish conquest in "The Conquistadors," from Pablo Neruda's *Canto General*, an epic about Latin America's history and people. Harrison embraces Neruda's cultural intervention against Capital as a politico-ethical expression of "brotherhood towards / men I do not know."[141]

Harrison has recently affirmed that where "the sufferer and the sympa-thizer are distinctly unrelated is the very essence of the idea of shared humanity and mortality."[142] This humanist fraternity is consistent with his identification with *négritude*, and is also signaled through an allusion to Joyce's *Ulysses*, one of Harrison's favorite works. Joyce's Irish Jew Leopold Bloom declares his political vision: "New worlds for old. Union of all, jew, moslem and gentile. Three acres and a cow for all children of nature."[143] Bloom is of a persecuted race but he prophesizes "the new Bloomusalem" and calls for a "universal brotherhood" in which all will prosper regardless of religion or race.[144] The Mob soon call for Bloom to be lynched and roasted,[145] but Harrison seconds his, and Joyce's, rejection of racial, sectarian, and national hatreds, and their love of the citizen for the city and for men. Harrison's anti-colonial humanism and cosmopolitan republicanism profoundly inform the political, historical, and literary dimensions of the poems which have been examined in this chapter. The next chapter offers a sequence of contextual readings of the African poems of Part Two of *Loiners*.

NOTES

1. "Interview," 236.
2. Letters to Jon Silkin (1962–64). See also "Tony Harrison: Work Chart," in *Bloodaxe 1*, 511.
3. Terry Eagleton, "Antagonisms: Tony Harrison's *v.*," in *Bloodaxe 1*, 348–350, 349.
4. Terry Eagleton, *Heathcliff and the Great Hunger: Studies in Irish Culture* (London: Verso, 1995), 241.
5. "Interview," 236.
6. *Permanently Bard*, 171.
7. "Introduction," 19.
8. Huk, "The 'Leeds Renaissance'," 81.
9. Letter to Silkin (28 February 1963).
10. Letter to Silkin (8 November 1964).
11. "Interview," 236.
12. Letter to Silkin (10 May 1964).
13. Tony Harrison, "Black and White and Red All Over: The Fiction of Empire', *London Magazine*, new series, vol. 12, no. 3 (August/September 1972), 90–103, 92.
14. Letter to Silkin (8 November 1964). Jean Paul Sartre, *Black Orpheus*, trans. Arthur Gillet, part one in *Stand*, vol. 5, no. 2, 1962; and part two in *Stand*, vol. 6, no. 1, 1962. Volume 5 also contains a short story by Harrison, "The Toothache."
15. Jean Paul Sartre, "Black Orpheus," trans. John MacCombie, *The Massachusetts Review*, vol. 6, no. 1 (1965), 13–52, 33–35.
16. "Preface," *Aikin Mata*', reprinted in *Bloodaxe 1*, 84–7, 86.
17. "Preface," *Aikin Mata*, 84.
18. For a discussion of *Aikin Mata* and its Nigerian themes see also Nicholson, "'Reciprocal Recognitions'," 64–6.
19. Letter to Silkin (4 December 1962).
20. Letter to Silkin (28th February 1963).
21. "Interview," 236. In response to my question whether Harrison could mean Harold Acton, in a personal communication (email, 14 June 2006) John Haffenden commented to me that Harrison was referring to Lord John Acton, who wrote on internal colonialism in the British Empire.
22. *v.*, *CP*, 264.

23. "Durham" was first published in the "Other Poems" section of *From "The School of Eloquence" and Other Poems* (1978) but moved to the *Loiners* section of the *Selected Poems* and *Collected Poems*.

24. "Durham," *CP*, 71.

25. *CP*, 72.

26. Friedrich Engels, *The Origin of the Family, Private Property and the State*, trans. E. Untermann (Chicago: C.H. Kerr, 1902), 157–158. Harrison elsewhere refers to "what Engels called the historical defeat of the female sex," i.e., to *The Origin of the Family, Private Property and the State*. See "Interview," 241.

27. *CP*, 71.

28. *CP*, 70.

29. Victor Hugo, *Notre-Dame de Paris*, trans. Alban Krailsheimer, Oxford World Classics, second ed. (Oxford and New York: Oxford University Press, 1999), 58.

30. Tony Harrison's *The Prince's Play* (1996) is a translation of Hugo's irreverent republican play *Le Roi s'amuse* [*The King's Fool*]. In conversation with Harrison at the National Theatre, in London on 11 April 2008, he also discussed his great interest in Hugo and his regard for Graham Robb's *Victor Hugo: A Biography* ((New York and London: W.W. Norton and Company, 1997).

31. Hugo, *Notre-Dame*, 128.

32. Hugo, *Notre-Dame*, 132.

33. *CP*, 71.

34. Hugo, *Notre-Dame*, 197.

35. *CP*, 71.

36. *CP*, 70. See also Article 1 of the *Declaration of the Rights of Man and Citizen* (1789); and *Declaration of the Rights of Man and Citizen, in The French Revolution and Human Rights: a Brief Documentary History*, ed. Lyn Hunt (Boston: Bedford Books, 1996), 77–9, 78.

37. *Permanently Bard*, 134.

38. *CP*, 71.

39. Hugo, *Notre-Dame*, 291.

40. Kathryn E. Wildgen, "Romance and Myth in *Notre–Dame de Paris*," *The French Review*, vol. 49, no.3 (1976), 319–27, 324.

41. Hugo, *Notre–Dame*, 189.

42. Hugo, *Notre–Dame*, 196.

43. *CP*, 72.

44. Hugo, *Notre-Dame*, 170.

45. Hugo, *Notre-Dame*, 195.
46. Hugo, *Notre-Dame*, 189 and 192.
47. Robert Recorde, "Preface," *The Grounde of Artes* (New York: Da Capo Press, 1969 [1542]). Noted in *Permanently Bard*, 143.
48. *CP*, 130.
49. Alexander J. Ellis, *On Early English Pronunciation*, vol. 1 (London: E.E.T.S., 1869–1936), 23. Quoted in A.C. Gimson, "The RP Accent," in *Language in the British Isles*, ed. Peter Trudgill (Cambridge: Cambridge University Press, 1984), 45–54, 45.
50. *Harrison: Poets and People*, Channel 4.
51. "Interview," 233; and "Them & [uz], II," *CP*, 134.
52. Hoggart, *The Uses of Literacy*, 62.
53. "Interview," 237.
54. "Tony Harrison in interview with John Tusa," BBC Radio 3 (March 2008).
55. "Them & [uz], I," *CP*, 133.
56. *CP*, 134.
57. Daniel Jones, *The Cambridge English Pronouncing Dictionary*, rev. Ed., ed. Peter Roach, James Hartman and Jane Setter (Cambridge: Cambridge University Press, 2006 [1917]).
58. *CP*, 133.
59. *CP*, 134.
60. *CP*, 133.
61. *Them & [uz]: A Portrait of Tony Harrison*, *Arena*, BBC TV (15 April 1985).
62. "On Not Being Milton," *CP*, 122.
63. Aimé Césaire, *Cahier d'un retour au pays natal* [*Notebook of A Return to the Native Land*], in *Aimé Césaire: The Collected Poetry*, trans. and with an Introduction by Clayton Eshleman and Annette Smith (Berkeley: University of California Press, 1983), 34–85. See also "Interview with Aimé Césaire," in Aimé Césaire, *Discourse on Colonialism*, trans. Joan Pinkham (New York: Monthly Review Press, 1972), 65–79.
64. "Interview," 236.
65. Ken Worpole, "Scholarship Boy: The Poetry of Tony Harrison," in *Bloodaxe 1*, 61–74, 61.
66. Worpole, "Scholarship Boy," 61.
67. "Lines to My Grandfathers, II," *CP*, 192.
68. *Them & [uz]: A Portrait*, BBC.
69. "Me Tarzan,"" *CP*, 126.
70. *CP*, 126.
71. Rick Rylance, "'On Not Being Milton'," in *Bloodaxe 1*, 114–128, 121.

72. "Me Tarzan," *CP*, 126.

73. David Kennedy, "Ideas of Community and Nation in the Poetry of the 'Middle Generation': Douglas Dunn, Tony Harrison, and Seamus Heaney" (Unpublished PhD thesis, University of Sheffield, 1999), 7–10.

74. Jean-Paul Sartre, "Preface," in Frantz Fanon, *The Wretched of the Earth*, trans. Constance Farrington (Harmondsworth: Penguin, 1965 [1961]), 7.

75. "All Out," review of *The Penguin Book of Socialist Verse*, London Magazine, new series, vol. 10, no. 12 (March 1971), 87–91, 90; and "Fiction of Empire," 90.

76. Césaire, *Notebook*, 67.

77. See also "Interview with Aimé Césaire," 78–79.

78. "Interview," 234.

79. "Interview with Aimé Césaire," 69.

80. *Permanently Bard*, 170.

81. "All Out," 87.

82. "All Out," 87.

83. Graca Machel, Minister for Education and Culture, Frelimo, quoted in Chris Searle, "The Mobilization of Words: Poetry and Resistance in Mozambique," in *Marxism and African Literature*, ed. Georg M. Gugelberge (Trenton: Africa World Press, 1985) 150–164, 159.

84. Searle, "The Mobilization of Words," 157.

85. *Them & [uz]: A Portrait*, BBC.

86. Searle, "The Mobilization of Words," 152.

87. Barry Munslow, *Mozambique: The Revolution and Its Origins* (London and New York: Longman, 1983), 133–134.

88. *"Dichtung und Wahrheit," CP*, 195.

89. Larry Kahaner, *AK-47: The Weapon That Changed the Face of the War* (New Jersey: John Wiley & Sons, 2007), 100.

90. Robert Fraser, *West African Poetry: A Critical History* (Cambridge: Cambridge University Press, 1986), 69

91. Letter to Silkin (28 February 1963).

92. Letter to Silkin (28 February 1963).

93. Léopold Senghor, quoted in Salah D. Hassan, "Inaugural Issues: The Cultural Politics of the Early *Présence Africaine*, 1947–55," *Research in African Literatures*, vol. 30, no. 2 (Summer 1999), 194–221, 195.

94. Abiola Irele, "*Négritude* or Black Cultural Nationalism," *Journal of Modern African Studies*, vol. 3, no. 3 (1965), 321–348.

95. "Fiction of Empire," 94.

96. Césaire, *Discourse on Colonialism*, 1.

97. "All Out," 88.

98. "All Out," 87–88.

99. Letter to Silkin (28 February 1963); and Sartre, *Black Orpheus*, 47.

100. See also Léopold Senghor, "What is '*Négritude*'?," in *The Idea of Race*, ed. Robert Bernasconi and Tommy Lee Lot (Cambridge: Hackett Publishing, 2000), 136–138.

101. "The White Queen 5: from *The Zeg-Zeg Postcards*, XVIII," *Loiners*, 43–44.

102. Huk, "The 'Leeds Renaissance'," 82.

103. Wole Soyinka, *Conversations With Wole Soyinka*, ed. Biodun Jeyifo (Jackson: University Press of Missouri, 2001), 10.

104. "Interview with Aimé Césaire," 27.

105. "Shango," 91.

106. "Interview with Aimé Césaire," 27.

107. "Shango," 90–91.

108. "travesty," *OED Online*, meaning *n.* 1.

109. "travesty," *OED Online*, meaning *n.* 2.

110. "Shango," 90. Nicolás Guillén (1902–1990) was regarded as the laureate of the Cuban Revolution and a significant "exponent of Black poetry in the Spanish-speaking world." See editorial note to "Shango," 90.

111. "Shango," 92.

112. "The White Queen 3: *Travesties*, II: *The Ancestor*," *Loiners*, 33.

113. "The White Queen 3: *Travesties*, III: *Rumba*," *Loiners*, 33–34.

114. *Loiners*, 34.

115. "Shango," 88.

116. "Shango," 103.

117. "The White Queen 3: *Travesties*, I," *Loiners*, 31.

118. *Syphilis: Or, A Poetical History of the French Disease*, written in Latin by Fracastorius, and now attempted in English by N.Tate (London: J. Tonson, 1686), 68. Harrison borrowed N.Tate's translation of *Syphilis* from the Robinson library at Newcastle University.

119. *Loiners*, 32.

120. Nicholson, "'Reciprocal Recognitions'," 69.

121. Woodrow Borah, "Introduction," in *Secret Judgements of God: Old World Disease in Colonial Spanish America*, ed. David Cook Noble and George W. Lovell (Norman: University of Oklahoma Press, 1992), 3–19, 11. See also David Cook Noble, "Sickness, Starvation, and Death in Early Hispaniola," *Journal of Interdisciplinary History*, vol. 32, no. 3 (Winter 2002), 349–386, 353.

122. *Loiners*, 32.

123. *The Book of Chronicles* II, 9: 10–22.

124. *Loiners*, 31.

125. Heinz Hofman, "*Adveniat tandem Typhis qui detegat orbes*: Columbus in Neo-Latin Epic Poetry," in *The Classical Tradition and the Americas*, ed. Wolfgang Haase, Meyer Reinhold, vol. 1, pt. 1 (Berlin and New York: W. de Gruyter, 1994), 420–656, 492.

126. Fracastorius, *Syphilis*, 68.

127. *Loiners*, 31–32.

128. José Rabasa, *Writing Violence on the Northern Frontier: the Historiography of Sixteenth-Century New Mexico and Florida and the Legacy of Conquest* (Durham: Duke University Press, 2000), 142.

129. Hofman, "*Adveniat tandem Typhis*," 426.

130. "Interview," 245.

131. Percy Bysshe Shelley, "A Defence of Poetry," in *Shelley's Prose, or The Trumpet of a Prophecy*, ed. with an Introduction and Notes by D.L. Clark (New York: New Amsterdam Books, 1988 [1955]), 275–297, 280.

132. "Piazza Sannazaro," *London Review of Books*, vol. 32, no. 20 (21 October 2010), 27.

133. Shelley, "A Defence," 285.

134. Shelley, "A Defence," 297.

135. Percy Bysshe Shelley, "The Mask of Anarchy," *Percy Bysshe Shelley: Selected Poetry and Prose*, ed. with and Introduction and Notes by K.N. Cameron (New York: Holt, Rinehart and Winston, 1951), l. 151, 40.

136. Shelley, "A Defence," 296–297.

137. *Poetry TH*, 30.

138. John Masefield, "Cargoes," *The Collected Poems of John Masefield* (London: William Heinemann, 1927 [1923]), l. 11 and ll. 13–14, 56.

139. "New Worlds for Old," review of four collections of Latin-American poetry, *London Magazine*, new series, vol. 10, no. 6 (September 1970), 81–85, 83.

140. "New Worlds for Old," 83.

141. "All Out," 89. The line is from Neruda's "To My Party" but in the translation of *Canto General* by Jack Schmitt the line is: "You have given me fraternity towards the / unknown man." Neruda, *Canto General*, 398.

142. "The Tears and the Trumpets," *Arion*, vol. 9, no. 2 (2001), 1–22, 18.

143. James Joyce, *Ulysses*, A critical and synoptic edition prepared by Hans Walter Gabler with Wolfhard Steppe and Claus Melchior (New York: Garland, 1984), 1061.

144. Joyce, *Ulysses*, 1049 and 1061.
145. Joyce, *Ulysses*, 1066–1067.

CHAPTER 4

AFRICAN POEMS OF
"SEX AND HISTORY"

The tour de force African poems of "sex and history,"[1] in Part Two of *Loiners*, "enact dramatically the confrontation of Europe and Africa" through the sexual lives of expatriate Loiners in West Africa.[2] These tragic-comic poems contain satirical exposés of European sexual exploits and explore "the interrelation of...exploitations, empire, cruelties, with the business of the loins."[3] The poems activate the colonial history and neocolonial predicaments of West Africa and understanding them requires an examination of their African contexts. But the dense allusive fields of the poems have hitherto been largely unremarked in the scholarship. This chapter presents contextual information necessary for understanding the political references in the poems and explains some of the "complicated social and historical reasons" which Harrison has said are important to his poetry, and which are most intricate in the major African poems.[4]

Harrison's witness of what he calls in a letter the "great mess" in Africa,[5] particularly Nigeria, is essential to understanding the African poems, including references to genocide, oil in the Niger Delta, and metaphorical signs of the looming Nigerian-Biafran War (1967–1970). Colonial cartography produced the conditions for conflict, amplifying ethnic, class, and regional tensions, when the British colonial administration divided Nigeria into three regions at Federation in 1954.[6] Each region was led by a governing party based on the major ethnic group: Hausa Fulani Muslims in the North, the Christian Igbo in the South, and the animist Yoruba in the West.[7] These highly referential poems also suggest that ethnic competition for the resources of capitalist modernity exacerbated traditional tribal divisions. Nigeria declared independence from Britain in 1960, and Harrison's observations in letters that foreign investors were scrambling for Nigeria's wealth in her first decade of independence elucidate political perspectives found in the poems.[8] Historic events such as military coups and pogroms, referred to in poems and letters,[9] and imminent war may have prompted Harrison's departure from Nigeria in 1966, and he did not pursue subsequent academic posts partly because of the wider chaos in Africa. [10]

The African poems use traditional versification, couplets, and iambics as the vehicle for scabrous, bawdy, and satiric content. Colloquial idioms and aggressive slang are combined with learned registers. The verses present a narrative of colonial excess and pathologies that unsparingly ridicules empire and its agents. While the subject matter is dark, the treatment is very funny. The poems exhibit an iconoclastic wit and ambitious range. The epigraph to Part Two of *Loiners* in the original edition is a quotation from the prose poem and meditative essay *Religio Medici* by Sir Thomas Browne: "*There is all Africa and her prodigies in us; we are that bold and adventurous piece of Nature.*"[11] Browne's Africa is a metaphor for the exotic and a hopeful, imaginative evocation of the potentialities of the self. But the verses that follow are preoccupied with the "infinite possibilities for crimes committed in the spirit of play" by colonial adventurers in Africa.[12]

The adventures on the "Dark Continent" begin with "The White Queen," a major poem sequence comprised of five sequences that each contain three or more poems or movements, only some of which are titled.

In the original publication of *Loiners* the first sequence in "The White Queen" is "*Satyrae,*" which has five movements; "*The Railroad Heroides*" has four movements; "*Travesties*" and "*Manica*" have three movements; and "from *The Zeg-Zeg Postcards*" has twenty-seven movements. The fictional, eponymous author of this complex sequence is the White Queen, a poet, translator, and professor from Yorkshire living in Africa and partly satirically identified with Harrison. "*Satyrae,* I," for example, is a dramatic monologue in the White Queen's voice, and the "*Postcards*" are short poems he pens and posts to an illiterate African lover. But in other poems the White Queen adopts different personas, such as an "*African Personality*" in "*Manica,*" or creates other characters, like the White Russian exile in "*Satyrae,* V." The other African poems in Part Two are "The Songs of the PWD Man, I, II," "The Death of the PWD Man, I, II," and "The Heart of Darkness." Conrad's famous novella and the Conradian theme of human "darkness" and tales of horror perpetrated in Africa are an important reference point for Harrison's African poems.

I

The title "The White Queen" refers to Queen Victoria, figurehead of the golden age of the British Empire. Harrison also refers to Victoria as "the great White Queen'" of Africa, India, and Northern England in a literature review from 1972.[13] The phrase is taken from Rudyard Kipling's "The Ballad of East and West," where an Indian native fighter conscripted into Victoria's service must "eat the White Queen's meat."[14] In Harrison's poems "ill-fed" African boys sexually service the White "Queen," a homosexual predator who holds "court / On expat pay, my courtiers all bought": "*One masta want / One boy—one boy for bed ....*"[15] In "*Postcard,* III" the words "expatriate" and "Cleopatra," the Egyptian Queen, form the contraction "Excleopatriates!"[16] In the satirical figure of the White Queen Harrison launches a scatological republican attack on the sexual crimes of the British Empire, and implicitly the privileges and hypocrisies of monarchy and the hereditary principle. These poems also reflect Harrison's republican contempt at the monarch-like pretensions of the colonial class and "inane" expatriate community (of which he was a highly disaffected member),[17] and how they were treated like white royalty in black Africa.

The title "*Satyrae*" alludes to the Roman satirist Juvenal's *Satyrae* and signals that some of these poems take up Juvenal's strident satiric stance, moral indignation, and use of demotic and obscene language in classical forms.[18] The White Queen's Dionysian enthusiasms might render him one of the celebrated satyr-like figures in Harrison's oeuvre, if he did not have a predilection for "frightened, black" boys.[19] In "*Satyrae*, I" the White Queen introduces himself as a "Professor! Poet! Provincial Dadaist!,"[20] a member of Europe's cultural elite. As the fictional author of these poems, his use of Sir Thomas Wyatt's "They flee from me" as a model of difference for the second last stanza of "*Satyrae*, I," and allusions to Dadaism, and T.S. Eliot and modernist poetics demonstrate his high cultural credentials.[21] His education allows him to analyse his actions but does not change his desires or decisions:

> Black. Black. What's the use? I can't escape
>
> Our foul conditioning that makes a rape
>
> Seem natural, if wrong, and love unclean
>
> Between some ill-fed blackboy and fat queen.

Colonial rape, particularly sodomy, is in the poems a trope and manifestation of the rapacity of Europe's impositions on Africa. When sodomizing African children the White Queen chooses *Vaseline Petroleum Jelly*, metonymically suggesting the oil industry's part in what Harrison described as "the pitiful lot of the general people" in oil-rich Nigeria.[22]

The poems reflect Harrison's observations, in letters, of foreign investors regarding African societies merely as economic markets: "And the 'great' powers pour in the money. Russians come, Americans, British,

Arabs from the U.A.R, Germans come, all wanting a pull of the string. And only a few seem to benefit from it all."[23] In the poems global Capital is stamping its brand names all over African urban landscapes: *Vaseline,*[24] *Shelltox,*[25] *Coca-Cola,*[26] *Dunlop,*[27] *Guinness,*[28] *Stars,*[29] *Black & White,*[30] *White Horse,*[31] *Peugeot,*[32] *Light Ale,*[33] Bitter,[34] *Somalgins,*[35] BUTOX,[36] *Phenobarbitone,*[37] *Dettol,*[38] *Od-o-ro-no,*[39] *Players,*[40] *Turkish Delight,*[41] *Volks,*[42] *Raleigh,*[43] VW,[44] and Chevie.[45] The recurring images of "a sharpened piece of Chevie"[46] and "flashy Chevie fins"[47] pun upon the colloquial term "capitalist shark" and suggest the emerging reign of multinationals as the basic units of neocolonialism and as powerful economic predators in fledgling republics.[48] The Chevie fins are taken from the chrome fenders of Chevrolet cars and "Honed up for knife blades or curled for muezzins / To megaphone the *Koran....*"[49] The fins are carried by Muslims calling others to prayers or to massacres.[50] In the poems a sharpened piece of Chevie being wielded by a Muslim as a make-shift machete, and "Dunlop sandals" worn to massacres, also suggests that competition for the commodities and wealth generated by capitalist modernity fuelled the ethnic-religious violence.[51]

"*Satyrae,* III" refers to the kleptocracy and two military coups in Nigeria in January and July 1966 and displays an oppressive military presence in civil society, with armoured trucks on the streets, curfews, patrols, shells, and shots.[52] A voice over a megaphone "promises corruption's dead and lies / Riddled with bullets in three mortuaries."[53] The killing of corruption and the bullet-riddled bodies refer to the motivations and methods of the coup conspirators. Harrison notes in letters the "cloak and dagger" character of Nigerian politics, and that the native elite were as willing to flagrantly rob the people as the old colonial masters, with "appropriated funds" and "Ministerial swindles as a matter of course."[54] The Igbo and later Biafran Chinua Achebe (whom Harrison was reading at this time) called the civil administration a "cesspool of corruption and misrule" that prompted the coups.[55] In "*Satyrae,* IV," which depicts an alcoholic English teacher, the White Queen observes that "*coups* / Can throw the whole white quarter on the booze."[56]

"*Satyrae*, III" also contrast the judicial murder of homosexuals in Northern Nigeria in the 1960s with their medical incarceration back in Britain when the White Queen, now "past fifty," was a younger man. A shaken White Queen hears the proclamation of the "*death!*" sentence for homosexuality in the Islamic North.[57] But in the last two last stanzas he remembers being one of the screaming "queers" who are "trussed" and "locked away" by "butch nurses" in London, suggesting standard "aversion therapies" like the administering of electric shocks. When the White Queen describes himself as "pathetic" because he is "pathic" he reflects the Western medical view that the "sexual invert" was morally and intellectually deformed.[58] In "*Satyrae*, I" he evades the Nigerian police raiding the gay bars and defiantly declares his homosexuality:

> I come back raddled to the campus bar
>
> And shout out how I laid a big, brute
>
> Negro in a tight, white cowboy suit.[59]

He admires the courage of this flamboyant black "queen" and prostitute who was "not scared,"[60] yet also regards the African as a "brute" to be laid or metaphorically slain by the white hunter.

"*Satyrae*, I, III" and entries in "from *The Zeg-Zeg* Postcards" are particularly preoccupied with what sexual liberty and violence mean in the context of colonial power relations. The persecuted homosexual and his prey are both allowed the moral concern due to victims. The White "Queen" is "Pathic, pathetic, half-blind and half-pissed / Most of these tours in Africa. A Corydon...' who will "sometimes cruise / For boys the blackness of a two–day bruise."[61] "*Satyrae*, I" and several of the "Post-cards" are fictional entries in the autobiographical genre of homosexual tourism, which is explicitly preoccupied with homoeroticism, sexual politics, and colonial exploitation.[62] These poems measure European homosexual liberation in Africa against the exploitation of the colonial other through *la lutte*, the struggle of opposite perspectives and needs conceived by André Gide.

The French man of letters and critic of colonialism was however, "*Satyrae*, I" suggests, an apologist for homosexual tourism in Africa. The White Queen is "a Corydon,"[63] an allusion to Virgil's pastoral in the second *Eclogue* but also to Gide's *Corydon*, an early defence of homosexuality in the aftermath of scandals in England, France, and Germany in the late nineteenth century which involved such writers as Rimbaud and Verlaine, and Oscar Wilde whom Gide knew. Wilde is described as a victim in *Corydon* and sympathetically portrayed in Gide's novel *The Immoralist* which, like the second part of *If it Die*, discusses European men's sexual encounters with Arab boys in the then French colony of Algeria.[64] Harrison invokes Gide's defence of homosexuality but contrapuntally suggests that the classical apologia for pederasty in *Corydon* is a sophisticated justification for the White Queen's "taste in little boys."[65]

Gide's *la lutte* is also significant for Harrison's wider sense of responsibility as an artist to give sincere rather than received accounts of the different voices in his work, but equally to be true to his historical criticisms of their viewpoints:

> It's a struggle and dialectic, what Gide called "*la lutte*." There are so many ironies in my work…because I keep all the responsibilities and wounds open: keeping them open is to refuse a compromise.[66]

The School of Eloquence sonnet "A Good Read" begins by naming Gide alongside Marx and Ibsen as formative intellectual influences for Harrison. It unfolds a Gidean dialogue in which the conflicted poet addresses his working-class father, conceding that "I've come round to your position on 'the Arts' / but put it down in poems, that's the bind."[67] *La lutte* is among the significant influences for the dialectic of irreconcilable tensions that informs Harrison's oeuvre.

Like the White Queen, the Public Works Department (PWD) man is a comic-tragic character in which Harrison satirizes an unofficial imperial history and tradition, "the sexual exploits of expatriate Englishmen doing things in Africa they wouldn't get an opportunity to do in a country where their own moral restraints were still in operation."[68] In "The Songs of the PWD Man, I, II" and "The Death of the PWD Man, I, II" Harrison brings some of the comic style and techniques of the Northern music hall stand-up comics into dramatic monologues. The unlikely speaker of the rhyming couplets is the PWD man, caught in a dialectic between Eros and Thanatos and "Laying roads and ladies up as far as Kano town":[69] "Out here I'm as sprightly as old George Formby's uke. / I think of Old Folk's England and, honest, I could puke." Peter Porter and Colin Nicholson have observed that the rhythms and style of these poems also derive from Kipling, and in turn from the music-hall songs and recitations Kipling made his own.[70] The crude, heterosexual, working-class PWD man is at one level an alter-ego for the highly cultured White Queen, and both seem to be self-parodied aspects of Harrison.

Godless, lecherous, hard drinking, and unwell old Loiners, the PWD man and the White Queen are also both "in their different ways haunted by the ghosts of imperialism, existentially and psychosomatically."[71] In "*The Foreign Body*" the White Queen's psycho-political pathologies manifest in nightmarish visions of imperial invasions mapped onto a human body that is swarming with parasites and riddled with disease, his veins likened to worms burrowing for blood.[72] The PWD man, like the White Queen, journeys from Leeds to Africa and circles back, and from London catches a train Northward bound. His medicated diseases include an anxiety whose accelerating intensity is likened to the hurtling rhythms of the train. The rhythmic repetition of the word "*anxious*" evokes the sound and movement of the train:

Anxious, anxious, anxious, anxious, perhaps the train'll crash.

Anxious, anxious, anxious, Doctor Adgie, there's a rash

The shape of bloody Britain and it's starting to spread.

My belly's like a blow-up globe all blotched with Empire red.

Chancres, chancres, Shetlands, spots, boils, Hebrides,

Atlasitis, Atlasitis, British Isles Disease![73]

"*Atlasitis*" can be construed as "an obsession with dominating the Atlas."[74] The PWD Man's "*British Isles Disease*" manifests in a "*rash / The shape of bloody Britain*," and this character too is a vehicle for Harrison's dramatization of "the Imperial Dream, a dream that turned into a sort of psychosomatic disorder."[75]

Harrison found a fictional prototype of the PWD Man in "Josephus Taedium Vitae," a character in *The Seductive Coast: Poems Lyrical and Seductive from Western Africa* (1909) by J.M. Stewart Young.[76] In a letter Harrison reproduces a few lines from *The Seductive Coast*:

Withal he has a wife at home: three black ones also here,

While two have earned him "black and tans," and a fourth may appear.[77]

Harrison's interest in Young's "Kiplingesque but subversively randy lyrics" is consistent with the bawdily humorous treatment of colonials "Shacking with natives" in the African poems.[78] He found Young's "beautiful book" in Manchester,[79] where Young was a low-paid clerk with social ambitions beyond his position, as well as a forger and "jailbird."[80] Young settled in Nigeria, where he became a wealthy businessman and established a partly fraudulent identity as a literary gentleman. His false claims of friendship with "Cousin Ruddy" Kipling enhanced his stature and in West Africa Young was labeled "the West African Kipling," though in Europe he has always been regarded as a minor poet.[81] Young is a nineteenth-century version of the PWD man in that he was a lower-class Englishman finding wealth, status, and sexual opportunities in

Africa. He was also regarded by other Europeans in Africa "as one of the many 'queer fellows' to find a home in the British Empire."[82] Young and "Josephus Taedium Vitae," like the PWD Man and the White Queen, are expat Englishmen escaping the limitations of class and the policing of sexual behavior in their home communities only, in the case of Harrison's Loiners, to abuse their relative anonymity and ambiguous liberty in Africa.

"Africa—London—Africa— / to get it away":[83] the White Queen's libidinous adventures in Africa, genocide, and the Nigerian-Biafran war are the main subjects of the twenty-seven short poems in the "from *The Zeg-Zeg Postcards*" sequence.[84] Zeg Zeg was the name historians and geographers of the Middle Ages gave to the region now known as Zaria, the state in Northern Nigeria where Harrison lived, and the title signals the knowledge of the region's history that is widely evident in *Loiners*. The White Queen, as the fictional author, wrote these poems about Africa on postcards of or from Europe, sending them to an uneducated African lover.[85] The mute Africans in these poems are only significant as the targets of the Englishman's unchecked carnal and aesthetic pleasures: "What begins in honest lust can end / with innocent blood on its hands."[86] With pornographic imagination, the White Queen depicts commodified black bodies, a black man in the shower becoming "cool *Coca-Cola*,"[87] or in fellatio "licked back bright" "*Turkish Delight*."[88] Some "*Postcards*" are simply bawdy puns upon "useful" Hausa words and phrases: "I'd like to / *sukuru* ["screw"] / you."[89]

In "*Postcard, XX*" erotic and political wit are married in a metaphorical appeal that requires knowledge of the map of Senegambia to be understood. In 1891 the British protectorate of Gambia became one of the few countries whose borders were almost entirely engulfed by another country.[90] The Donne-like conceit identifying sexual with colonial conquest refers to the cartographic image of a phallic Gambia inside the feminized Senegal:

Mon *égal!*

Let me be the Gambia

in your Senegal.[91]

The pornographic use of the map has a political point to make about European cartography and the invasive colonial enterprise. The address in French to "*Mon égal*" ["my equal"] ironically registers the French Revolution's republican ideals of *liberté, égalité, fraternité* in the context of colonial partition and slavery in the former Senegambia. Similarly, in "*The Railroad Heroides*," which is partially set in Senegambia, the principles of human liberty, equality, and fraternity are used to indict French colonialism and participation in the slave trade. Both poems very much reflect Harrison's anti-colonialist and republican stance.

In "*Postcard*, XV" genocide is an activity of ordinary people using improvised machetes against former neighbors and, for the White Queen, it is a disturbing recreational activity of the natives. He is distracted from his latest dose of "clap" by "terrifying cries" outside his secure residence:[92]

I stagger up and see

through mesh and acacia sharp metal flash,

my steward, still in white uniform and sash,

waving a sharpened piece of Chevie, ride

his old *Raleigh* to the genocide.[93]

The poem synthesizes African and European histories of genocide with a brilliant pun. *Raleigh* is the brand name of an English bicycle and also the name of the English poet and voyager Sir Walter Raleigh, who wrote an account of "The Discovery of the Large, Rich and Beautiful Empire of Guiana,"[94] and is one of the knight-errants at the start of Conrad's

Heart of Darkness. The contemporary historical moment of "*Postcard,*
XV" is 1966, after the Igbo-led military coup in January was followed by a
counter-coup in July, and the slaughter of Igbos living in enclaves in the
Islamic North. Achebe believed that the Igbo were also targeted because
of their achievements in education and business and that these were
"carefully planned" "mass killings which the Government—the Army, the
Police, the people who were there to protect life and property—brought
against the people they were supposed to protect."[95]

In the wake of retribution the mass exodus of the Igbo led to the
establishment of a new homeland in the East, the secessionist Republic
of Biafra. The history of the conflict and the genocide in Biafra are
of great but critically unrecognized importance for *Loiners.*[96] Some of
the poems were still being written as the Nigerian state's war against
Biafra was being waged (1967–1970), and *Loiners* was published the same
year the Republic collapsed. In "Newcastle is Peru" Harrison is back in
Newcastle-upon-Tyne and sees newspaper coverage of the "massacre"
and a photograph of "lobbed mortar bombs / smashing down Onitsha
homes."[97] Before being reproduced in *Loiners* "Newcastle is Peru" was
published as a pamphlet in 1968, the year the Igbo town of Onitsha, a key
battleground in the war, was captured by the Nigerian army.[98] In "The
Excursion" Harrison visits Hexham Cathedral in Northumberland, which
has temporarily marked the donations box with *Biafra,* the cause of the
day,[99] and he regards Biafra as another victim of "empire we can't get
away from."[100] The Christian Biafrans understood the war as a religious
struggle and identified with the Israelites, who flee enslavement and seek
a homeland in the *Book of Exodus.*[101] By 1970 a million Biafrans had died,
mainly because of the famine produced by the Nigerian military blockade.
The Christian narrative through which Biafra expressed its struggle to
the world is picked up by Harrison and he depicts the genocide through
age-old biblical mythologies in several of the African poems, including
"*Postcard,* XI" and "The Heart of Darkness."

"*Postcard*, XI" alludes to the frightening prophesies of war and famine in the *Book of Revelations* to apprehend the magnitude of what was unfolding in Biafra. The alcoholic speaker's "hell" is an empty *White Horse* whisky bottle, but the evocation of the biblical Apocalypse has an historical application in the poem:

> My *White Horse* plastic horses carousel
>
> whirls round an empty and my hell,
>
> when the last neat whisky passes my cracked lips,
>
> is a riderless Apocalypse.[102]

The speaker is literally referring to the "merry go round of the little plastic horses" on the seal of *White Horse*, which "he has balanced on the empty bottle."[103] The poem is also alluding to the white horse in the *Book of Revelations*. The "riderless Apocalypse" is an allusion to the biblical Apocalypse, another name for the *Book of Revelations*, which contains Saint John's vision of the Four Horsemen. The first horse is white and symbolizes conquest, the red horse symbolizes war, the black horse symbolizes famine, and the fourth is pale, ridden by Death, and followed by Hell:[104] "And I saw, and behold, a white horse, and hee that sate on him had a bowe, and a crowne was giuen vnto him, and hee went foorth conquering, and to conquere."[105] In "*Postcard*, XI" revelations are secular and whisky is the means by which a man becomes a seer. Harrison's *White Horse* of the Apocalypse is an omen of portent for the hell unleashed in the Christian Igbo's homeland. His familiarity with the *Book of Revelations*, and Christian Apocalypse mythology in social and political thinking, is explicit in the later poem "The Pomegranates of Patmos" (1989), where Saint John's doomsday visions are dispelled by a defiantly sensual and secular narrator.[106]

II

In "The Heart of Darkness" and "*The Elephant and the Kangaroo*" Harrison draws on the rhetoric and mythology of the *Book of Genesis* and adapts Conrad's *Heart of Darkness* as literary lenses through which to dramatize Biafra's tragedy. The home of the speaker in "The Heart of Darkness" is like an "aquarium" and a "glass-house,"[107] suggesting a protected environment like an expatriate compound. The situation in the poem seems modeled on Harrison's while he was teaching at Ahmadu Bello University in Samaru, Zaria, including the detail of "Tuareg guards" whose "swords" are eerie reminders of dangers in the society outside.[108] The wireless set provides the only source of news but a heavy storm has interfered with transmission:

> This means
>
> no news from England, no new war
>
> to heighten the familiar:
>
> Nigeria's Niger is not yet
>
> harnessed to our wireless set.[109]

The reference to "no new war" registers wars already underway like the Vietnam War, which many politicized Western writers focused on in this period. Harrison's concern is the war in "Nigeria's Niger," the oil-rich Nigerian region of the Niger Delta where Biafra was established.[110] The poem associates the Nigerian state's war against Biafra with Belgian atrocities in the Congo as presented by Conrad's *Heart of Darkness*.[111] What the Nigerians did in Biafra is presented to the reader as another "heart of darkness," a tale of horror in Africa.

"The Heart of Darkness" and "*The Elephant and the Kangaroo*" allude to the Deluge in the *Book of Genesis*, an archetype of mass-extermination, to speak of the terrible vengeance unleashed in Biafra. In "The Heart of Darkness" the rains are so heavy "it seems a whole sea must pour through / our all-glass house at Samaru," and nightfall is a metaphor for the "darkness" descending in "Nigeria's Niger." In '*The Elephant and the Kangaroo*', which refers to the bawdy bar-room song "We're off to see the Wild West show," an Englishman drinks brandy on his verandah and likens the heavy rains to "Noah's weather":

A clean green everywhere and it still pours.

This is Noah's weather. All will drown –

But I'll escape by crawling on all fours.[112]

"Noah's weather" made the earth "clean" by killing all who can't "escape."[113] These poems metaphorically suggest ethnic "cleansing" through allusions to the purification wrought by the great Flood. As Claude Rawson observes, the destruction of the cities of the Plain in the *Book of Genesis* has "a grim and quizzical relation to the mass-slaughters of human history...."[114] The line "But I'll escape by crawling on all fours" alludes to Marlow's witness, in Conrad's *Heart of Darkness*, of Kurtz "crawling on all-fours" back to the African encampment to escape being returned to Europe.[115] Harrison places his speakers in the long imaginative shadow cast by Kurtz, the imperial idealist and ivory trader who dealt in mass murder. The biblical rhetoric of mass extermination in the poems and the allusions to Kurtz, whose famous call was to "exterminate all the brutes," have historical application to the genocide in Biafra.

The humanist concern with Biafra and the nature of politics in Nigeria is also articulated through a poignant allusion in "*The Railroad Heroides*" to Achebe's *Things Fall Apart*, which Harrison describes in a letter as "a most moving and well written novel":[116] "After the bloodshed, if your tribe survives, / Pounding a big man's yams among young wives."[117] The line concisely refers to the measures of a man in the traditional Igbo society recreated in Achebe's novel: bloodshed, paternity, and yams. A man's possession of fertile wives depended on his reputation as a warrior and his wealth, measured primarily by yams: "Yam, the king of crops, was a man's crop."[118] The poem alludes to Achebe's tragic warrior Okonkwo but also refers colloquially to the contemporary "big man" quasi-feudal oligarchies of the "African strongmen." In "*The Railroad Heroides*" Harrison poetically addresses the Igbo and Biafran Achebe and wonders if his people will survive a genocidal war: "After the bloodshed, if your tribe survives."

In these poems biblical mythologies of conquest and extermination stand behind the history of empire and genocide in Africa. Harrison, like Achebe in *Things Fall Apart*, and like Conrad in *Heart of Darkness*, regards Christianity as dangerous. In *Things Fall Apart* the Christian missionaries are the ideological spearhead for the colonial economic and military invasion. Conrad in his critique of imperialism exposes the complicity of Christianity in the horrors that he describes. Harrison is also concerned with Christianity as a sacrificial religion: "Harrowing Christ! O Superlamb, / grown lupine, luminous—*Shazam!*'[119] Christ has come to mystify, harrow, rob, and plunder Africa in the name of God. Harrison's focus on religion here is relevant because the Nigerian-Biafran War was also a religious war between Christianity and Islam. The preoccupations of "*The Origin of the Beery Way*," a significant and neglected poem, include the history of Islamic *jihad* in West Africa. "The Heart of Darkness" and "*The Elephant and the Kangaroo*" were set in Nigeria, while "*The Origin of the Beery Way*" is set in the Senegambian region of West Africa.

III

"*The Origin of the Beery Way*" is a wonderful, zestful example of the creatively detailed and nuanced engagement with history in Harrison's poetry. The subjects of the poem include Islamic empire-building and confrontations with French and British imperialism, and the relationship between the *colon* and the Africans. "*The Origin of the Beery Way*" is the first of three poems grouped under the main title "*Manica*," which is the fourth poem sequence within "The White Queen." The second poem from "*Manica*," "*The Elephant and the Kangaroo*," has a shared concern with Christian wars of empire, and the third poem, "*The Foreign Body*," with imperial psycho-political pathologies. The title "*Manica*" clearly invites wordplays like manic(a) and mani(c)a, with reference to the psychopathologies of empire and the crazed behavior of the colonial class. Manica is also the name of a province in Mozambique but the three poems in the "*Manica*" sequence are set in some of the other many African locations traversed in *Loiners*. A meaning of the classical Latin word "*manica*" is "handcuffs, manacles," and the main title "*Manica*" signals that a subject of "*The Origin of the Beery Way*" is slavery.[120] The madness suggested by "*Manica*" also puns upon the "mad" Islamic *jihadists* we meet in "*The Origin of the Beery Way*."[121]

Harrison's interest in the history of alcohol is also signaled by the titles "*manica*," because a "*Manica Hippocrates*" was a white cotton bag used in a seventeenth-century distillation process,[122] and "*The Origin of the Beery Way*." The alcoholism rampant amongst the *colon* and the Islamic prohibition against alcohol receive humorous treatment in "*The Origin of the Beery Way*." The disjointed surface of "*The Origin of the Beery Way*" creates a manic effect that is appropriate to its preoccupation with madness and drunkenness, and that effect is partly created by dense allusions whose connections are not obvious. "*The Origin of the Beery Way*" is an ambitious poem that cannot be plausibly explained without some critical account of the complex history that its dense references and allusions open up from title to closing couplet.

The settings of "*The Origin of the Beery Way*" shift between the mid-nineteenth and twentieth centuries and suggest fundamental continuities in this period. The time slippage in the poem is first signaled by the combination of the epigraph to "*Manica*" and the first line of "*The Origin of the Beery Way*." 1960 is the publication date provided for the medical science book from which the epigraph is drawn:

"An experienced doctor has said that he has never seen tropical
neurasthenia develop in a man with a sound philosophy of life."
—Notes on the Preservation of Personal Health in Warm
Climates
The Ross Institute of Tropical Hygiene, London, 3rd edn,
1960.[123]

Then the first line of "*The Origin of the Beery Way*" tells us that the scene
is "The Coast, the Coast, a hundred years ago!"[124] The poem implicitly
begins with the White Queen in 1960s Senegambia imagining the arrival
a hundred years ago of British merchants in "Victorian hearse-plumes" on
"the Coast", referring to "the Coast" off St Louis, a large town in colonial
Senegal. In the mid-nineteenth century British and French trading centres
were located along the Senegal River or near the Coast off St Louis.[125]

The first of the two stanzas in "*The Origin of the Beery Way*" recre-
ates with historical accuracy the scene of British and French merchant
communities on the Senegambian coast in the mid-nineteenth century.
The first stanza is preoccupied with the experience of the *colon*, particu-
larly their sexual and economic relations with the Africans and the role
of alcohol. The stanza refers to "reports" that "put down" boozing and
"Shacking with natives," and draws the reports and memoirs that histo-
rians have also used to reconstruct the lives of the merchants on the Coast.
Directors of the *Compagnie des Indes* reported that the merchants "lived
in extravagance and drunkenness" and when not working were "drinking
and womanizing."[126] "*The Origin of the Beery Way*" refers ambiguously
to "Boozers with riff-raff in their *British* arms,"[127] or Englishmen freed
in Africa from the strict moral codes of Victorian England. Colonials
"murmur *beau, beau, beau* / Like some daft baby at your Mandingo."
The Englishman is ridiculed as a "daft baby" sucking the breast of "your
Mandingo," the major ethnic group in the region, suggesting that some
local women became the property and playthings of European men.
The poem performs a purposefully riotous staging of drunkenness and
lechery to satirize the "big *colon*." Harrison uses "*colon*," the French word

for "colonialist," for purposes of explicit wordplay. A colon follows the word "*colon:*," typographically and punningly presenting the colonial class as colons, rectums, sodomites, and complete arses.

The epigraph, quoted above, reproduces a medical view of tropical neurasthenia, neurotic disorders developed by Europeans living in tropical climates, as a psychosomatic condition made possible by the absence of "a sound philosophy of life." In the poem the colonialists are not ill but actively exploiting their distance from the moral codes and expectations of their own Victorian society. Harrison wryly implies that "tropical neurasthenia" is a convenient medical excuse or euphemism for the lack of moral restraint among Europeans in Africa. The poem also indicates that the Coast was no paradise for the Europeans when it refers to *El Vomito*, evocative Spanish for yellow fever, which killed large numbers of Europeans in the Senegambian region.[128] Alcohol abuse and sexual relations with local women were also among the reasons given in reports for the strikingly high mortality rate among the Europeans.[129]

In the first stanza of "*The Origin of the Beery Way*" the colonials give *cadeau* to their Mandingo *beaus*. There are line end rhymes on *beau* / Mandingo /*cadeau* which emphasize overlapping economic and sexual relations between Europeans and Africans. The poem refers particularly to the alliances between European merchants and *signares*, local women merchants. The *signares* having sexual relationships with European merchants were regarded by company officials in Paris as smugglers using their sexual charms to obtain goods, but smuggling proved to be a mutually profitable alliance for *signares* and Europeans.[130] In the poem the White Queen continues in the 1960s the unofficial colonial tradition of swilling whisky and having sex with Africans, and imagines that he is a nineteenth-century pirate, a profession associated with smuggling. He describes himself as:

A real beaubarian and buckaneer, that's me, Yo Ho,

Bottles of *Black & White* do me for rum.[131]

A buccaneer is a pirate and "Yo Ho" is a colloquial exclamation with a
nautical provenance associated with sailors and pirates and rum, a trade
commodity.[132] Harrison spells "buccaneer" as "buckaneer" to link the
White Queen's piracy to his sexual exploitation of Africans. "Buckaneer"
integrates the word "buck," here a colloquial variation on "fuck", into
"buccaneer," merging sexual and economic piracy. *Black & White* is the
brand name of a blended Scotch whisky and in the poem also a pun upon
black and white racial relations and miscegenation. The entwined sexual
and economic relationships between the colonial class and the Africans
is a preoccupation of the first stanza, and indeed of many poems in "The
White Queen" sequence.

The White Queen also describes himself as "A real beaubarian" who
needs to "forage among francophones."[133] "Beaubarian" is Harrison's pun
upon "Rhubarbarians," a term he coins in *The School of Eloquence* sonnet
"Rhubarbarians, I" to describe a "barbarian" from Leeds, examined in
chapter 7. In "*The Origin of the Beery Way*" the White Queen, Harrison's
fictional alter-ego, is a barbarian from Leeds playing at being a French
beau in Africa. He is a *beau* in the sense of being a cultivated dandy
and also in the sense of courting beautiful black boys. The beaubarian
employs "a bit of the old Francais finesse" in his dubious seduction of
Africans. He does "Not work at your ballocks like a kid's yo-yo, / then
buck you off them like a rodeo." The beaubarian's sex-life is "manic like
a bad rondeau."[134] This reference to the rondeau, a French poetic form
dating from the fourteenth century, associates the French with sexual
and cultural arrogance, which is satirized in "*The Origin of the Beery
Way.*" Its references to French language and culture also signal that the
White Queen is now in French as well as British colonial Africa.

The English White Queen is adopting a French personality and also
an *African Personality* in "*The Origin of the Beery Way.*" He is "Armed
with my *Dettol*, my *Od-o-ro-no*, / My *African Personality.*"[135] *African*

Personality was the name of a locally traded talcum powder. "African Personality" was also an African anti-colonial political concept and the poem's punning implies the commodification of the concept. The African Personality had a cultural parallel in *négritude*,[136] and similarly "*Zeg-Zeg Postcard*, XVIII" satirizes the commodification of *négritude*. "*The Origin of the Beery Way*" suggests the continuing political, economic, and sexual exploitation of Africans by Europeans despite the successes of the anti-colonial movements, and the epigraph highlights the date 1960 partly because it was the year Independence was declared in Senegal and Gambia.

In the second stanza of "*The Origin of the Beery Way*" the White Queen imagines the historical confrontation between Islamic forces and the French and British in the Senegambian region, and raises the history of Islamic dynasty and empire building. The first line of the second stanza refers to an historical figure, the Muslim Marabout El Hadj Omar Tall: "Omar, not Khayam, the Gambia's mad Marabout."[137] Omar waged a *jihad* of the sword from 1852–1860 to establish Islamic states and resist French and British commercial control of the region.[138] Omar Tall is an ancestor of Ahmadu Bello and the son of Usman dan Fodio, and the poem alludes to Omar's Islamic and ethnic empire building and implies its continuation and contemporary resurfacing in Bello's Nigeria. The movement in the poem between the nineteenth and twentieth centuries also invites the reader to compare these two figures from the same Islamic dynasty. "*The Origin of the Beery Way*" implicitly and irreverently traces the "origins" of Bello's "way," his Islamic crusade for religious and racial supremacy during the First Republic, to the political and historical context of nineteenth-century *jihad*.

The "off the page" background to "*The Origin of the Beery Way*" includes Bello's pronouncements that ancestral lineage and Allah legitimized his political agenda for a greater Islamic state. Harrison too emphasizes the presence of historical and cultural past, but to satirize rather than sanction Bello's Holy War. In his autobiography *My Life* (1962) Bello writes: "My ancestor was chosen to lead the Holy War which set up his empire. I have been chosen by a free electorate to help build a modern state."[139] Bello constantly reminded his audience "that he had been entrusted, by Allah, with the responsibility for maintaining the well-being of the Sokoto caliphate established in 1804 by his noble ancestor of revered name, Usman dan Fodio."[140] Fodio led a *jihad* which established a political-religious hegemony in much of what became Northern Nigeria, including Zaria.[141]

The use of Zaria's ancient name Zeg Zeg in the title "*Zeg-Zeg Postcards*" also shows that the African poems are preoccupied with Nigerian history, a history characterized by conquests in which Fodio and Omar were leaders. From 1852 Omar led a series of *jihads* in what is today Mali against the predominantly non-Muslim Bambara and Mandingo, the ethnic group referred to in the first stanza of "*The Origin of the Beery Way*."[142] Omar also inspired the Marabout-Soninke Wars (1850–1901), which resulted in the Islamic conversion of many of the Mandingo.[143] The Mandingo Kingdoms were mainly located on the Gambia River, which is one reason Omar is "The Gambia's mad Marabout."

"*The Origin of the Beery Way*" is also concerned with the "mad" or angry Omar's militant resistance to European empires, and refers to the legend of the Sufi opposing the British with his mystical powers:

> Omar, not Khayam, the Gambia's mad Marabout
>
> Changed the Commissioners' bullets into water;[144]

There was a popular belief that marabouts had magical powers,[145] and Omar reportedly cultivated the local legend that he could turn bullets into water.[146] Omar's act of transubstantiation is clearly regarded as apocryphal in the poem, which does however take seriously Omar's military attacks on British settlements in Gambia in 1855.[147] Harrison's beaubarian, assuming the role of the French *colon*, in stanza two imagines doing battle with Omar's scimitar-wielding warriors in order to "put

Islam to rout," and this refers to the historical conflict between Omar and the French.

The allusions in *"The Origin of the Beery Way"* to Omar's conflicts with the British, the French, and the Mandingo raises the history of the rise and fall and re-emergence of religious and mercantilist empires in West Africa. It was Omar's ephemeral empire that was being divided into European spheres of influence in the nineteenth century but the poem also points to the transience of European empires in the region. The beaubarian does a "soft-shoe shuffle on the white man's bones,"[148] referring particularly to the recent demise of a number of French and British colonies in Africa, notably countries Harrison visited during the 1960s when he was writing *Loiners*, such as Gambia, Senegal, and Nigeria. However, the poem's reminder that empires will fall comes in the wake of re-emerging Islamic empires, implicitly represented by Omar's descendant Bello, and neo-colonial economic empires, represented by the beaubarian.

Omar is most immediately presented as a "mad" or crazy Islamic warrior-mystic who magically liquefies the French army's bullets, but the poem has a serious interest in Omar's Holy War against nineteenth-century colonial expansion. Several historical angles upon Omar's campaigns and legacy are registered in the poem, including accounts of him as a great Islamic leader and hero of anti-colonial resistance, and alternately as an invader who forced Islam on non-Muslims or upon Muslims who practiced a different form of Islam.[149] The poem registers Omar as a Janus-faced figure of empire, a leader of failed Islamic opposition to the expanding French commercial and military presence, but who was able to force Islam on indigenous animist tribes like the Mandingo in a culturally diverse region.[150]

The description of Omar as "the Gambia's mad Marabout" also refers to the massive destruction his *jihads* wrought in the region. Omar's armies of *taalibe* and *sofa* ("slave warriors") devastated the middle Niger.[151] The poem is informed by the history of Islamic political revolutions in

Senegambia, from which Omar emerges in the nineteenth century as a great warrior for the establishment of new Islamic states and empire in the region.[152] In "*The Origin of the Beery Way*" Omar is an icon of the regional history and lineage of *jihad* and the Islamic state. Most historical accounts present Omar's *jihads* as attempts to establish new Islamic states in the tradition of the Fulbe state's empire building and, under Omar's leadership, especially the Tokolor who shared the same language with the Fulbe.[153] It has alternately been argued that Omar was most concerned to promote Fulbe ethnic privilege and colonization in an ethnically diverse region, rather than being dedicated to the institutions of Islamization and attendant political and social objectives.[154] However, in the poem Omar is identified by his religious vocation as a marabout, and his battles to enforce the Muslim prohibition against alcohol consumption, which was very important in his *jihads* against black infidels. "*The Origin of the Beery Way*" refers irreverently to Omar's holy war against alcohol consumption, but does so alongside explicit references to "pissed," lecherous, and racist colonials swilling *Star* beer, *Black & White* rum, and *Guinness*, and offers a nuanced consideration of the significance of alcohol in the complex history of the region.

Ambivalently satirizing European hedonism unleashed in the colonies, "*The Origin of the Beery Way*" more subtly draws on the relationship of alcohol to *jihad* in nineteenth-century Senegambia. Alcohol consumption was not only a line of demarcation between European and Islamic cultures but a point of confrontation between the Marabouts and the Mandingos, the Soninke and their kings.[155] The Mandingo, the Soninke, the royal courts, and the majority of commoners incurred the wrath of Islam because of their alcohol consumption. Omar's warriors fought the monarchy's *ceddo*, "plundering warriors who drank alcohol."[156] When Omar's Muslim armies adopted the ways of the warrior they "even imitated the ritual drinking bouts of the *ceddo* before battle but replaced the cursed alcoholic libations of the *ceddo* with tamarind juice."[157] This history is a subtext and inspiration behind Harrison's imaginative angle upon alcohol, Islam, and empire in "*The Origin of the Beery Way*."

In the drunken visions of the twentieth-century beaubarian, Omar's holy wars against the French Empire and alcohol are merged. The beaubarian imagines that his alcohol consumption has incurred Omar's wrath and, in the scatological second stanza, imagines himself as an infidel warrior vanquishing Omar's *mujahidin* with urination and masturbation:

> Omar, not Khayam, the Gambia's mad Marabout
>
> Changed the Commissioners' bullets into water;
>
> Into water being Moslem. I, being atheist,
>
> Am full of more potent potions when I'm pissed.
>
> A century later, full of *Guinnesses* and *Stars*,
>
> I'm God's own Heaven, and as I slash I shout:
>
> *The white man's water turns back into fire!*
>
> Braving castration at their scimitars,
>
> And single-handed put Islam to rout,
>
> And vanquish the missions with my bent desire,
>
> Spouting a semen capable of slaughter.[158]

The alcohol-charged urine and semen of the very drunk atheist are weapons that "slash" and "vanquish" Islam and also the Christian missions. The beaubarian's macho performance is mocked and his masculinity satirically encoded as militarism. However, the caricature of the sloshed and sexually "foraging" colonial macho simultaneously celebrates libertinism in a boisterously energetic language which enthralls the reader in its wild affront to Allah and God. The beaubarian is at one level the barbarian poet scatologically masturbating and urinating over religion, and anarchically embracing sexual license and alcohol in defiance of religious prohibitions.

Harrison's argument with a repressive Islam stands alongside his regard for an alternative tradition of liberalism and secularism within Islamic societies. The poem specifies the marabout Omar Tall by ostensibly directing our attention away from the Persian poet Omar Khayam: "Omar, not Khayam." Khayam was made famous in Europe through Edward Fitzgerald's free translation of his *Rubaiyyat* (1859).[159] The oriental poet who celebrated wine as the water of life and an antidote to sorrow is juxtaposed with an Omar who slaughters wine-drinkers, an Omar less palatable and lesser-known in Europe.

An admiration for the sensual, secular humanist vision expressed in Khayam's translated verse is implicit in "*The Origin of the Beery Way*," and later celebrated in *The Blasphemer's Banquet* (1989). In both poems Khayam, who lived in an Islamic society but was viewed with suspicion by Orthodox Muslims, represents an alternative tradition of liberalism within Islamic society. The scholar and poet Khayam is contrasted to lifeless Victorians and to a violently oppressive Islam in "The Origin of the Beery Way," and in *The Blasphemers' Banquet* is contrasted to Muslim bigots burning Salman Rushdie's *The Satanic Verses*. In Harrison's poetry drinking wine often represents, Khayam-like, a secular philosophical commitment to the pleasures of "this fleeting life."

The celebration of alcohol in "*The Origin of the Beery Way*" is a symbolic refusal of the repressions of Islam, Christianity, and the Victorians, and is in tension with the place of alcohol in the *colons'* exploitative relations with Africans. The first stanza presents the colonial "Boozers" "Shacking with natives" in the nineteenth century and in the second stanza, "A century later," the beaubarian is "full of *Guinnesses* and *Stars*." By the closing couplet he is "Flat on my back, beneath the Galaxy, I fear / This burning in my groin is gonorrhoea."[160] In the poem's theatre of inebriation, however humorous, grim matters of alcoholism and sexual disease are associated with the *colon*.

This association is continued with the pun upon "firewater," a colloquial Native American term for the alcohol given to them by the colonists, which also suggests the burning sensation experienced by sufferers of gonorrhoea whilst urinating. The beaubarian drinks so much alcohol that he imagines a miracle occurring as he urinates: "*The white man's water turns back into fire!*" The pun is on firewater but also "fire-power." The "fire" here suggests that the atheist beaubarian, waging imaginary battle with the *mujahidin*, has transubstantiated "water" into "fire-power," or bullets, a miraculous reversal of Omar's transubstantiation of French bullets into water. The references to "fire-water" and gonorrhoea recall that alcohol and sexually transmitted diseases were elements in the cultural disorientation and degradation of indigenous peoples. The beaubarian's boozing and murderous sexuality, slaughtering with his semen, refers to the role of alcohol and sexual disease in the decimation of many native peoples.

"*The Origin of the Beery Way*" mocks Omar's holy war against alcohol but the anti-colonial politics evident in *Loiners* suggest Harrison would not be entirely unsympathetic to Omar's *jihad* against "free trade."[161] Harrison intends to be historically specific when he signals the date 1860 at the start of the poem. As noted, the epigraph for "Manica" is dated 1960 and the first line of the first poem in the sequence, "*The Origin of the Beery Way*," is "The Coast, the Coast, a hundred years ago!" 1860 was also the year that Omar Tall ceased his fight with the French, marking the triumph of the French commercial empire.[162] The poem's ostensible dismissal of Omar as "mad" is tempered because it issues from the speaker taking on the role of the *colon*. The French in Saint Louis dismissed Omar and his followers as "fanatics" because they were *jihadists* committed to the Islamic state,[163] and because they resisted French commercial control of the region.[164] 1860 is also a key date because it marks the end of the old eighteenth-century system, the beginnings of the new commercial empire, and the point of movement towards greater French territorial empire later in the 1860s.

The eighteenth-century system had been based on slavery and this signaled in the title "*Manica*," whose meanings, as noted, include manacles and shackles. Another meaning of manica is the garment of a sleeve, and by association the cloth that was used for the garments. It was Senegambian slaves who wove the cotton to make the cloth, the women spinning cotton fibre into thread and the men weaving the thread into cloth.[165] Cloth was also used as a form of money that could be traded easily, so that in a poem concerned with systems of commerce "manica" also stands for money.[166] The poem's allusions to manacles, owned Mandingos, and "the Coast, a hundred years ago" also recalls the slave pens on the coastal islands of St Louis and Gorée, where Africans were held before being exported as slaves to American sugar plantations.[167]

Harrison was focused on the issue of slavery when he was composing *Loiners*. He was considering writing a slave novel and did write an unpublished review of *The Biography of a Runaway Slave*, a testimonial narrative about slavery in a Latin American context.[168] Histories of slavery are alluded to several times in *Loiners*, most lightly and with satirical humour in "The Death of the PWD Man, I." Wandering in a graveyard in Bathurst, Gambia, the PWD man observes the headstone of a commissioner whose dying chant, the local people said, was "*A coffle of fourteen asses bound for Sansanding!*"[169] This chant is an abbreviated quotation from the nineteenth-century Scottish explorer and surgeon Mungo Park's "*moral* and *physical*" geography of Africa.[170] In his *Travels in the Interior Districts of Africa* Park describes setting off "accompanied by a coffle of fourteen asses, loaded with salt, bound for Sansanding," in Mali.[171] In *Travels* he refers to coffles of both asses and slaves, both beasts of burden, and discusses how slaves were traded and exported from Gambia. Park laments that the slaves (like the asses) are chained together and that "the poor wretches are kept constantly fettered."[172] The African poems show a deep engagement with colonial history and contemporary events in West Africa. After "exploring" Africa, Harrison returned to England and settled in the Northern city of Newcastle-upon-Tyne, which is the setting for "Ghosts: Some Words before Breakfast." In the next chapter "Ghosts" is interpreted by making visible the haunting of Harrison by Rimbaud.

Notes

1. "Interview," 231.
2. Tony Harrison's papers relating to *Loiners*, London Magazine Editions, 73 uncatalogued and unnumbered items, Special Collections, Brotherton Library, University of Leeds (abbreviated throughout the book as *THP*).
3. *THP*, uncatalogued and unnumbered.
4. *Harrison: Poets and People*, Channel 4.
5. Letter to Silkin (25 August 1967).
6. Barbara Bush, *Imperialism, Race and Resistance: Africa and Britain, 1919–1945* (London: Routledge, 1999), 125.
7. Larry Diamond, "Class, Ethnicity, and the Democratic State: Nigeria, 1950–1966," *Comparative Studies in Society and History*, vol. 25, no. 3 (1983), 457–489, 457–59.
8. Letter to Silkin (8 November 1964).
9. Letter to Silkin (4 December 1962 and 28 February 1963). For a discussion of the political situation in Nigeria in the period leading to the civil war see for example S.K. Panter–Brick, ed., *Nigerian Politics and Military Rule: Prelude to the Civil War* (London: Athlone Press, 1970).
10. Letter to Jon Silkin (25 August 1967).
11. Thomas Browne, *Religio Medici*, ed. Jean-Jacques Denonain (Cambridge: Cambridge University Press, 1953 [1642]) l. 15, 24.
12. Hannah Arendt, *The Origins of Totalitarianism* (New York: Harcourt, Brace and Company, 1951), 191.
13. "Black and White and Red All Over: The Fiction of Empire," *London Magazine*, new series, vol. 12, no. 3 (August / September 1972), 90–103, 94.
14. Rudyard Kipling, "The Ballad of East and West," in *Rudyard Kipling: Complete Verse* (New York: Anchor Press, 1989 [1889]), 233. See also Nicholson, "'Reciprocal recognitions'," 75.
15. "The White Queen 1: *Satyrae*, I," *Loiners*, 20–21.
16. "*Postcard*, III," *Loiners*, 40. This verse was dropped from the *Selected Poems* and *Collected Poems*.
17. Letter to Silkin (28 February 1963)
18. Juvenal, *Satyrae*, trans. John Ferguson (Basingstoke: Macmillan, 1979).
19. *Loiners*, 21. See also, for example, Harrison's Satyr play, *The Trackers of Oxyrhynchus*, based upon the remaining fragments of a lost satyr play Sophocles wrote on papyrus.

20. "The White Queen 1: *Satyrae*, I," *Loiners*, 20.
21. "*Satyrae*, I," *Loiners*, 20, 22; and "*The Foreign Body*," *Loiners*, 2. See also Sandie Byrne, *H, v. & O: The Poetry of Tony Harrison* (Manchester: Manchester University Press, 1998), 10–11; and Nicholson, "'Reciprocal recognitions'," 66–67.
22. Letter to Silkin (28 February 1963). See also for example Chibuike Uche, "Oil, British Interests and the Nigerian Civil War," *Journal of African History*, vol. 49, no. 1 (2008), 111–135.
23. Letter to Silkin (28 January 1963).
24. "*Satyrae*, I," *Loiners*, 21.
25. "The White Queen 2: *The Railroad Heroides*, II," *Loiners*, 29.
26. "The White Queen 5: from *The Zeg-Zeg Postcards*, XVI," *Loiners*, 43.
27. "*Postcard*, XV," *Loiners*, 43. "Dunlop" is one of several brand names that are not italicized in *Loiners*.
28. "The White Queen 4: *Manica*, I: *The Origin of the Beery Way*," *Loiners*, 36.
29. "*Origin of the Beery Way*," *Loiners*, 36.
30. "*Origin of the Beery Way*," *Loiners*, 35.
31. "*Postcard*, XI," *Loiners*, 42; and "*Satyrae*, III," *Loiners*, 23.
32. "*Satyrae*, IV," *Loiners*, 26.
33. "The Death of the PWD Man, II," *Loiners*, 55.
34. "The Death of the PWD Man, II," *Loiners*, 56.
35. "The Death of the PWD Man, II," *Loiners*, 56.
36. "*Postcard*, XVIII," *Loiners*, 44.
37. "The Death of the PWD Man, II," *Loiners*, 56.
38. "*The Origin of the Beery Way*," *Loiners*, 35.
39. "*The Origin of the Beery Way*," *Loiners*, 35.
40. "*Postcard*, XI," *Loiners*, 41.
41. "*Postcard*, XVII," *Loiners*, 43.
42. "*Satyrae*, I," *Loiners*, 20.
43. "*Postcard*, XV," *Loiners*, 43.
44. "*Postcard*, XXII," *Loiners*, 44.
45. "*Postcard*, XV," *Loiners*, 43.
46. "*Postcard*, XV," *Loiners*, 43.
47. "The Songs of the PWD Man, II," *Loiners*, 52.
48. See for example Bade Onimode, "Imperialism and Multinational Corporations: A Case Study of Nigeria," *Journal of Black Studies*, vol. 9, no. 2 (1978), 207–232, 207.
49. "The Songs of the PWD Man, II," *Loiners*, 52.
50. "*Postcard*, XV," *Loiners*, 43.

51. *"Postcard, XV,"* Loiners, 43. The violent ethnic competition for the resources of modernization in Nigeria in the 1960s is discussed in Diamond, "Class, Ethnicity, and the Democratic State," 460.
52. For a discussion of the political situation in Nigeria in the period leading to the civil war see, for example, *Nigerian Politics and Military Rule: Prelude to the Civil War*, ed. S.K. Panter-Brick (London: Athlone Press, 1970).
53. *"Satyrae, III,"* Loiners, 24.
54. Letter to Silkin (28 February 1963). The appropriated funds Harrison refers to include the substantial bribes paid by private business interests to government officials in return for lucrative contracts and licenses and the diversion of vast amounts of public money, mainly oil profits, into private accounts. See Diamond, "Class, Ethnicity, and the Democratic State," 462.
55. Chinua Achebe, "The African Writer and the Biafran Cause," in *Morning Yet on Creation Day: Essays* (London: Heinemann Educational, 1975), 78–84.
56. *"Satyrae, IV,"* Loiners, 26.
57. *"Satyrae, III,"* Loiners, 24.
58. *"Satyrae, I,"* Loiners, 20. See also for example André Gide, *Corydon* (New York: Octagon Books, 1977 [1950]), 22.
59. *"Satyrae, I,"* Loiners, 22.
60. *"Satyrae, I,"* Loiners, 21.
61. *"Satyrae, I,"* Loiners, 20.
62. Judith Still, "Not Really Prostitution: The Political Economy of Sexual Tourism in Gide's *Si Le Grain Ne Meurt*," *French Studies*, vol. 54, no. 1 (2000), 17–34. Famous authors in the autobiographical genre of homosexual tourism include Gide, Wilde, Flaubert, Barthes, Foucault and Orton.
63. *Loiners*, 20.
64. André Gide, *The Immoralist*, trans. Dorothy Bussy (New York: Alfred A. Knopf, 1948 [1930]). The character of Menalque is based on Wilde and has been the subject of a scandal and lawsuit. See also André Gide, *If It Die: An Autobiography*, trans. Dorothy Bussy (New York: Vintage Books, 2001 [1935]), 287–88.
65. "Interview," 245.
66. "Interview," 245–246.
67. *CP*, 152.
68. *Them & [uz]: A Portrait*, BBC.
69. "The Songs of the PWD Man, I," *Loiners*, 51.

70. Nicholson, "'Reciprocal recognitions'," 75. See also Peter Porter, "In the Bosom of Family," *London Magazine*, new series, vol. 10, no. 5 (1970), 72–8, 75; and Rudyard Kipling, *Complete Verse* (New York: Anchor Press, 1989 [1940]).

71. *THP*, uncatalogued and unnumbered.

72. "The White Queen 4: *Manica*, III: *The Foreign Body*," *Loiners*, 38.

73. "The Death of the PWD Man, II," *Loiners*, 55.

74. Woodcock, "Is Tony Harrison a post-colonial poet?," 82.

75. "Fiction of Empire," 92.

76. Letter to Ross (16 February 1970). *The Seductive Coast: Poems Lyrical and Seductive from Western Africa* was published under the name O. Dazi Oka but the author is generally thought to be J.M. Stewart-Young and this is who Harrison refers to as the author. See also George Lang, "Ghana and Nigeria," in *European-Language Writing in Sub-Saharan Africa*, vol. 1, ed. Albert S. Gérard (Budapest: Akadémiai Kiado, 1986), 108–115, 108.

77. Letter to Ross (16 February 1970).

78. Letter to Ross (16 February 1970); and "The White Queen 4: *Manica*, I: *The Origin of the Beery Way*," *Loiners*, 35.

79. Letter to Ross (16 February 1970).

80. Stephanie Newell, *The Forger's Tale: The Search for Odeziaku* (Athens: Ohio University Press, 2006), 29–30.

81. Newell, *The Forger's Tale*, 139-140.

82. Newell, *The Forger's Tale*, 3.

83. "*Postcard*, I," *Loiners*, 40.

84. There are twenty-seven entries in "from *The Zeg-Zeg* Postcards" in the original publication of *Loiners*, with only fifteen "*Postcards*" retained and accordingly renumbered in later *Selected Poems* and *Collected Poems*.

85. "Note" accompanying the "*Postcards*," *Loiners*, 46.

86. "*Postcard*, IX," *Loiners*, 41. This "*Postcard*" was dropped from *Selected Poems* and *Collected Poems*.

87. "*Postcard*, XVI," *Loiners*, 43.

88. "*Postcard*, XVII," *Loiners*, 43

89. "*Postcard*, X," *Loiners*, 41. The footnote explains: "*sukuru*: Hausa> English screw, as *sukurudireba* > English screwdriver. A useful portmanteau word." See *Loiners*, 46

90. Arnold Hughes and David Perfect, eds., *Historical Dictionary of the Gambia* (Lanham: Rowman & Littlefield, 2008), xxiii. See also Ewan W. Anderson, *International Boundaries: A Geopolitical Atlas* (New York: Routledge, 2003), 306–08.

91. *"Postcard, XX," Loiners*, 44.

92. "The Heart of Darkness," *Loiners*, 49.

93. *"Postcard, XV," Loiners*, 43.

94. Sir Walter Raleigh, "The Discovery of the Large, Rich and Beautiful Empire of Guiana, With a relation of the Great and Golden City of Manoa (which the Spaniards call El Dorado) And the provinces of Emeria, Arromaia, Amapaia and other Countries, with their rivers, adjoining." This is the Epistle Dedicatory preceding "The Discovery of Guiana," in *Sir Walter Raleigh: Selected Writings*, ed. Gerald Hammond (Manchester: Carcanet, 1984), 76–123.

95. Achebe, "The African Writer and the Biafran Cause," 83.

96. Antony Rowland excavates holocaust as one of the great themes of Harrison's poetry but his focus is the Jewish Holocaust, the bombing of Hiroshima and Nagasaki, a projected nuclear holocaust, and some other European wars. See Antony Rowland, *Tony Harrison and the Holocaust* (Liverpool: Liverpool University Press, 2001).

97. "Newcastle is Peru," *Loiners*, 84.

98. Chinua Achebe, "Onitsha, Gift of the Niger," *Morning Yet on Creation Day: Essays* (London: Heinemann Educational, 1975), 90–92.

99. "The Excursion," *Loiners*, 71.

100. *Loiners*, 71.

101. Palmer-Fernandez, *Encyclopaedia of Religion and War*, 329–30.

102. *"Postcard, XI," Loiners*, 42.

103. Letter to Vivienne Lewis (15 March 1970), BC MS 20c *London Magazine*, Special Collections, Brotherton Library, University of Leeds.

104. *Revelations*, 6: 2–8.

105. *Revelations*, 6: 2.

106. "The Pomegranates of Patmos," *CP*, 291–99.

107. "The Heart of Darkness," *Loiners*, 49.

108. *Loiners*, 49. See also Letter to Silkin (8 November 1964).

109. *Loiners*, 49.

110. Ann Genova, "Nigeria's Biafran War: State, Oil Companies, and Confusion," *XIV International Economic History Congress*, Helsinki, 2006.

111. Joseph Conrad, *Heart of Darkness: Background and Criticisms*, ed. Leonard F. Dean (New Jersey: Prentice Hall, 1960). See also Patrick Brantlinger, *Rule of Darkness: British Literature and Imperialism, 1830–1914* (Ithaca: Cornell University Press, 1988), 255–74.

112. *"The Elephant and the Kangaroo," Loiners*, 37.

113. *Loiners*, 37.

114. Claude Rawson, *God, Gulliver and Genocide: Barbarism and the European Imagination, 1492 – 1945* (Oxford: Oxford University Press, 2001), viii. The period Rawson concentrates upon is from the fifteenth century to WWII but his argument can be applied to conquest and genocide in post-war history.

115. Conrad, *Heart of Darkness*, 54.

116. Letter to Silkin (28 February 1963).

117. *Loiners*, 30.

118. Chinua Achebe, *Things Fall Apart* (Oxford: Heinemann Educational, 1996 [1964]), 16.

119. *Loiners*, 49.

120. "*manica*," *OED Online*.

121. "The White Queen 4: *Manica*, I: *The Origin of the Beery Way*," *Loiners*, 36.

122. John French, *The Art of Distillation. Or, A Treatise of the Choicest Spagyrical Preparations Performed by Way of Distillation, Being Partly Taken Out of the Most Select Chemical Authors of the Diverse languages and Partly Out of the Author's Manual Experience together with, The Description of the Chiefest Furnaces and Vessels Used by Ancient and Modern Chemists, also A Discourse on Diverse Spagyrical Experiments and Curiosities, and of the Anatomy of Gold and Silver, with The Chiefest Preparations and Curiosities Thereof, and Virtues of Them All.* London. Printed by Richard Cotes, 1651.

123. *Loiners*, 35.

124. *Loiners*, 35.

125. David Robinson, "French 'Islamic' Policy and Practice in Late Nineteenth-Century Senegal," *Journal of African History*, vol. 29, no. 3 (1988), 415–435, 418.

126. James F. Searing, *West African Slavery and Atlantic Commerce: The Senegal River Valley, 1700–1860* (Cambridge: Cambridge University Press, 1993), 66.

127. *Loiners*, 35.

128. See Philip Curtin, *Economic Change in Precolonial Africa: Senegambia in the Era of the Slave Trade* (Madison: University of Wisconsin Press, 1975), 5.

129. Searing, *West African Slavery*, 97.

130. Searing, *West African Slavery*, 98–99 and 164.

131. *Loiners*, 35.

132. Curtin, *Economic Change in Precolonial Africa*, 59 and 68.

133. *Loiners*, 35.
134. *Loiners*, 35.
135. *Loiners*, 36.
136. Abiola Irele, "*Négritude* or Black Cultural Nationalism," *Journal of Modern African Studies*, vol. 3, no. 3 (1965), 321–348, 321.
137. *Loiners*, 36.
138. Robinson, "French 'Islamic' Policy," 419–20. El Hadj Omar Tall is alternately known as Al Hajj Umar. *The Epic of El Hadj Omar* is the most famous religious epic in West African literature. See Samba Diop, "The Wolof Epic: From Spoken Word to Written Text," *Research in African Literatures*, vol. 37, no. 3 (2006), 120–132, 4.
139. Ahmadu Bello, *My Life* (London: Cambridge University Press, 1962), viii.
140. A.H.M. Kirke-Greene, "His Eternity, His Eccentricity, or His Exemplarity? A Further Contribution to the Study of H.E. the African Head of State', *African Affairs* (1991), vol. 90, 163–187, 174.
141. Kirke-Greene, "His Eccentricity," 174.
142. Robinson, "French 'Islamic' Policy," 419.
143. Omar A. Touray, *The Gambia and the World: A History of the Foreign Policy of Africa's Smallest State, 1965–1995* (Hamburg: Institute of African Affairs, 2000), 15.
144. *Loiners*, 36.
145. Lucy Behrman, "The Political Significance of the Wolof Adherence to Muslim Brotherhoods in the Nineteenth Century," *African Historical Studies*, vol. 1, no. 1 (1968), 60–78, 62.
146. See J.M. Gray, *History of the Gambia* (Cambridge: Cambridge University Press, 1940), 391. Quoted in Nicholson, "'Reciprocal recognitions'," 70.
147. Gray, *History of the Gambia*, 391. Quoted in Nicholson, "'Reciprocal recognitions'," 70.
148. *Loiners*, 36.
149. Martin A. Klein, "Social and Economic Factors in the Muslim Revolution in Senegambia," *Journal of African History*, vol. 13, no. 3 (1972), 419–41, 431. See also B. Olatunji Oloruntimehin, "Resistance Movements in the Tukulor Empire," *Cahier d'Études Africaines*, vol. 8, *Cahier* 29 (1968), 123–43, 126.
150. Robinson, "French 'Islamic' Policy," 41.
151. Searing, *West African Slavery*, 162.
152. Searing, *West African Slavery*, 88–89.

153. Robinson, 'French 'Islamic' Policy', 419.

154. Robinson, "French 'Islamic' Policy," 419.

155. Elizabeth Allo Isichei, *A History of African Societies to 1870* (Cambridge: Cambridge University Press, 1997), 308.

156. Searing, *West African Slavery*, 24.

157. Searing, *West African Slavery*, 162.

158. *Loiners*, 36.

159. Omar Khayyam, *Rubaiyyat of Omar Khayyam*, trans. Edward Fitzgerald (London: Bernard Quaritate, 1859).

160. *Loiners*, 36.

161. Robinson, "French 'Islamic' Policy," 419–420.

162. Robinson, "French 'Islamic' Policy," 418.

163. David Robinson, "France as a Muslim Power in West Africa," *Africa Today*, vol. 46, no. 3 (1999), 105–127, 108.

164. Robinson, "French 'Islamic' Policy," 418–19.

165. Searing, *West African Slavery*, 176.

166. Searing, *West African Slavery*, 69.

167. Searing, *West African Slavery*, ix.

168. Letter to Vivienne Lewis (19 September 1970), in BC MS 20c London Magazine, Special Collections, Brotherton Library, University of Leeds.

169. *Loiners*, 47.

170. Mungo Park, *Travels in the Interior Districts of Africa,* vol. 1, with an Appendix and illustrations by Major Rennell (London: W. Bulmer & Co., 1799), iii.

171. Park, *Travels in Africa*, 54.

172. Park, *Travels in Africa*, 26.

CHAPTER 5

GHOSTS

Harrison described "Ghosts: Some Words before Breakfast," in an unpublished description of *Loiners*, as "a bitter, ironic affirmation of the need for poetry on many levels, a grudging autobiographical credo, the need for love, a celebration, an art, however difficult."[1] The ironies of the poem's affirmation of poetry and love are illuminated through the life, letters, and poetry of Rimbaud, whose importance for "Ghosts" is signaled by an epigraph, a quotation from one of Rimbaud's last letters: "*C'est mon unique soutien au monde, à présent!*" Arthur Rimbaud, 2nd July, 1891 (*Oeuvres*, p. 528).[2] Harrison has read Rimbaud's letters and knows his biography, and the legend of his rupture with poetry and Paul Verlaine, and that he travelled the world, transforming himself into a trader and explorer in colonial Africa. It is Rimbaud's struggle to survive as a poet, his decisive poetic silence, his freedom, and the manner of his dying that haunt Harrison in "Ghosts." Rimbaud holds the key to understanding new and intimate dimensions of an enigmatic poem, whose autobiographically based aspects are elucidated by Harrison's personal correspondence. Reading "Ghosts" alongside Harrison's and Rimbaud's letters, and observing the poem's resonances with Rimbaud's *Une saison en enfer* [*A Season in Hell*], we also discover one of the great unrecognized literary friendships between the dead and the living.

"Ghosts" is a monologue in octosyllabic couplets. The speaker is, implicitly, the persona "Tony Harrison," a haunted figure in a poem heavy with personal and literary memories and "ghosts." The title "Ghosts" also alludes to the play *Ghosts* by Henrik Ibsen, the nineteenth-century Norwegian dramatist, and it identifies Harrison's poem as being like Ibsen's play: a modern tragedy with features of the fatalistic Greek tragedy. A miscarriage, the maiming of a child, and the retributive religion of a mother in the poem symbolically suggest the cycle of tragedy in which the young are destroyed by their parents. Harrison's poem and Ibsen's play share a focus upon the power of heredity and the dramatization of inherited ideas as destructive "ghosts." The poem, like the play, attacks the moral authority of the family and the church, and does so partly by dramatizing the disintegration of a son: in the play it is the dying Oswald and more subtly in the poem it is Harrison. A very different version of "Ghosts" was first published in *Poetry and Audience* but one phrase is retained in the poem as it appears in *Loiners*, where Harrison is "still afraid" "about the next descent of night,"[3] which echoes how the doomed Oswald is "haunted by this ghastly fear" in Ibsen's play.[4]

The epigraph to the first version of "Ghosts" is "I gave you life" and it is taken from Ibsen's play. Oswald tells his mother Mrs Alving that he has hereditary patrilineal syphilis, and asks her to kill him, but she suggests that this would pervert a natural moral order: "But I gave you your life."[5] Harrison slightly alters the line and uses it as the epigraph to indicate the poem's concern with a mother's moral claim of control over her son's life, manifest in her bitter opposition to a love affair. Although the epigraph from Ibsen is dropped, these preoccupations persist into the *Loiners'* version of "Ghosts," where he attributes responsibility for his mother's view that a miscarriage was divine retribution for conception outside of wedlock to Queen Victoria's virulent puritanism. Addressing a statue of the "Queen / here slender, beddable," he attacks a hypocritical

public code of morality and its poisoning of private relationships, and
the inhumanities of a Christian theology:

> your clean-
>
> living family image drove
>
> my mother venomously anti love,
>
> and made her think the stillbirth just
>
> retribution for our filthy lust;
>
> our first (the one we married for)
>
> red splashes on a LADIES floor...
>
> *inter urinam et faeces nasc-*
>
> *imur...*issues of blood.[6]

Harrison recalls the birth and death scene of his first child and he
remembers the Latin words of Saint Augustine that we are born between
urine and faeces. The Church Father's words, and the reference to
"issues of blood" on the floor of the "LADIES" toilet, seems to reprise
his mother's view of the indecent filthiness of his poetry. In "Ghosts"
his mother's puritanism is a metaphorical "disease" and a matrilineal
version of the patrilineal syphilis in Ibsen's play, which is also part of
the literature of syphilis recurrently alluded to in *Loiners*. The poem
takes up the metaphorical dimension of Ibsen's use of "disease," and of
"ghosts" as metaphors for "dead beliefs" that are passed from generation
to generation and cause great suffering.

"Ghosts" is dedicated to Jane, Harrison's first surviving child, and in
the poem the young daughter, "Jane," lies in a paediatric ward with "legs
splayed outwards" and "crushed bones."[7] The first of the two epigraphs
to "Ghosts" is taken from an inscription in *The League of Friends* rest
room, at the Royal Victoria Infirmary in Newcastle-upon-Tyne where,

in the poem and in life, the poet keeps a vigil by his daughter's hospital bed.[8] The epigraph is:

> These rooms have been furnished by the League of Friends
>
> For your comfort and rest while illness portends.
>
> Take care of the things which from us you borrow
>
> For others are certain to need them tomorrow.[9]

Harrison explains the terrible accident that is a catalyst for the poem in a letter to Alan Ross, the editor of *London Magazine* which published *Loiners*, and an early supporter in the literary world. In a dark coincidence, on the same day that Harrison posted the manuscript of *Loiners* to Ross, 5 April 1968, "my daughter, who is rare and beautiful, had both legs crushed under a ten ton lorry on the Great North Road."[10] A month later he writes that "the threat of amputation is still not removed."[11]

Harrison's poem for Jane recalls Rimbaud because a comparable tragedy befell the French poet. Rimbaud's leg was surgically amputated on 27 May 1891. Little more than a month later, 2 July 1891, Rimbaud writes the line that becomes the second epigraph of a poem occasioned by the crushing of Jane's legs: "*C'est mon unique soutien au monde, à présent!*" ["It's the only support I have in the world right now!"].[12] Rimbaud was literally referring to his left leg as his only physical support after the amputation of his right leg. Rimbaud's advice, if he were to be consulted by someone in a similar condition, was to die rather than allow the terrible suffering brought by amputation.[13] In "Ghosts," Harrison anticipates for his small daughter "almost a lifetime's crippledom" and wonders if he should "cut off / your breathing with a last wet cough."[14] Harrison once described Jane as "my only solace,"[15] and of the accident wrote that "no-one could have devised anything more horrible to tear me apart."[16] He finds support in the sincerity of Rimbaud's letters, which have intimate resonances with the biographical experiences and melancholy layers of memory that

"Ghosts" is poetically composed of. Reading the dead poet's letters and poems helps the living poet's spirit survive "this newest sorrow."[17]

Harrison's sense of himself as a haunted figure, an "anxious ghost" on the move,[18] a "weightless" "shadow man,"[19] is intensified in the hellish time that "Ghosts" is about, and recalls Rimbaud's sense of himself as a walking ghost in *A Season in Hell*: "*Au matin j'avais le regard si perdu et la contenance si morte, que ceux que j'ai rencontrés ne m'ont peut-être pas vu*" ["In the morning I had so vacant a look and so dead an expression, that those I met *perhaps did not see me*"].[20] The autobiographically-based narrators of Rimbaud's and Harrison's poems are in the throes of "*Le combat spirituel*" ["a spiritual battle"], one lost in "*patrie de l'ombre*" ["a land of darkness"],[21] the other walking in circles in "the dark."[22] In *A Season in Hell* poetry and love are treasured sources of Beauty, but poetry also brings poverty and madness, while love brings sorrow and isolation, and here an essentially similar vision underlies "Ghosts." But where Rimbaud's prose poem foresees burying his dead, his poetic ambitions and the relationship with Verlaine, Harrison's verse poem subtly reflects a despairing struggle to sustain his poetry and his family. *A Season in Hell* and "Ghosts" also share a personal and political refusal of the received religious and moral order, a republican contempt for empires, a yearning for exploration in Africa, and an "aesthetic of intoxication" and solitary walking.

The dying Rimbaud also expresses his sense of being a still breathing ghost, and the suffering that possesses him, in a letter to his sister Isabelle: "*Pour moi, je ne fais que pleurer jour et nuit, je suis un homme mort*" ["All I do is weep day and night. I have ceased living."][23] In "Ghosts" Harrison speaks through Rimbaud's letters to express his grief and fading emotional grip on life in the time the poem is about, which is remembered in "A Kumquat for John Keats" (1981):

days, when the very sunlight made me weep,

> days, spent like the nights in deep, drugged sleep,
>
> days in Newcastle by my daughter's bed,
>
> wondering if she, or I, weren't better dead,[24]

When he writes in "Ghosts" that "I'm still afraid' he also echoes letters where Rimbaud wrote that "I am very afraid."[25] The poem evokes correspondences between Rimbaud's fear and sleeplessness as he lies in the *Hôpital de la Conception* in Marseille, and the fear that has Harrison haunting hospital wards and striding through the streets "while Newcastle sleeps."[26]

Harrison soothes his spirit by walking but the poem intimates his metaphorical identification with the maiming of Rimbaud's and Jane's bodies, which become at one level objective correlatives of a wounded interiority. The poem implicitly likens the reclusiveness of the writer's life to the spiritual sanctuary of the "priory" and the marginality of the vulnerable, here the child he silently addresses: "You'll live, / like your father, a contemplative."[27] Harrison also presents a symbolic affinity between his mind and Jane's body, though this time in a humorous register, in the short prose piece "Shango the Shaky Fairy" (1971). He pairs "the unbalanced poet and the lame daughter," playfully concurring with the general view that poets are mad, or mentally "unbalanced."[28] The image of the unbalanced poet also suggests Harrison's imaginative identification with Rimbaud's "lack of balance" after his leg is amputated very high up, and his fear of falling.[29] "Shango" also describes how Jane and an injured friend "compared sufferings and became immediately close."[30] One of the poet's gifts to his daughter in this poem dedicated to her is the quiet identification of a kindredness of sorrows between Rimbaud and Jane, and Rimbaud's being both "crippled" and a poet makes him a brother in spirit to father and daughter.

"Ghosts" conceives of writing poetry as "the laying of ghosts,"[31] as a way to make peace particularly with the complex legacies of Harrison's relationships with the three generations of women addressed in the poem: "Mother, wife and daughter, ghost – / I've laid, laid, laid, laid / you, but I'm still afraid."[32] One "ghost" addressed here is the stillborn child laid to rest and another is the poet himself, an intimate yet enigmatic figure in "Ghosts." The partially occluded causes of his anxiety in the poem include the difficult rapprochement between familial love and the solitude needed to write the poetry that his life importantly depends upon. Domestic life is subtly contrasted with the world of writing and it is in the quiet hours "before Breakfast" that he can write "some Words." In a letter Harrison describes "a life of quiet despair, as before," alluding to Thoreau.[33] On the day of Jane's accident he wrote that "I seek cures elsewhere than booze and blue pills (I mean work)." In "Ghosts" poetry is metaphorically likened to the blood transfusions keeping his daughter alive in the RVI:

> Blood transfusion, saline drip,
>
> 'this fiddle' and 'stiff upper lip'
>
> Have seen us so far."[34]

"This fiddle" refers to "Poetry," appropriating the words of the American modernist poet Marianne Moore.[35] For Harrison poetry and its metrical rhythms are "like the pulse" and "like a life support system."[36] He regards the tragic vision found in Greek drama as the nearest to "an accurate vision of our lives."[37] "Ghosts" reflects his humanist view that art can give greater form and solace to the human spirit than religion, and that "poetry has to try to help us."

The letter that Harrison quotes from in the epigraph to "Ghosts" was written about fifteen years after Rimbaud had severed himself from poetry and it is a grief-stricken cry of being without support, emotional and physical: "*C'est mon unique soutien au monde, à présent !*" ["It's the only support I have in the world right now!"]. Rimbaud was terrified that his remaining leg would also be amputated.[38] The biographer Graham

Robb writes that "for Rimbaud, amputation was the worst thing that could have happened" because "his size-41 feet had always been...a means of escape...."[39] From late childhood until the "hammer blow" below the knee,[40] the illness that presaged his death, much of Rimbaud's travel involved walking extraordinary distances, sometimes hundreds of kilometers between European cities and across African deserts, because walking was both free and freeing. Walking also figures importantly in many of Rimbaud's poems, and *A Season in Hell* remembers his childhood of vagabondage, of being "*Sur les routes, par des nuits d'hiver, sans gîte, sans habit, sans pain*" ["On the roads, on winter nights, without clothes, without bread"].[41] But in "*Ma Bohéme (Fantaisie)*" ["My Bohemian Life (Fantasy)"] the poet as tramp mends his tattered clothes with his rhymes and "*Comme des lyres, je tirais les élastiques / De mes souliers blessés, un pied près de mon coeur!*" ["Like lyres I plucked the elastics / Of my wounded shoes, one foot near my heart!"].[42] Rimbaud's loss of the ability to walk and lost connection to poetry haunt Harrison in "Ghosts," where walking and poetry are similarly depicted as what is sustaining and freeing for him.

In "Ghosts" Harrison is, implicitly, mentally composing the lines of his verse while walking the city's darkened streets, an urban parallel to Wordsworth's composing lines while walking in daylight and in nature. Walking through the bleak cityscape becomes an objective correlative for the internal journey involved in writing a poem to lay the ghosts that still walk. Like the circular nature of his physical path through the city, however, "Ghosts" closes with the resurfacing of anticipatory fear "about the next descent of night."[43] Harrison says that "it's an existential need, the metrical form, for me,"[44] and he associates metrical rhythm "with the heartbeat, with the sexual instinct, with all those physical rhythms which go on despite the moments when you feel suicidal."[45] This sense of the physicality and momentum of poetic metre is part of its connection to walking and exploration in the imaginations and lives of these two poets. Rimbaud's journeys by foot, horseback, train, and ship were also driven by his wish to become "someone else," "*Je est un autre*" ["I is someone else"], a poetic concept whose meanings include escaping himself and the causes of his suffering through seeming transformations of identity in the series of lives that he lived.[46] In "Ghosts" Harrison is also walking away, in nocturnal interludes, from his own history and identity, and his grim striding through the dark gives physical expression to an urgent quest for an elusive inner peace.

The poem meditates upon Rimbaud's poetic silence, and upon a line of prose that he wrote when he was alone in the *Hôpital de la Conception*, the line quoted in the epigraph to "Ghosts." A tragic irony implicit in the poem is that one of the greatest poets in Harrison's and in European literature's canon was without poetry in a time of desperate need. However, "Ghosts" also reflects upon the powerlessness of poetry and love, and their roots in the tragedy of our mortality. Helplessly observing how his child's exhaled breaths resemble "death throes," he knows neither poetry nor love can make her any "less / the helpless prey of Nothingness—."[47] He grieves for Rimbaud's loss of poetry and his loneliness in, ironically, a poem about the impotency of poetry and about struggling to survive "issues of blood" and love. The intense independence of Rimbaud emerges as, in ways, a bleakly attractive alternative to "Harrison's" experience, in "Ghosts," of being "a stranger caught / loosely flapping on my mother's grate," isolated in a life partly scripted and framed by the expectations of a loving family.[48]

Harrison's struggle to stay connected to the "life support system" of poetry, while honoring the now consuming dues of love, is intimated in "Ghosts." The subtextual anxiety about writing in the poem is clarified by letters lamenting how little he has written, and explaining that "all my energy is going into Jane's restoration and I find little left for poems."[49] When he describes being "caught / loosely flapping on my mother's grate" he metaphorically likens himself to paper thrown on the hearth. He again equates himself with failed drafts of poems, this time consigned to rubbish bags:

> — In each black
>
> PVC disposal sack,
>
> I see two of my dimensions gone
>
> into a flat oblivion.[50]

The poet's identity is largely defined by his writing, but his capacity to sustain the poetry is constrained by familial circumstances. The implications of his predicament resonate with Rimbaud's acknowledgement in *A Season in Hell*, that "*Je suis trop dissipé, trop faible*" ["I am too worn out, too weak"] for "*domestique*" "*bonheur*" ["domestic" "happiness"], but, redemptively, that "*La vie fleurit par le travail, vieille vérité*" ["Life flowers through work, an old truth"].[51]

Essential affinities exist between Harrison and Rimbaud, across spatial and temporal distances, but a defining difference in the choices they make is that one stays and the other leaves poetry and loved ones. Yet, ironically, both find themselves "strangers" essentially alone in their different situations, and this is an aspect of his identification with Rimbaud in "Ghosts." However, Harrison makes a mysterious symbolic reference to a ghostly pedestrian who shadows him when he walks at night:

> The black spot crossing; on both sides
>
> a blank male silhouette still strides.[52]

Rimbaud regarded himself as "*un piéton, rien de plus*" ["a pedestrian, nothing more than that"],[53] presenting himself as simply a working man through a metaphor that also conveys the importance of walking for the kind of person and poet he was. Mirroring Rimbaud's aesthetic of the solitary walker is one of the ways Harrison conjures his presence in "Ghosts." But it is as if the ghost of Rimbaud is one of the dead friends accompanying Harrison through the dark.[54]

"Ghosts," and the epigraph taken from Rimbaud's letter, together suggest the different choices made, the different prices paid, and how the memory of Rimbaud's freedom more fully explains Harrison's brooding ambivalence in the poem: "Air! Air! There's not enough / air in this small world."[55] Suburban claustrophobia could only be heightened by reading Rimbaud's letters from foreign lands, describing how "the world is very big and full of magnificent places."[56] Rimbaud needed his "wandering free existence," while Harrison found that travel "is the only thing that brings me out of myself."[57] In "Ghosts" his cry, "O caravanserais!," likens a pair of tankers transporting Newcastle beer to desert caravans,[58] and recalls the caravans that Rimbaud travelled and traded with in Africa. For Harrison opportunities for more travel in Africa through academic positions were tempting but familial and wider circumstances meant "we have to stay put, like it or not."[59]

Familial love is honored in "Ghosts" for being as fundamental as food and characterized by visceral courage, for being "this / brave trophallaxis of a kiss."[60] This line, and the quiet desperation permeating "Ghosts," bespeak the poet's material struggle "so that food is again in the gobs of the children."[61] Harrison "scratched" a sparse living together at this time mainly, the letters indicate, with intermittent teaching, book readings, and payments for poems.[62] The year *Loiners* was published he wrote that "it has been really bad this year, and in the end so bad I couldn't work properly...."[63] In a wryer tone he reports that the only break from "enforced slimming" was a basket of food delivered by a local charity worker, a little old lady who said "we heard about you." A displaced commentary about his experiences of poverty can be found in Harrison's 1975 translations of Palladae of Alexandria, epigrammatist of the fourth century A.D. and one of "the world's great pessimists,"[64] where with wrathful irony "poverty" is praised as "the soul / of temperance and self-control."[65]

In "Ghosts" Harrison identifies with Rimbaud as a poor man from a provincial region who struggled for material survival as a poet, and as an outsider in the literary world. Rimbaud's reputedly inexplicable farewell to poetry must be considered in the context of his fierce efforts to survive as a poet, and the poems and letters refer to his recurring experiences of hunger, homelessness, and a pariah status. In *A Season in Hell* he exclaims that *"J'exècre la misère"* ["I despise poverty"]: *"Eh bien! je dois enterrer mon imagination et mes souvenirs! Une belle gloire d'artiste et de conteur emportée!"* ["Well! I have to bury my imagination and my memories! A fine reputation of an artist and story-teller lost sight of!"].[66] Rimbaud was a revolutionary poet in both the content and forms of his work and was ahead of his time.[67] One of the few people of his day capable of understanding his poetry was Verlaine, whom he refers to as *"seulami"* ["my one friend"]. But with the collapse of that relationship Rimbaud lost his most important reader, and the material support Verlaine had given.[68] Rimbaud was also ostracized by powerful figures in the French literary community, and left without publishers, because, as Verlaine remembered, "some stupid hacks thought you a" "drunken schoolboy, a disgrace."[69] Rimbaud was aware his poetic silence was a tragedy, and Harrison sees this loss of poetry in a similar way.

The example of Rimbaud, the *"Shakespeare enfant"* as Victor Hugo dubbed him, is for Harrison one of literary history's most devastating "threat[s] to the most hubristic poetic self confidence."[70] Although *A Season in Hell* and *Illuminations*, masterpieces of modern European literature, were written before Rimbaud had turned twenty, he was unable to survive as a poet. Before *Loiners* was published an impoverished and little known Harrison repeatedly vowed that he had "irrevocably given up writing."[71] Rimbaud wrote that he was born a poet,[72] and in *A Season in Hell*, anticipating his anguished leave taking of poetry, asks *"Un homme qui veut se mutiler est bien damné, n'est-ce pas?"* ["A man who tries to mutilate himself is surely damned, isn't he?"].[73] "Ghosts" discloses Harrison's troubled empathy with Rimbaud's prophetic doubts, and his fear that he too may be driven into the self-mutilation entailed by such unnatural poetic silences.

"Ghosts" is also a memorial to Rimbaud as a figure of great poetic and personal importance for Harrison. Rimbaud's last letter is addressed to the director of a shipping company and enquires about the price for travel from Aphinar to the Suez. By now completely paralyzed, Rimbaud dictates a letter that shows his extraordinary will to keep moving and his inescapable artistry:

> Tous ces services sont là partout, et moi, impotent, malheureux, je ne peux rien trouver, le premier chien dans la rue vous dira cela.
>
> Envoyez-moi donc le prix des services d'Aphinar à Suez. Je suis complètement paralysé: donc je désire me trouver de bonne heure à bord. Dites-moi à quelle heure je dois être transporté à bord.
>
> [All the services there are everywhere, and I, infirm, miserable, I cannot find anything, the first dog in the street will tell you so. Please send me the price for services from Aphinar to Suez. I am completely paralyzed. I would therefore like to be on board well in advance. Tell me at what time I should be carried aboard.][74]

Aphinar does not exist on any maps and the letter refers to one of many journeys Rimbaud imagined as he lay dying. The letter was dictated to his sister Isabelle, who describes how Arthur was ending his life in a "deliberate dream" and "with art."[75] Rimbaud was once again artfully escaping reality and finding support in an imaginary story which affirmed his essential identity as a poet and traveller. Harrison came to "love Rimbaud" through his poetry and letters,[76] and the epigraph to "Ghosts" is also an epitaph for the man and the poet, celebrating and mourning Rimbaud's poetics of exploration and "departure into new affection and sound."[77]

Another poem "*Fonte Luminosa*" is also haunted by Rimbaud and centers round the crushing of Jane's legs and Harrison's need to walk. His daughter's tears "as once more you start coming through" "your seventh anaesthesia" remind him of the *fonte luminosa*, a luminous fountain in Brazil.[78] "*Fonte Luminosa*" is the second of the four parts comprising the long poem "Sentences" and was first published in 1978, but it draws on Harrison's travels in Brazil and Cuba in 1969, and his life in Africa and England in the 1960s. Back in Newcastle-upon-Tyne, he walks past "the crossing / where you had your legs crushed":

> Walking on the Great North Road
>
> with my back towards London
>
> through showers of watery sleet,
>
> my cracked rubber boot soles
>
> croak like African bullfrogs.[79]

The poem associates Harrison's walking on the Great North Road with his travels in Africa, and the associative image of the poet walking also recalls Rimbaud, "*le piéton de la grand'route*" ["the wanderer along the main road"],[80] often journeying by foot through Europe and Africa. The Northern poet turning his back on the Southern metropolis and its literary coteries also mirrors Rimbaud's rejection of Parisian literary milieus. In "*Fonte Luminosa*" Harrison's determined singularity, sorrows, and existential need to move are again shadowed by Rimbaud.

The importance of walking in "*Fonte Luminosa*" and "Ghosts" includes its continuity with other forms of exploration undertaken by Loiners in other poems from *Loiners*. As the PWD man, a Loiner who has travelled from Leeds to Lagos, explains, "Life's movement and life's danger and not a sit-down post."[81] Rimbaud's need to move was so great that he combined tramping with measures like legal expulsion as a foreign immigrant, and joined merchant navies in order to travel extensively without money through Europe and Africa.[82] There is uncertainty about what caused the paralysis that ended Rimbaud's journeys but he may privately have suspected syphilis, which he contracted in Africa while playing a part in French geographical exploration and economic imperialism.[83] Rimbaud's presence in "Ghosts" is consistent with the interest in *Loiners* in the intertwined literary history of empire and of syphilis. Rimbaud the great outsider was an involuntary member of a nineteenth-century French literary club of syphilitics, whose other "cursed poets" included two whom Rimbaud regarded as rare seers, Baudelaire and Verlaine.[84] In the last poem of *Loiners*, Harrison summons into the present the ghost of Rimbaud who still walks, "his long legs moving calmly and regularly...his beautiful eyes fixed on the distance, and his face entirely filled with a look of resigned defiance, an air of expectation—ready for everything, without anger, without fear."[85] Rimbaud haunts the imagination of Tony Harrison, Loiner.

NOTES

1. Original book description for *Loiners*, Tony Harrison's papers relating to *Loiners*, London Magazine Editions, 73 uncatalogued and unnumbered items, Special Collections, Brotherton Library, University of Leeds (abbreviated throughout this book as *THP*).

2. "Ghosts: Some Words before Breakfast," *Loiners* (London: London Magazine Editions, 1970), 96. See also Letter to Isabelle Rimbaud (2 July 1891), *I Promise to be Good: The Letters of Arthur Rimbaud*, trans. and ed. Wyatt Mason (New York and Toronto: Modern Library, 2004), 347.

3. *Poetry and Audience*, vol. 7, no. 22 (20 May 1960), 6–7. See also *Loiners*, 96.

4. Henrik Ibsen, *Ghosts; A Public Enemy; When We Dead Awake*, trans. Peter Watts (Harmondsworth: Penguin, 1964), 98.

5. Ibsen, *Ghosts*, 100.

6. *Loiners*, 91.

7. *Loiners*, 94.

8. See for example, Letter to Ross (4 May 1968), *THP*.

9. *Loiners*, 96.

10. Letter to Ross (4 May 1968), *THP*.

11. Letter to Silkin (16 June 1968).

12. Letter to Isabelle (2 July 1891), *I Promise to be Good*, 347.

13. Letter to Isabelle (15 July 1891), *I Promise to be Good*, 354.

14. *Loiners*, 94.

15. Letter to Silkin (28 February 1963).

16. Letter to Ross (4 May 1968).

17. *Loiners*, 95.

18. "The Death of The PWD Man," Northern Arts Ms. Collection Vol. 6, "Tony Harrison," The Literary and Philosophical Society, Newcastle-upon-Tyne.

19. *Loiners*, 93.

20. Arthur Rimbaud, *"Une saison en enfer"* [*"A Season in Hell"*], *Rimbaud: Complete Works, Selected Letters*, trans. Wallace Fowlie (Chicago: University of Chicago Press, 2005 [1966]), 270–271 (abbreviated as *RCWSL*). All quotations from Rimbaud's poems and letters are from *RCWSL* unless otherwise indicated.

21. *RCWSL*, 302–03, and 294–95).

22. *Loiners*, 94.

23. Letter to Isabelle (23 June 1891), *RCWSL*, 446–447.
24. "A Kumquat for John Keats," *CP*, 222.
25. Letter to Isabelle (2 July 1891), *I Promise to be Good*, 347.
26. *Loiners*, 94.
27. *Loiners*, 96.
28. "Shango," 89.
29. Letter to Isabelle (2 July 1891), *I Promise to be Good*, 347.
30. "Shango," 99.
31. *THP*, uncatalogued and unnumbered.
32. *Loiners*, 96.
33. Letter to Ross (21 July 1973), *THP*.
34. *Loiners*, 95.
35. Marianne Moore, "Poetry," *The Complete Poems* (London: Faber and Faber, 1968), 36.
36. "Conversation," 43.
37. "Interview with Bragg."
38. Letter to Isabelle (2 July 1891), *I Promise to be Good*, 347.
39. Graham Robb, *Rimbaud* (London: Picador, 2000), 426.
40. Letter to Isabelle (15 July 1891), in Arthur Rimbaud, *Selected Poems and Letters*, ed., trans., and with an Introduction by Jeremy Harding and John Sturrock (London: Penguin, 2004), 414.
41. *RCWSL*, 270–271.
42. "My Bohemian Life (Fantasy)," *RCWSL*, 66–67.
43. *Loiners*, 95.
44. "Conversation," 43.
45. "Interview," 236.
46. As emphasized, for example, in Charles Nicholl, *Somebody Else: Arthur Rimbaud in Africa 1880–1891* (London: Jonathan Cape, 1997). See also Rimbaud, Letter to Paul Demeny (15 May 1871), *RCWSL*, 374–375.
47. *Loiners*, 92.
48. *Loiners*, 93.
49. Letter to Silkin (16 June 1968).
50. *Loiners*, 93.
51. *RCWSL*, 272–273.
52. *Loiners*, 94.
53. Letter to Paul Demeny (28 August 1871), *RCWSL*, 386–387.
54. "Interview," 245.
55. *Loiners*, 93.
56. Letter to his Family (15 January 1885), *RCWSL*, 430–431.

57. Letter to Ross (21 July 1973), *THP*.

58. *Loiners*, 95.

59. Letter to Ross (4 May 1968 and 5 April 1968).

60. *Loiners*, 92–93.

61. Letter to Jeffrey Wainwright (18 December 1980), BC Ms 20c Wainwright, Special Collections, Brotherton Library, University of Leeds.

62. Letter to Silkin (22 October 1968).

63. Letter to Ross (7 October 1970).

64. "Preface," *Palladas: Poems, Bloodaxe 1*, 133–135, 133.

65. See epigram 21, *Palladas: Poems, CP*, 83.

66. *RCWSL*, 302–303.

67. The revolutionary trajectory of Rimbaud's poetry is discussed in Chapter 8.

68. Letter to Verlaine (4–5 July 1873), *RCWSL*, 396–397.

69. Paul Verlaine, "To Arthur Rimbaud," *Paul Verlaine: Selected Poems*, trans. Martin Sorrell (New York: Oxford University Press, 1999), 217.

70. "Inkwell," 34.

71. Letter to Silken (22 October 1968).

72. Letter to Paul Demeny (13 May 1871), *RCWSL*, 371.

73. *RCWSL*, 274–275.

74. Letter to the Director of the Messageries Maritimes (9 November 1891), *RCWSL*, 446–448.

75. Isabelle Rimbaud, Letter to her Mother (28 October 1891), *Selected Poems and Letters*, ed. Harding and Sturrock, 423.

76. In conversation with the poet at the National Theatre, in London on 11 April 2008, Harrison affirmed his love of Rimbaud.

77. Rimbaud, "*Départ*" ["Departure"], *Illuminations, RCWSL*, 320–321.

78. "*Fonte Luminosa*," *CP*, 107.

79. *CP*, 107.

80. Rimbaud, "*Enfance*, IV" ["Childhood, IV"], *Illuminations, RCWSL*, 312–313.

81. "The Songs of the PWD Man, II," *Loiners*, 52.

82. See for example Robb, *Rimbaud*, 162; and Enid Starkie, "On the Trail of Arthur Rimbaud," *The Modern Language Review*, vol. 38, no. 3 (1943), 206–216.

83. See Robb, *Rimbaud*, 418, 322 and 425. See also Isabelle Rimbaud, Letter to her Mother (22 September 1891), *Selected Poems and Letters*, ed. Harding and Sturrock, 419.

84. See Letter to Paul Demeny (15 May 1871), *RCWSL*, 380–381.

85. Ernest Delahaye, Letter to Berrichon (21 August 1896), in *Delahaye, Temoin de Rimbaud*, ed. F. Eigeldinger and A. Gendre (Neuchatel: La Baconniére, 1974), 155. Quoted in Harding and Sturrock, "Introduction," *Selected Poems and Letters*, xviii–xliii, xxxviii.

CHAPTER 6

ILLUMINATIONS

The importance of Rimbaud's life and work for Harrison's identity and poetic has not been recognized in the scholarship. Yet the identification is explicitly made by Harrison in *v.*, where he identifies with Rimbaud "the hoodlum poet," and is implicitly registered in "Ghosts: Some Words before Breakfast," where there is an underlying preoccupation with Rimbaud's poetic silence and the manner of his dying. This chapter examines Rimbaud's presence in some of Harrison's other writings. It explores the traces of Rimbaud's African years infused through the literary and historical terrain of the African poems in *Loiners*, and Harrison's implicit adoption of Rimbaud's identity as the white "*nègre.*" I also argue that Rimbaud's interest in Illuminism influences Harrison's elegiac vision in *The School of Eloquence*. The importance of "illuminations," in the sense of epiphanies and visions, for Harrison's poetry registers the influence of Rimbaud, and is also enriched by the writings of Percy Bysshe Shelley, James Joyce, and Walter Benjamin. Harrison's highly visual poetic also takes as one of its models Rimbaud's aesthetic of verbal photography or "illuminations."

Harrison's elective affinity with Rimbaud is signaled by the quotation from one of Rimbaud's earliest letters in *v.* and from one of his last letters in "Ghosts," a poem written more than fifteen years earlier, and three decades later the poet confirmed his enduring love of Rimbaud.[1] "The example of Rimbaud" is one of both emulation and difference for Harrison.[2] His identification with the white "*nègre*," a poetic identity dramatizing Rimbaud's roots in an inferior white domestic class, is discernable in "The Inkwell of Dr Agrippa" (1971). The title of this short autobiographical statement alludes to "The Story of the Inky Boys," a German children's tale about white boys who are turned black in the inkwell of Dr Agrippa for teasing a blackamoor. Agrippa chastises the boys to "leave the Black-a-moor alone!" because "He cannot change from black to white."[3] Harrison, however, has changed from white to "black," the color of ink and of Africans. Metaphorically blackened in Agrippa's inkwell of learning, he discovers that his class subjugation is the basis of an affinity with Africans. "Inkwell" is the story of the inky "black" poet, and his dip into Agrippa's inkwell is also linked to his "growing black" and his *négritude* in "On Not Being Milton." The allusion in the sonnet to Aimé Césaire's iconic poem of *négritude*, *Cahier d'un retour au pays natal* [*Notebook of a return to the native land*] signals Harrison's parallel development of an aesthetic to ennoble Northern working class experience.[4] It has not been noticed in the scholarship on Harrison, however, that he implicitly adopts Rimbaud's poetic identity as the white "*nègre*."

Césaire regarded Rimbaud as his most important inspiration, and Rimbaud and Césaire are powerful interrelated influences on Harrison.[5] In *Cahier d'un retour au pays natal* Césaire coined the defiant term *négritude*, which is derived from the racist "*nègre*" or "nigger," as "a violent affirmation" in a world where to be black was to be ashamed.[6] Rimbaud also identified himself as a "*nègre*" but translated this, as Harrison does, into the class degradation of a poor white man. Harrison's *négritude* is implicitly an adoption of Rimbaud's self-conception as a white "nigger." In the prose poem "*Mauvais Sang*" ["Bad Blood"], from *Une saison en enfer* [*A Season in Hell*], Rimbaud's white narrator says "*Je suis de race inférieure*" ["I am of an inferior race"],[7] and uses the derogatory term "*nègre*" subversively to express his origins in an inferior white domestic class. Rimbaud originally considered the titles *Livre nègre* [*The Book of the Nigger*] and *Livre païen* [*The Book of the pagan*] for "Bad Blood,"[8] and its narrator affirms that he is a "*nègre*," and imagines travelling to the primitive tropics and returning to Europe with darkened skin.[9] In a poetic eulogy Verlaine described Rimbaud as the "*nègre blanc*" ["white Negro"].[10]

Harrison and Rimbaud dramatize their origins in the inferior white domestic classes through a poetic identification with enslaved Africans. Rimbaud's narrator in "Bad Blood" declares that he has never belonged to Christian Europe and that "*J'entre au vrai royaume des enfants de Cham*" ["I am entering upon the true kingdom of the children of Ham"].[11] The last line of "On Not Being Milton" includes the words "*I Ham*."[12] Ham was the second son of Noah, and the curse of Ham is the curse of servitude Noah laid upon his son in the *Book of Genesis*.[13] The descendants of Ham came to be regarded as the enslaved Africans, with whom both Rimbaud and Harrison identify. Harrison's familiarity with the legend of Ham's African descendants is evident in the allusion to "the sable sons of Ham" in "Voortrekker."[14] In "On Not Being Milton" "*I Ham*" is part of a quotation of the last words of Richard Tidd, the Cato Street conspirator hanged as an enemy of the state in 1820: "*Sir, I Ham a very Bad Hand at Righting*." In the sonnet the quotation refers to the history of English working-class radicalism and the standardization of English, but the punning allusion to Ham also links Harrison and the Northern working class with enslaved Africans. Harrison's identification with Africans is also mediated through Rimbaud.

Harrison's reclamation of his "black" barbarian roots in "Inkwell" and "On Not Being Milton" parallels Rimbaud's establishment of his "black" barbarian history in "Bad Blood." In "On Not Being Milton" Harrison declares, upon returning to England from Africa, that he is "growing black enough to fit my boots," black "boots" connoting black "roots."[15] In a reverse trajectory Rimbaud leaves Europe to return to his black roots. Rimbaud also suggests solidarity between Africans and French

Communards in "*Qu'est-ce pour nous, mon coeur*" ["What does it matter for us, my heart"], reaching out to his "*frères: Noirs inconnus*" ["brothers: / Dark strangers"], in despair after the bloody destruction of the Paris Commune in 1871.[16] Harrison shares this sense of brotherhood with Africans and forges a class-based identification with the black race Rimbaud's narrator declares he belongs to in "Bad Blood." In both poets there is an empowering association of the white lower classes with the reviled black race, an association that ironically and subversively recalls the common presentation of the lumpenproletariat as a depraved tribe in nineteenth-century bourgeois social analysis.[17] In *v.* Harrison identifies with Rimbaud, understanding him as an explosive blend of poet, lumpenproletarian skinhead, and white "nigger." The exploration in *Loiners* of lower-class Europeans gaining class and racial ascendancy in Africa, and becoming "someone else," recalls Rimbaud's life in Africa, and Harrison paraphrases Rimbaud's famous poetic dictum in *v.*.

Rimbaud is also important for one of Harrison's greatest obsessions, the struggle for personal and historical articulation versus a silence bespeaking powerlessness. In "Inkwell" he traces his unlikely formation as a poet by traversing ostensibly disparate stages of his life, from WWII to Leeds Grammar to Africa to his own reading and translation. The underlying uniting theme of these experiences is Harrison's definitive struggle for expression despite biographical and historical pressures to be silent. His "bouts of speechlessness" began in his WWII childhood, where images of Belsen and VJ day bonfires to celebrate Hiroshima still "casts dark shadows in my skull."[18] "Haunted by recent history on which speech gags," and with the examples of Rimbaud, Hieronymus Fracastorius, and Virgil in mind, Harrison wavered between the effort to keep writing and a vow of silence.[19] Harrison's silences are part of his empathetic identification with Rimbaud, Fracastorius, and Virgil, major poets in his personal canon. Fracastorius "was born literally without a mouth and died speechless," Virgil requested that his "botched" masterpiece *The Aeneid* be burned at his death, and Rimbaud's poetic silence "is also disturbing."

Poetic silences and Africa are entwined dimensions of Rimbaud's importance for Harrison. An impoverished poet who fell silent and sought his fortune as a trader in Africa,[20] one legend has it that Africa destroyed Rimbaud's poetic voice. In his letters from Nigeria, Harrison similarly conceives of Africa as a place that causes creative "aridity" because it "burnt out" the senses. Europeans "cut off their awareness because it is hard on the mind and the senses to take in Africa."[21] He thought that he would write about Africa after he left,[22] but instead wrote and staged *Aikin Mata* and began writing *Loiners* in Nigeria.[23] Rimbaud and Joseph Conrad have been seen as major figures in conflicting mythologies of Africa as a place that reduces European writers to silence, or a place of literary inspiration.[24] Mythologies of Africa as dissolving or inspiring European creativity as mediated by Rimbaud and Conrad have resonances in Harrison's letters and in African poems like "Heart of Darkness." In "*Satyrae*, V" a European stranded between "miles of churning sea" and the African Sahara is silenced by a Sartrean sense of nothingness and nausea.[25] Africa, silences, *négritude*, and the age of exploration and empire are preoccupations in "Inkwell" and the African poems of *Loiners*.

Rimbaud is a ghost in the imaginative landscape of the African poems. He played a part in many of the historical scenes referred to in the poems, and sometimes translated into a twentieth-century setting, including the migration of European men making their fortune in "the scramble for Africa," and engaging in sexual and domestic relationships with the Africans.[26] *Loiners*' focus on Africa, sex, empire, and *Heart of Darkness* emanates from historical terrain inhabited by Rimbaud. Ideas associated with Rimbaud in Africa are also explored by Conrad in *Heart of Darkness*, such as escaping the constraints of "civilization" and becoming "someone else." It has been argued that there are broad parallels between the legend of Rimbaud the poet and Communard sympathizer now "lost in the midst of Negroes,"[27] and Kurtz the poet and political radical who "went native" in Africa, though the comparison stops there.[28] Rimbaud was dead by the time Conrad began writing in the mid 1890s, but in the year *Heart of Darkness* (1899) was published Conrad said he was familiar with

Rimbaud's verses.[29] Harrison's entwined fascination with Africa, *Heart of Darkness*, and Rimbaud finds imaginative expression in *Loiners*.

Harrison imaginatively conceives of himself as a poet-explorer, a "poet / Pissarro" with an "El Dorado in my head,"[30] and global geographical movement is a basis of *Loiners* and subsequent poems. His most important model for the poet-explorer is Rimbaud, a poet whose travels were also very important to his poetry and letters, and who metamorphosed into an explorer in Africa. Graham Robb describes Rimbaud as "the Dr Livingstone of French literature,"[31] and Harrison aspired to be the Dr Livingstone of English literature: "Somehow it seems that my two early ambitions to be Dr Livingstone and George Formby, were compromised in the role of poet, half missionary, half comic, Bible and banjolele, the Renaissance *ut doceat, ut placeat.*"[32] He shares with Rimbaud an enduring interest in the accounts of nineteenth-century explorers. Like the young Harrison reading *Livingstone's Travels*, Rimbaud's early writings were inspired by adventure novels like *Robinson Crusoe* but also *Discovery of the Source of the Nile* by the nineteenth-century explorers Speke and Grant.[33] Harrison also refers to travelers' accounts, including those of Livingstone and Francis Galton, and *FRAM* (2008) is about the nineteenth century Norwegian explorer Fridtjof Nansen, another man of adventure devoted to art who captured Harrison's imagination.[34]

Some of Rimbaud's letters were an explorer's account of Africa, in the sense that they describe foreign lands and his expeditions into uncharted territories, and they are part of the travel literature Harrison reads. Rimbaud published a very influential essay about one of his expeditions, and it "helped to shape French policy and thus the modern history of East Africa."[35] Robb's view is that "apart from Victor Hugo, no French poet of the late nineteenth century had a greater impact on imperial politics or earned more money" than Rimbaud.[36] Harrison's interest in Hugo's life and times, and his reading of Robb's biography *Victor Hugo*, in which the life is understood in its historical context, also evidences his interest in the nineteenth-century imperial history of which Rimbaud was a part.

Harrison's poems often subtly invite the reader to see his poetry as verbal photography about his travels and wider experience, and this too seems to have been inspired by Rimbaud. A number of the poems liken Harrison's craft to visual forms, are concerned with how word and image illuminate each other, and show the poet reflecting upon photographs, paintings, drawings, films, and postcards, a form which highlights the importance of travel in his life and work. Literary geography and place names are important to many of his poems, including in *Loiners*, and are also important to Rimbaud's poems, particularly in *Illuminations*. The *"Zeg-Zeg Postcards"* in *Loiners* foreground the poet as a verbal photographer in the context of travel. The title presents the poems as *"Postcards"* in which the visual and linguistic elements are literally and semantically inseparable. The note at the end of the *"Zeg-Zeg Postcards"* sequence explains: *"The postcards are all from, or of, places in Europe visited by the 'White Queen' on leaves from Africa, and the poems on them are, almost without exception, about Africa. Picture and poem are often strangely interrelated."*[37] Using the satirical persona of a gay white poet living in Africa, "the White Queen," as his fictional author, Harrison writes poems that he titles *"Postcards."* The concept of *"Zeg-Zeg Postcards"* recalls Rimbaud, who in one of his many lives was a gay white poet who tried to establish himself as a photographer in Africa, and sent letters and black and white photographs back to Europe. In the photographic self-portraits Rimbaud, as he prophesied in "Bad Blood," has skin so dark he might almost be of a different race,[38] so dark that he is "tanned almost to *négritude.*"[39]

Many of the *"Zeg-Zeg Postcards"* contain risqué or pornographic homosexual images that have parodic elements, and the sequence seems inspired by the *Album Zutique*, a series of homo-erotic parodic poems circulated as playful correspondence between Rimbaud, Verlaine, and a group of poets collectively known as the *Vilain Bonhommes* and later as the *Zutist Circle*. The *"Postcards"* share the spirit of the *Album Zutique*, whose title is derived from the slang *"zut,"* a stronger version of "damn," and is redolent of the aggression signified by Harrison's polyvalent *v.*

sign. The title *Album Zutique* also invites the reader to conceive of the poems as a collection of photographs in a photo album. Similarly, the title and "Note" to *"Zeg-Zeg Postcards"* invites the reader to conceive of these poems as *"a collection written on the backs of postcards and gradually accumulated over the years in a card-index cabinet."*[40] Harrison also collects postcards and considered having reproductions of postcard images accompany the text of *"Zeg-Zeg Postcards."*[41]

The trope of photography for poetry is found in a number of the elegiac sonnets from *The School of Eloquence*, where the contemplation of photos and also films and paintings reveals metaphysical truths manifest in the material. The title of the sonnet "Still," for example, literally refers to a movie still or photograph of Rudolph Valentino, and to the stillness of death, and metaphysically to the continuation of the poet's relationship to his dead father, who admired Valentino. The title of "Gaps" refers to the physical gap left between Harrison's father and son when he moved to photograph them, and metaphorically to the gap left in his life by his father's death and by his son's absence through madness, specifically schizophrenia,[42] "his visions frightening as the First Gulf War's."[43] Ironically, the person not in the "snap" of "a snatched but happy family scene" is the only one still fully present. The subtle intimation of private grief in "Gaps" is quietly framed by public mourning, and its reference to individual insanity is framed by historic madness, which anticipates the gaping hole in New York City's landscape after the terrorist attacks in 2001, and which the sonnet links to American foreign policy in the Middle East, like the Gulf Wars. The background in the photo is "the World Trade Centre's unbombarded towers."[44] In another *School of Eloquence* sonnet "Background Material" the poet photographing his parents can be discerned as a background reflection. Several of the Sonnets for August 1945, "Black & White," "Snap," and "The Figure," also use the trope of photographs for poems. The important relationship between word and image in Harrison's poetry is also evident is his being a poet of the stage and the screen, where his verse literally accompanies visual mediums. He has observed how "the scansions of the screen and the prosodies of poetry" together create the "mutually illuminating momentum" of the film-poem.[45]

In "Bridlington" Harrison sketches in words the scene of his portrait being sketched by the Yorkshire artist David Hockney, and mirrors their arts: "Him drawing those lines me composing these."[46] "Skywriting," dedicated to Hockney, likens and contrasts their visual and linguistic arts: "My desk top's like a Californian pool,"[47] an allusion to Hockney's famous paintings which take pleasure in that environment and lifestyle even as they observe its superficiality. "Skywriting" suggests Harrison's art and temperament is antithetical to a "HAPPY" Californian culture that is oblivious to the "dark depths" of experience.[48] The sonnet punningly chastises Californian narcissism by alluding to the myth of Narcissus, which had tragic subjects like unrequited love, retribution, and death. It identifies the poet as a "blackface Narcissus" who does not limit his gaze to reflections but metaphorically enters the waters and the underworld. "Skywriting' is a later sonnet that also shows the continuation of Harrison's metaphorical identification as "black": "The tarred creator stares at seas of ink." "Skywriting" presents the synaesthetic poet as a visual artist giving voice to human "cries."

Harrison's conception of his poetry as verbal photography and the influence of Rimbaud are also suggested by *The School of Eloquence* sonnets "Illuminations I, II, III," which allude to Rimbaud's *Illuminations*, his collection of highly visual prose poems.[49] The title of Rimbaud's *Illuminations* meant "coloured plates," referring to the method of photography then used, and his interest in photography dated back to *Illuminations*.[50] He also conceives of his poetry as verbal hallucinations in "*Alchimie du verbe*" ["Alchemy of the Word"], from *A Season in Hell*.[51] In "*Voyelles*" ["Vowels"] Rimbaud uses vowels to symbolize colors whose correspondences he has chosen, such as "O blue," so that the poet can imaginatively paint visual scenes.[52] The title *Illuminations* signifies the verbal photography of Rimbaud's poetry and also metaphorical "visions," intuitions, or epiphanies. Harrison also refers, in "Initial Illuminations," both literally to the coloring and embellishment of letters in the *Lindis-farne Gospels* and metaphorically to poetic vision and epiphany. The title of Harrison's "Illuminations" also has the sense of verbal portraiture and of epiphany and registers his reading of Joyce, Benjamin and Shelley.

The concept of "illuminations" begins and ends the sonnets "Illuminations, I, II." The Blackpool lights are a quotidian objective correlative for the metaphysical light or epiphany articulated in both these sonnets. The last sentence of "Illuminations, I" is: "The penny dropped in time! Wish you were here!"[53] The poet wishes that his dead father was with him now, and that he had realized while there was still time together the nature of his life and his love, but "it took me until now to understand." Instead there are late illuminations and the sonnet itself. Like a penny dropping in the "machines on Blackpool's Central Pier," illuminations are truths that shine through ordinary experience. Harrison's early unpublished prose was influenced by Joyce,[54] and the illuminations in his later sonnets are redolent of Joyce's epiphanies, where the "soul of the commonest object...seems to us radiant" and shines through the material and the ordinary.[55] Harrison seems to follow Joyce in his secular understanding of illuminations as heightened moments of perception, when visual contemplation of common people, objects, and situations reveals profound meanings radiating through the appearance.

The title of Harrison's "Illuminations," and its signification of meanings which transcend time and the material world, may also allude to Hannah Arendt's classic selection of essays by the Jewish-German literary critic Walter Benjamin entitled *Illuminations*. Harrison has read Benjamin's essays and *Illuminations* is probably the edition he read or would certainly be aware of.[56] "Illuminations I, II" are set in "that post-war year" and the "millions of ghosts in the machine" encompass the millions of Jewish lives taken, like Benjamin's, by Nazism.[57] "*The Haunted House*" is a machine on the pier but also in the sonnet a symbol of the collective cultural imagination haunted by the terrors of recent history. The Nazis' industrialization of genocide is signified by five references in a fourteen line sonnet to "machines." The "50 weeks of ovens, and 6 years of war" refers to the ovens his father baked bread in, but also the incineration of inmates in the concentration camps. Arendt chose *Illuminations* as the title because this word was used by Benjamin to describe his work. Harrison's metaphorical "illuminations," such as the Blackpool lights, may reflect his reading of Benjamin because they lend a material form to the immaterial, and draw connections between distinct experiences and spheres. Benjamin's conception of metaphorical language as "the means by which the oneness of the world is poetically brought about,"[58]and the constellation of past, present, and future, also illuminates the electricity metaphor charging "Illuminations, II." The sonnet's reference to "Ohm's Law" metaphorically suggests that the invisible flow of electrons is "that small bright charge of life" where his parents meet in their son. The metaphor articulates the oneness of past, present, and future generations as genetic, mnemonic, and poetic, where illumination is also the apprehension of the possibility of "eternity" and a reality that is not discernible to the world of the senses.

Harrison's "illuminations" also involve wonder, with Keatsian negative capability, about the philosophical idea that there is a pure reality behind the visible world and this idea was important to Rimbaud, who was fascinated with the works of the nineteenth-century Illuminists and their belief "that behind the stage-set of sensory impressions lies a pure, absolute reality."[59] Illuminism influences the metaphysics behind a number of Rimbaud's poems such as "Vowels," *A Season in Hell*, and some of the prose poems in *Illuminations*. In "Illuminations, II" Harrison questioningly juxtaposes "eternity, annihilation, me," intuiting a continuing connection between himself and his dead parents:

Two dead, but current still flows through us three

though the circle takes forever to complete—

eternity, annihilation, me,

that small bright charge of life where they both meet.[60]

The sonnet corporealizes the intangible sense of connection with the dead beloved as the poet's begetting by his parents. He also though evokes "eternity" and an invisible current of connection with the dead, as live as electricity. In a number of the filial sonnets his rational atheism co-exists with a suspension of disbelief and hope of reunion with the dearly departed. "Under the Clock," for example, evokes a conception of time, figured as "Father Time," wherein the moment of the poet's own death will be the time of "our rendezvous."[61] The ambiguous sense of eternity in the elegiac filial sonnets may owe much to Rimbaud's interest in Illuminism.

In "Continuous" Harrison senses the presence of his dead father and intimations of a reality beyond the material world, which is mediated through Shelley's interest in Illuminism and a James Cagney gangster film.[62] Describing Cagney's as "the only art we ever shared," the sonnet connects the film noir flicks with the learned culture that separated the poet from his father, but which now illuminates his continuing sense of connection to him despite death. Remembering childhood jaunts with his father to see Cagney films, Harrison continues their outings on his own but wears the gold ring his father gave him, and still buys the childhood treat of a choc-ice: "I wear it now to Cagneys on my own / and sense my father's hands cupped round my treat." The gold ring is a symbol of eternal connection in "Continuous" and in other filial sonnets collected in *Continuous.* In the sonnet Mr Harrison's cremation is imagined taking place on the stage of the old-style cinema they went to together, where the movie-house organists played live music between features. The poet-son also hears a looped recording that figuratively suggests a continuous mnemonic connection to his father, and that obsessive replaying of memories associated with irresolvable conflicts and grief. The imagined theatrical cremation of Mr Harrison in the cinema recalls the last scene of Cagney's *White Heat,* when the character played by Cagney, Coady Jarret, commits suicide by causing a conflagration. Coady is a psychopathic criminal with an Oedipal complex, and tells an associate that he still talks to his dead "ma" and has a comforting sense of her presence, and asks if this seems insane. Harrison's sonnet about sensing his dead father's presence explores Coady's question through the larger mystery of what might lie on the other side of life.

Harrison turns for possible answers to Shelley's elegy for John Keats, "Adonais," which reflects Shelley's interest in Illuminism. In "Continuous" the "blinding light" of the crematorium flames annihilating Mr Harrison's body is also a metaphorical intimation of eternity. Introducing "Continuous," Harrison explains that *White Heat* refers to the film but also to "what Shelley called 'the white radiance of eternity'."[63] He is quoting a line from "Adonais," which ends with the soul of Keats figured as Adonais continuing "where the Eternal are":[64] "Life, like a dome of many-coloured glass, / Stains the white radiance of Eternity."[65] Shelley's conception of life and eternity bears some resemblance to Rimbaud's ideas about "illuminations," "coloured plates," and an absolute reality behind the visible world in, for example, "*Les Ponts*" ["Bridges"], from *Illuminations*: "*Un rayon blanc, tombant du haut du ciel, anéantit cette comédie.*" ["A white ray, falling from the top of the sky, blots out this dumb comedy."][66] In the prose poem the skies are like "Gray crystal," the pattern of bridges is mirrored in the lighted canal like a mirage, and the city is a sideshow and an illusion dispelled by a white ray of light.

Shelley also argued that the "poet participates in the eternal, the infinite, and the one," and that poetry must work through images of life to intimate transcendence in "A Defence of Poetry,"[67] which Harrison has read.[68] In "Continuous" film is a metaphor for life understood as a stage-set of images, through which the metaphysical radiance of "eternity" can be glimpsed. The idea is also present in "Testing the Reality," a sonnet about the death of Harrison's mother, where the instinctual flocking of birds intimates transcendence but has "blacked Beeston's sky."[69] The world of the senses, "all sight, all hearing, taste, smell, touch" has also "blocked the light," and her son is "the last soul still unhatched left in the clutch." Death is intimated as a birth into a reality associated with light beyond the material world and embodied self, in which he will be reunited with his mother. The allusion in "Continuous" to Shelley, an atheist like Harrison and Rimbaud, mediates an instinctual sense of eternity behind the transient stage-set of the senses, symbolized by the metaphor of film and cremation's flames.

While there may be several sources for Harrison's "illuminations," the presence of Rimbaud seems of primary significance. Harrison and Rimbaud conceive of a number of their poems as "illuminations" or "coloured plates," intensely observed verbal "photographs" of the sensory, material world, through which epiphanies or "illuminations" are sometimes manifest. There are enigmatic traces of Rimbaud's significance for Harrison wherever he uses photography as a trope for poetry, in the highly visual character of his verse for the page, stage, and screen, in the relationship between his poetry and travel, in the possibility of eternity he allows as an elegist, and in the authenticity of a brilliant and angry poor boy, the white *nègre* who gives voice to his rage in *v.*.

NOTES

1. In my conversation with the poet at the National Theatre in 2008, Harrison affirmed that "I love Rimbaud."
2. "Inkwell," 34.
3. Heinrich Hoffman-Donner, "The Inky Boys," in *Struwwelpeter, or, Merry Rhymes and Funny Pictures* (London: Blackie, 1900), 8–11, 9.
4. *Permanently Bard*, 171.
5. Clayton Eshleman and Annette Smith, "Introduction," in *Aimé Césaire: The Collected Poetry*, trans. Clayton Eshleman and Annette Smith (Berkeley: University of California Press, 1983), 1–31, 16.
6. "Interview with Aimé Césaire," in Aimé Césaire, *Discourse on Colonialism*, trans. Joan Pinkham (New York: Monthly Review Press, 1972), 65–79, 69. Also noted for a different purpose in Chapter 3.
7. "*Mauvais Sang*" ["Bad Blood"], *RCWSL*, 268–269.
8. Letter to Ernest Delahaye (May 1873), *RCWSL*, 392–393.
9. *RCWSL*, 268–269.
10. Paul Verlaine, "To Arthur Rimbaud," *Paul Verlaine: Selected Poems*, trans. Martin Sorrell (Oxford: Oxford University Press, 1999), 219.
11. *RCWSL*, 270–271.
12. "On Not Being Milton," *CP*, 122.
13. Genesis: 18–25, in *The Bible: Authorized King James Version*, ed. Robert Carroll and Stephen Prickett (Oxford and New York: Oxford University Press, 1997).
14. "Voortrekker," *CP*, 111.
15. *CP*, 122.
16. "*Qu'est-ce pour nous, mon coeur*" ["What does it matter for us, my heart"], *RCWSL*, 214–215.
17. Peter Stallybrass, "Marx and Heterogeneity: Thinking the Lumpenproletariat," *Representations*, no. 31 (Summer 1990), 69–95, 70.
18. "Inkwell," 32.
19. "Inkwell," 34.
20. See for example Letter to his Family (15 January 1885), *RCWSL*, 428–431. See also Robb, *Rimbaud*, 335–336.
21. Letter to Silkin (8 November 1964; and 4 December 1962).
22. Letter to Silkin (28 February 1963).
23. "Inkwell," 32.

24. Christopher L. Miller, *Blank Darkness: Africanist Discourse in French* (Chicago: University of Chicago Press, 1985), 181.

25. "The White Queen 1: *Satyrae*, V," *Loiners*, 26.

26. See Enid Starkie, *Arthur Rimbaud in Abyssinia* (Oxford: Clarendon Press, 1937); Robb, *Rimbaud*; and Charles Nicholl, *Somebody Else: Arthur Rimbaud in Africa 1880–91* (London: Jonathan Cape, 1997).

27. Letter to his Family (4 August 1888), *RCWSL*, 437.

28. Ian Watts, *Conrad in the Nineteenth Century* (London: Chatto and Windus, 1980), 164.

29. Joseph Conrad, Letter to William Blackwood (8 February 1899), *The Collected Letters of Joseph Conrad*, vol. 2, ed. Laurence Davies and Gene M. Moore (Cambridge: Cambridge University Press, 2005), 162.

30. "Fig on the Tyne," *CP*, 392. The poem puns upon the colloquial term "piss," or alcohol, and the conquistador Francisco Pizarro. See also "New Worlds for Old," 83.

31. Robb, *Rimbaud*, 399.

32. "Inkwell," 33.

33. Robb, *Rimbaud*, 20.

34. Harrison refers to Francis Galton's travels in South Africa, for example, in the "Preface" to *The Misanthrope*, reprinted in *Bloodaxe 1*, 138–53, 139–140. See also Francis Galton, *The Narrative of an Explorer in Tropical South Africa* (London: John Murray, 1853).

35. See *Le Bosphore égyptien* (25 and 27 August 1887). See also Robb, *Rimbaud*, 384.

36. Robb, *Rimbaud*, xvi.

37. "The White Queen 5: from *The Zeg-Zeg Postcards*," "Note," *Loiners*, 46.

38. *RCWSL*, 268–269.

39. "Newcastle is Peru," *Loiners*, 87. For examples of Rimbaud's photographic self-portraits see Robb, *Rimbaud*, photographs inserted between 364–365; and Nicholl, *Somebody Else*, photographs inserted between 241–242.

40. *Loiners*, 46.

41. Letter to Alan Ross (30 December 1969).

42. "Two Poems for My Son in his Sickness: 1. Rice-Paper Man," *CP*, 344.

43. "Gaps," *CP*, 215.

44. *CP*, 215.

45. "Flicks and This Fleeting Life," in *Collected Film Poetry* (London: Faber and Faber, 2007), vii–xxx, xxx.

46. "Bridlington," *CP*, 374.

47. "Skywriting," *CP*, 226.

48. *CP*, 228.

49. *Illuminations, RCWSL*, 309–357.

50. In an introduction to *Illuminations*, when the poems were first published in *La Vogue* in 1886, Verlaine explained the title: "The word *Illuminations* is English and means coloured engravings,*coloured plates*: it is even the subtitle that Mr Rimbaud had given to his manuscript."

51. "*Alchimie du verbe*" ["Alchemy of the Word"], *RCWSL*, 288–289.

52. "*Voyelles*" ["Vowels"], *RCWSL*, 140–141.

53. "Illuminations, I," *CP*, 157.

54. "Conversation," 40.

55. James Joyce, *Stephen Hero: part of the first draft of "A Portrait of the Artist as a Young Man"*, ed. T. Spencer, rev. ed. (London: Jonathon Cape, 1969), 213.

56. Harrison refers to Benjamin's essay "The Task of the Translator" in "Preface" to *The Misanthrope*, reprinted in *Bloodaxe 1*, 138–153.

57. Walter Benjamin took his own life to avoid capture by the Gestapo. See Hannah Arendt, "Walter Benjamin: 1892–1940," in Walter Benjamin, *Illuminations*, ed. Hannah Arendt, trans. Harry Zohn (New York: Schocken, 1969), 1–58, 18.

58. Arendt, "Walter Benjamin," 14.

59. Robb, *Rimbaud*, 159. Enid Starkie also discusses Rimbaud's interest in occult and Illuminist philosophy and his reading of other poets influenced by Illuminism like Charles Baudelaire. See Enid Starkie, *Arthur Rimbaud* (London: Hamish Hamilton, 1947 [1938]), 100–103.

60. "Illuminations, II," *CP*, 158.

61. "Under the Clock," *CP*, 180.

62. "Continuous," *CP*, 154.

63. Harrison, "Poets on Screen," <http://lion.chadwyck.com/poetsonscreen/showclip>.

64. Percy Bysshe Shelley, "Adonais," *Percy Bysshe Shelley: Selected Poetry and Prose*, ed. K.N. Cameron (New York: Holt, Rinehart and Winston, 1951), l. 495, 278.

65. Shelley, "Adonais," ll. 462–463, 277.

66. "*Les Ponts*" ["Bridges"], *RCWSL*, 326–327.

67. Percy Bysshe Shelley, "A Defence of Poetry," *Shelley's Prose, or The Trumpet of a Prophecy*, ed. D.L. Clark (New York: New Amsterdam Books, 1988 [1955]), 279. See also John Hardy and Nicholas Brown,

'Shelley's "Dome of Many-Coloured Glass." *Sydney Studies*, 103–106, 105.

68. The epigraph to "The White Queen 3: *Travesties*, I" is from Shelley's "A Defence of Poetry."

69. "Testing the Reality," *CP*, 173.

CHAPTER 7

THE POLITICS OF ELOQUENCE

The School of Eloquence (1978–) is Harrison's major ongoing sonnet sequence, and it contains further sequences of political-historical sonnets and of filial sonnets. *The School of Eloquence* is his most discussed work and it is the filial sonnets which have attracted extensive commentary. Widely regarded as being among the most moving poems in the language, the filial sonnets have also been criticized for sentimentality.[1] It has been observed that the focus upon the sentiment of these sonnets has obscured their political concerns.[2] What has not been noticed is the sonnets' politics of sentiment. The way Harrison's republicanism and socialism are refracted in the sonnets about his family is illuminated by "Marked with D," the great elegiac sonnet for Mr Harold Harrison. "Marked with D" remembers his uneducated father's "feeling of being worthless...,"[3] and grieves for "the baker's man that no one will see rise / and England made to feel like some dull oaf."[4] The political implications of merging the rising of the baker's man with mastery of language are clear in poetry preoccupied with linguistic and political suppression. Harrison's deeply felt and highly crafted bid for the heart is a humanist political weapon of poetic dissent against the British class system. The filial sonnets have attracted distinguished commentary. In this chapter

I will be discussing the political sonnets, the creation of a republican political mythology, and the identification with John Milton that lies at the heart of Harrison's republicanism.

I

The School of Eloquence is an unfinished "work in progress" and seemingly will only end with the poet's death.[5] The sonnet sequence to date has an unusual and complex publication history, and has progressively appeared in a variety of publications. The first publication of *The School of Eloquence* was a private edition containing ten sonnets and published by Rex Collings as a Christmas Book (1976), with 150 copies made.[6] Eighteen sonnets appeared in *From "The School of Eloquence" and Other Poems* (1978), and the sequence expanded again in *Continuous: Fifty Sonnets from "The School of Eloquence"* (1981). Sixty-four sonnets appeared in the first edition of the *Selected Poems* (1984). *Ten Sonnets from "The School of Eloquence"* (1987) was published in the same year that seventy-six sonnets appeared in the second edition of the *Selected Poems.* Five new sonnets appeared alongside other poems in *Under the Clock* (2005), and the *Collected Poems* (2007) contains ninety-five sonnets. A number of the sonnets were collected in anthologies, and also progressively published individually in magazines and newspapers before being collected together in the more permanent book form. The sonnet sequence, as it appears in *Continuous* and in later *Selected* and *Collected* editions, has a tri-partite structure, with the political sonnets in part one, the filial sonnets in part two, and sonnets on a range of themes in part three. The word "*Continuous*" in the title of the 1981 edition conveys that Harrison regards the sequence as "a continual enterprise."[7]

Harrison's use of the unfinished sonnet sequence is not without precedent. Literary pretexts for the sequence include George Meredith's *Modern Love* (1862), which anticipates the sixteen line sonnet form used by Harrison. Although *Modern Love* is not an unfinished sequence it is a series of fifty connected sonnets, just as *School* is a long series of connected sonnets which though are also grouped into sequences. Harrison uses a variable sixteen-line Meredithian sonnet, rather than the fourteen-line Shakespearian sonnet, for its metrical and narrative possibilities:

> I decided on the sixteen-line sonnet because not only can you make it do what the traditional octet-sestet fourteen-liner can do but also because you can use it, for example, as two octets— so that the dialectic can be stronger. It also has...the narrative possibilities of Meredith as well as all the single, one-off strengths of the traditional sonnet.[8]

Another literary antecedent for *The School of Eloquence* sonnet sequence is the American modernist poet Ezra Pound's *Cantos*. Like *School*, Pound's *Cantos* is an unfinished personal mythology with political commentary, with the centrality of the poet-persona and his vocation. Harrison comments that "Pound was important to me" because he called "the bluff of all that sort of artificial English,"[9] but thinks that Pound "virtually lost the struggle with comprehensibility."[10] In Harrison's quatrain poem "Summoned by Bells" it is Pound's fascism and elitism that helped "rebotch" what Pound had called in *Hugh Selwyn Mauberley* "a botched civilization."[11] Harrison rejects Pounds politics but is interested in his ideas about literature, and *Cantos* is a model for *The School of Eloquence*.

An important question which needs to be addressed is why Harrison, a politically engaged poet, chooses an apparently apolitical form, the sonnet, in *The School of Eloquence*. He knows most people don't read poetry and certainly not sonnets. Given the centrality of political ideas to his poetry, it would seem a more obvious choice for Harrison to only write public verse or forms of poetry that have more often been used as vehicles for political ideas. John Donne, for example, uses the sonnet to talk about religion and love. Shakespeare and Sir Philip Sidney are of a tradition in which the sonnet is used to talk about love. Although traditionally and in more recent times the sonnet has been seen to be an apolitical form, there is an earlier tradition of republican writers who chose the sonnet form for political discussion.

In *The School of Eloquence* Harrison follows Milton in using the sonnet to talk about politics. He is also interested in Milton's ideas. Milton used the sonnet as a vehicle for his republican politics in, for example, "Sonnet XVI: To the Lord General Cromwell," or "Sonnet XVIII: On the Late Massacre in Piedmont." Harrison has taken the formal sixteen-line sonnet used by Meredith in *Modern Love* and uses it for political commentary. Milton also used the sixteen-line sonnet but Milton is not the only model for a political sonneteer. Another important poet for Harrison who used the sonnet to talk about politics and one influenced by Milton's example is Shelley in, for example, "England in 1819" or "Feelings of a Republican on the Fall of Bonaparte." Authors of modern political sonnets whom Harrison reads include W.H. Auden and Dylan Thomas.[12] Other poets such as Andrew Marvell and John Keats are also significant political writers for Harrison. But Milton's use of the sonnet for a wide range of topics was clearly inspirational for Harrison. He has identified Milton's sonnets X to XXIII, "ranging from the public statement of 'A book was writ of late called *Tetrachordon*' to that tender, inward sonnet, 'Methought I saw my late espoused saint'" as the most important literary influences for his sonnets.[13]

An important historical source for *The School of Eloquence* is E.P. Thompson's *The Making of the English Working Class*, a humanist Marxist account of working-class consciousness, politics, and culture in the period 1780–1832. This "history from below" is referred to in Harrison's "poetry from below," which similarly seeks to rescue the artisans and working class from historical occlusion and "condescension." The title and an epigraph in *The School of Eloquence* are taken from a passage in Thompson about the introduction of special legislation in 1799 "utterly suppressing" the London Corresponding Society (LCS) and the United Englishmen. These working men's political organizations were targeted as part of the wider suppression of reformers, who were uniformly vilified as "Jacobins" with links to French republicanism following the 1789 Revolution. The epigraph is a quotation from Thompson about an "indefatigable conspirator" who, when arrested, "was found in possession of a ticket which was perhaps one of the last 'covers' for the old L.C.S.: *Admit for the Season to the School of Eloquence.*[14] Harrison explains that the corresponding societies gave working people access to political and cultural education: "in the eighteenth century working people would meet and one literate person would read to a room, and working people would discuss literature and politics."[15] *The School of Eloquence* begins Harrison's commitment to bring his education and poetry that discusses politics, literature, and history back to the working "people you were brought up with."[16] Even in the most challenging political sonnets he achieves a conversational idiom and wants "to be the poet my father reads," and to be accessible to his father's class, albeit with awareness of the limitations inherent in his liminal position.[17] His politico-poetic project in *The School of Eloquence* is in keeping with the spirit of the L.C.S. and reflects great regard for the egalitarian republican and reformist traditions of the English working class.

Classical republicanism is also an important influence in *The School of Eloquence.* In Harrison's lexicon "eloquence'" refers to poetry, "the word at its most eloquent,"[18] and to rhetoric, the persuasive function of language as it addresses public life. John Stuart Mill famously argued that poetry and eloquence were in part antithetical modes of expression, that "eloquence is *heard*, poetry is *over*heard. Eloquence supposes an audience...Poetry is feeling confessing itself to itself, in moments of solitude."[19] Harrison's lyric voice has a public, dramatic dimension. *The School of Eloquence* participates in a pre-Romantic, classical tradition of which Milton's poetry is a part, and which saw poetry integrated into the important spheres of public life in Ancient Greece. The political sonnets present Harrison's poetic vision of great public matters of politics and history, including internal colonialism in the United Kingdom, nineteenth-century Luddite resistance to capital, and the seventeenth-century English republican revolution.

II

In the political sonnets Harrison writes out in republican verse, like Milton, Blake, Yeats, and other political mythologers before him, the oppression and aspirations of a people, offering consolation and cultural weaponry, and celebrating their revolutionary traditions of resistance to kings and capital.[20] Harrison faces North in *The School of Eloquence*, towards his community of origin and "the tradition of all the dead generations [that] weighs like a nightmare on the brains of the living."[21] These sonnets also bring together histories of class and colonization from Leeds to the Caribbean, Cornwall to Wales, from the tenth century to the twentieth century. As a political mythology, the sonnets dramatize the shared substance of different struggles, illuminating the deeper political history that unites them.[22] "On Not Being Milton" and "Rhubarbarians, I," the first and second sonnets in the sequence, are heavily allusive incantations wherein the poet-mythologer champions the seventeenth-century republican revolution against monarchy, divine right, and the hereditary principle, and the Luddites' direct action against capital and its subordination of human need to profit. "National Trust" and "t' Ark" are also political sonnets and public elegies, and are concerned with the history of linguistic and political disempowerment in other regions of the United Kingdom.

Harrison has commented that there are a number of reasons why "On Not Being Milton" is the leading sonnet in *The School of Eloquence.*[23] "On Not Being Milton" is in a sense his poetic manifesto because it presents his larger vision of issues of history and politics, and his republicanism and humanist Marxism, the two major intellectual traditions he is shaped by. The character of Harrison's republicanism is established in the sonnet in relation to the ambivalent presence of Milton. The sonnet activates chains of association through a series of historical and cultural markers, most prominently Milton himself. The republican poet, political writer, and revolutionary is an icon of republicanism in the sonnet and through him Harrison taps into republican mythology. Harrison seems to regard

Milton as a bourgeois republican revolutionary, following the view found in Marxist historians like E. P. Thompson and Christopher Hill.

Harrison's allusions to Milton are always to the republican revolutionary. He shows little interest in Milton's religion. Harrison's silence on Milton's religion signals his rejection of Milton's independent Puritanism. There is a humorous register to the title's identification with and negation of Milton. It is impossible to separate Milton's theology and his politics. However, Milton comes to Harrison via Blake, Marx, and Shelley. Harrison is interested in Milton's radical republicanism. David Norbrook comments that Harrison is one of the contemporary republican poets who have "had to do a certain amount of excavating to establish their tradition, for literary history in the twentieth century has often had a strongly monarchist bias."[24] Norbrook and Oliver Taplin observe that an early essay by Harrison, on verse translations of Virgil's *Aeneid*, shows an awareness unusual for its time of "the Whiggish and republican cult of Lucan, Milton and Marvell."[25] Milton is attractive to Harrison as a republican political writer and he locates Milton and himself in a radical republican literary lineage.

Harrison reclaims Milton the republican revolutionary from appropriation by various critical orthodoxies. In the eighteenth century Joseph Addison was a key figure who attempted to sanitize Milton for a gentlemanly Whiggism. Addison erased the identity of the radical Puritan inspired by the "Inner Light," and substituted the sublime poet which dominates mainstream criticism today.[26] Thomas Gray, an important figure in Harrison's canon, also appropriated Milton for Whig political purposes. T.S. Eliot, the self-described high Anglican in religion and Royalist in politics, maligned the reputation of the radical Puritan and republican heavyweight. Eliot, Leavis, the New Critics, and C.S. Lewis led the twentieth-century critical offensive to lower Milton's profile in the canon. Harrison would agree with his fellow classicist T.S Eliot, however, that the civil war "has never been concluded."[27] Harrison is on the side of the republicans and he wants to claim Milton for his particular brand of republicanism.

The critical contestation waged in the Milton industry over his identity and meanings is part of the legacy inherited by Harrison, whose evocations involve a range of left-wing perspectives on this major precursor. Christopher Hill does acknowledge Milton's problematic relationship with the English people. Milton did not support theories of democratic representation,[28] for example, and in this Harrison differs sharply from Milton. However, the paramount importance of the individual conscience in the Protestant tradition and rejection of ecclesiastical hierarchies suggest an egalitarian theology which it is often noted influenced Milton's politics. Hill discusses the enormous emphasis Milton placed on personal discipline as the basis for individual liberty and the fitness of the citizenry to be the foundation of the republic. Hill finally regards Milton Agonistes, the autobiographical dimension of *Samson Agonistes*, as an authentic portrait of the blinded, imprisoned, and unyielding giant who fought for his God and his people. Milton is also an imperfect but daunting and heroic figure in Harrison's imaginary.

Harrison sees the English civil war as a class war, and in class terms he is not on the same side as the bourgeois republican Milton. Milton rejected the divine right of kings and the hereditary principle, as Harrison does. "A Celebratory Ode on the Abdication of King Charles III" honors "Milton, whose Latin justified / to Europe Britain's regicide," though Harrison would prefer Charles III to resign.[29] Unlike Harrison, Milton wanted power limited to an educated and propertied elite. One way Harrison signals his distance from Milton is through the reference to the London Corresponding Society in the epigraph to *The School of Eloquence*. Harrison aligns himself with the L.C.S., who continued the demands of the democratic republican Levellers, whom Milton was to the "right" of. The L.C.S. was against "the century-old identification of political with property rights," and this same challenge had "been voiced before —by the seventeenth-century Levellers."[30] Milton did not speak against

Cromwell's crushing of the Levellers. In class terms, Milton was part of the *status quo* challenged by the Levellers, by the London Corresponding Society and, in a twentieth and twenty-first century context, by Harrison.

Harrison's republicanism and the way it shapes his conception of his poetic role resonates most with the Milton of *Areopagitica*, who casts himself as a classical orator standing before the people in the Areopagus, the high court of Athenian justice.[31] *Areopagitica* was a printed "speech" to the Parliament of England in 1644 for the liberty of unlicensed printing. This was a time when Parliamentary speeches were printed for reading by the general public, so that Milton's polemical tract *Areopagitica* addresses Parliament and the people.[32] Milton and other writers of the English revolution turned rhetoric "away from its courtly setting and towards the true Ciceronian mode of rhetoric where orators served the state by first serving the people."[33] In "Rhubarbarians, I" Harrison aspires to play the part of the "tribune," one of those elected by the people to represent their interests in the Roman Republic, suggesting by analogy that the poet would like to place his eloquence at the service of his people.

In "On Not Being Milton" the poet is an artisan working alongside other artisans, his pen like "a swung, cast-iron" "sledge-hammer," forging a voice for his class. This vision recalls that in *Areopagitica* of artists, intellectuals, and workers side by side in the republican city, where the hammer is also placed alongside the pen. In *Areopagitica*'s republic at war artisans and scholars in their workshops are at one:

> the shop of warre hath not there more anvils and hammers waking, to fashion out the plates and instruments of armed Justice in defence of beleaguer'd Truth, then there be pens and heads there, sitting by their studious lamps, musing....[34]

In "On Not Being Milton" too writers and others artisans place their skills at the service, in a sense, of a shared struggle. "On Not Being Milton," like "Rhubarbarians, I," invites the reader to see parallels between Harrison's poetic project and the guerrilla struggle of the Luddites, who were mainly textile artisans. In "On Not Being Milton" the poet's linguistic materials and metrical craft are merged with the materials and crafts of the Luddites. Harrison's struggle to shape a Leeds voice using traditional poetic meter and make a place for "uz" in the sonnet form is dramatically cast in terms of the Luddites struggle to continue practicing their crafts and to stay in their workshops. The Luddites were skilled men in small workshops like printers and weavers, resisting mechanization of their trades and being forced into factories.[35] Harrison's conception of the poet as an artisan also recalls Blake's. "On Not Being Milton" projects the poet alongside workers in struggle, with reference to *Areopagitica*, and also resonates with the revolutionary events of Paris in 1968 which seem to have influenced Hill's and Harrison's portraits of Milton.

Areopagitica's intervention against censorship in the form of pre-publication licensing and defence of intellectual autonomy for the republic's citizens, and Milton's wider attacks on priestcraft and the clergy's control over thought, is an important part of Harrison's regard for him. Harrison also alludes to *Areopagitica* in a literature review, relishing its rejection of the "excremental whiteness" of a cloistered poetry.[36] However, in *The Blasphemer's Banquet* Harrison presents a "great men of history" account of the fight for freedom of speech and publication, and the fight against priestcraft and bigots who kill authors and burn books. Milton, who became a censor, is not mentioned in *The Blasphemer's Banquet*, perhaps because he was not against burning books once they had been published, nor prosecuting their authors as *Areopagitica* makes clear.

Harrison's identification with a republican literary lineage is also evident in the classical republican texts that he has chosen to translate. Harrison's translations of classical republican texts may also be a way in which he sees his work as continuous with Milton's, and he comments that "Milton used classical texts as a revolutionary."[37] For the epigraph to *Areopagitica* Milton translates a passage from Euripides' *The Suppliant Women*, a passage which presents the right of all men to speak freely in public as central to the "true Liberty" of a republic.[38] Euripides' plays "epitomized the spirit of bold thinking and speaking."[39] Harrison translated Euripides' *Hecuba* and also Aeschylus's trilogy of republican Greek tragedies, *The Oresteia*. Like Milton in *Areopagitica*, in *The Oresteia* Aeschylus lays claim to the Areopagus as a republican form of government and as part of the Greeks' democratic heritage.[40] Harrison's allusions to Milton and his translations of Euripides and Aeschylus are part of his identification with a republican literary lineage which advocates bold and free speech for all men in the public sphere, and a republican form of government in which there is participatory democracy.

This identification can also be seen in one of the epigrams Harrison translates from the *Greek Anthology*, "Hypatia," in *Palladas: Poems*.[41] Harrison selects for translation seventy of the 151 epigrams by Palladas preserved in the *Greek Anthology*. Hypatia (355–415 CE) was a renowned scholar who taught mathematics and natural philosophy at the great school at the Alexandrine library. Milton's publisher, John Toland, an anti-clerical Protestant, had an interest in Hypatia because she was assassinated by Christians. Toland published an essay in 1753 titled *Hypatia, or the history of an in everyway accomplished lady, who was torn to pieces by the clergy of Alexandria*.[42] Harrison also draws attention in his "Preface" to the lynching of Hypatia "by Christians wielding oyster shells like razors."[43] "Hypatia," unlike other epigrams in *Palladas: Poems*, also honors its subject, "revered Hypatia": "knowing your province is really the heavens, / finding your brilliance everywhere I look."[44] Hypatia may be attractive to Harrison as a martyr against religious extremism admired by republicans like Milton's publisher.

In "On Not Being Milton" Harrison is cheering for the "tongue-tied" working class, encouraging high political and cultural aspirations—but it is John Milton, the bourgeois scrivener's son, who is the supreme measure of achievement. Harrison's cry, "Three cheers for mute ingloriousness!," alludes to a line in Thomas Gray's *Elegy Written in a Country Churchyard*: "Some mute inglorious Milton here may rest."[45] Gray's "Milton" is mute because he was from the illiterate rural laboring class, and is buried among the anonymous peasants dead in the country churchyard: "But Knowledge to their eyes her ample page / Rich with the spoils of time did ne'er unroll."[46] The *Elegy* suggests that the potential of even the prodigiously gifted Milton would have been wasted if he had been born into the rural poor. But the *Elegy* naturalizes and aestheticizes this denial of human potential, comparing the gifted poor to flowers "born to blush unseen."[47] "On Not Being Milton" concurs that an exhausted laboring class has potential contenders for glorious achievements, but is cheering for the mute Milton's to overcome adversity: "Articulation is the tongue-tied's fighting." The sonnet also points to the importance of language in political struggle and calls on the working class to fortify its cultural weaponry.

The allusion to Gray's *Elegy* in "On Not Being Milton" provides an example of the convention Harrison transgresses: the gentleman bard speaking about the silent, uneducated majority. The last line of the sonnet is also a direct quotation of the last written words of Richard Tidd, shoemaker and Cato Street conspirator:[48]

> Articulation is the tongue-tied's fighting.
>
> In the silence round all poetry we quote
>
> Tidd the Cato Street conspirator who wrote:
>
> *Sir, I Ham a very Bad Hand at Righting.*[49]

Tidd was among the least literate of the hapless conspirators. His last words were written before his execution for the failed attempt to assassinate the British cabinet in 1820. Harrison has elsewhere observed that "what is recorded in history and literature is the political speeches of the ruling class in one way or another."[50] By contrast, "the language of the working class is considered important enough to record if they are on the point of being executed." Harrison, who takes the quotation of this illiterate man from Thompson's "history from below," is contravening literary collusion in the systemic censorship of the uneducated class.

Little is known about the Cato Street conspiracy but it had republican links, connections to Yorkshire, and began after the 1819 Six Acts, which launched an offensive against the Radical press, and radical lecture-meetings like those held by the London Corresponding Society.[51]

"On Not Being Milton" puns upon Tidd's "Righting" to suggest that writing is the poet's way of "righting" political wrongs. In this sense the sonnet is paralleled to Tidd's direct action. "Articulation is the tongue-tied's fighting," and the eloquent poet's way of fighting for them. Tidd's "Bad" writing, his illiteracy, and his affirmation that his failed action was "Right" in its motivations are honored in the supreme mode of eloquence, poetry. "On Not Being Milton" merges the poet's voice with the collective voice of Harrison's desired constituency, the laboring classes. "Three cheers" is a collective cry. In the sonnet's first line the poet speaks as "I" but by the closing lines it is "we": "In the silence round all poetry we quote" those excluded from the poetry and history books, and "the ghosts of the inarticulate."[52]

"On Not Being Milton" also draws attention to the standardization of English that was being introduced in this period in Britain by quoting and italicizing Tidd's vernacular. Harrison follows historians like Thompson in understanding the establishment of a universal standard of spoken and written English, based on the dialect of the southern-English ruling class, as a method of excluding working-class and regional vernaculars from public life.[53] "On Not Being Milton," by honoring Tidd's words, raises the larger question of whose speech is admissible in cultural and political discourse.

The "Ludding morphemes" of Harrison's Leeds voice come down like an Enoch sledge-hammer on Milton's "frames of Art" in "On Not Being Milton." Harrison's linguistic sabotage of inherited poetic forms, which have conventionally excluded the vernacular, is paralleled to the Luddites industrial sabotage of textile machines being introduced into the Northern mills during the Industrial Revolution, machines that would render their trades obsolete:

The stutter of the scold out of the branks

of condescension, class and counter-class

thickens with glottals to a lumpen mass

of Ludding morphemes closing up their ranks.

Each swung cast-iron Enoch of Leeds stress

clangs a forged music on the frames of Art,

the looms of owned language smashed apart![54]

Harrison's "hammer," his voice, has the force of history and the Luddite's rightful struggle behind it. Luddism is also a metaphor in the sonnet for his effort to forge a political voice for his class in poetry, and his aesthetic defence of the vernacular. But his attack on "the looms of owned language" is imagined so vividly it is as if he is present when the Luddites storm the mills and "clang" their hammers down on the mechanized looms. "On Not Being Milton," like "Rhubarbarians, I," the sonnet which will be discussed next, shifts between centuries, and past and present tense. Both sonnets also imagine that Harrison is present at meetings of underground radicals like the London Corresponding Society and the Cato Street conspirators, the poet having "read and committed to the flames" all secret correspondence.

In "Rhubarbarians, I" Northern barbarian speech will be raised up and brought into elite poetic and political discourses, and the Luddites are again centre stage in the project. The poet's *raison d'être* is to "raise / 'mob' *rhubarb-rhubarb* to a tribune's speech."[55] "Rhubarbarians" is Harrison's neologism for barbarians of Leeds, coined by combining the words "rhubarb" and "barbarians." "Rhubarb" is the word actors mutter to create inaudible "mob" noises in the theatre, and Harrison adapts the term to the Northern mob. "Rhubarb" became associated with Northern speech for Harrison after his father told him that 98 per cent of British rhubarb was grown in Leeds.[56] "*Tusky*," as a note to the sonnet tells us, is the Leeds dialect term for rhubarb. *Tusky* is associated in the sonnet with the Yorkshire Luddites speech, and also associatively links Harrison's father's generation of the Northern working-class with the Luddite resistance.

"Rhubarbarians, I" begins with Harrison's remembered sense of inadequacy about his Leeds voice, heavy with rebarbative consonants and glottals. He comes to realize though that his is the right poetic voice in which to remember and honor the Yorkshire Luddites:

> Those glottals glugged like poured pop, each
>
> rebarbative syllable, remembrancer, raise
>
> 'mob' *rhubarb-rhubarb* to a tribune's speech
>
> crossing the crackle as the hayricks blaze.[57]

The remembrancer bard seems to be present as the "mob" is crossing the blazing hayricks, and the sonnet offers us a poetic witness and chronicle of Luddite history. "Rhubarbarians, I" dramatizes a Yorkshire Luddite attack on a mill, and may refer to the legendary attack on Cartwright's mill at Rawfolds in 1812, which is detailed in Thompson.[58] Cartwright's mill was guarded by the soldiers, armed strike-breakers, and sentinels referred to in the sonnet.[59] The Luddites did not attack the mill of Horsfall of Ottiwells, who is named in the sonnet for other reasons. The incantatory third stanza, heavily assonant, evokes the danger of the midnight attack and the ghostly, metaphysical presence of the Luddites in the hills and in the sonnet:

> What t'mob said to the cannons on the mills,
>
> shouted to soldier, scab and sentinel
>
> 's silence, parries and hush on whistling hills,

shadows in moonlight playing knurr and spell.[60]

The allusion to the Northern game of knurr and spell, or Northern spell (which resembles the modern games of trap-ball and golf), reminds us that these ghostly, guerilla Luddites are Yorkshiremen.[61] The sound of the "mob" is "silence" because of the illegal nature of the Luddites' activities,[62] just as little is known of the Cato Street conspiracy. The sonnet offers poetic witness of the true purpose and bravery of the Luddites because, it strongly suggests, their story has not been fully or truly told in the history books.

"Rhubarbarians, I" contrasts the historical silence surrounding the Luddites and their attacks on property with the historical recording of bloody threats against the Luddites' persons by a mill-owner, who can speak out loud because capital is supported by the law and military in the sonnet. Historical records have preserved the exact words of Horsfall of Ottiwells, another large mill-owner who disregarded the Luddites' demands:

> Horsfall of Ottiwells, if the bugger could,
>
> 'd've liked to (exact words recorded) *ride*
>
> *up to my saddle-girths in Luddite blood.*[63]

"Rhubarbarians, I" impresses upon us the bloody intentions of the mill-owners and makes clear the alignment of the state and military with capital. Soldiers guard gaffers or bosses, and blacklegs or scabs. In the sonnet the army aim cannon at civilians, the Luddites, who are armed only with pikes. "The *tusky-tusky* of the pikes" suggests it is Yorkshiremen carrying the pikes. "Rhubarbarians, I" endorses direct action and armed struggle against oppression as just and necessary. The poet valorizes the Luddites, as he does the Cato Street conspirators and the London Corresponding Society

"Rhubarbarians, I," like "On Not Being Milton," participates in the cultural production of the mythology of Luddism. The Luddite counter-offensives against the large mill-owners were celebrated in local folk culture, such as in the croppers' song, which Harrison would have read in Thompson:

> And night by night when all is still,
>
> And the moon is hid behind the hill,
>
> We forward march to do our will
>
> With hatchet, pike and gun![64]

The third quatrain of "Rhubarbarians, I" recalls the croppers' song perhaps, especially in its "mills" / "hills" rhyme:

> What t'mob said to the cannons on the mills,
>
> shouted to soldier, scab and sentinel
>
> 's silence, parries and hush on whistling hills,[65]

Thompson observes that "the folk-traditions of the Rawfold's attack emphasized the heroism of the Luddites and the callousness of the defenders."[66] "Rhubarbarians, I" also evokes the heroism of the men who attacked the mill, and emphasizes the bloody force used against them. In the sonnet the Luddites only carry pikes while in the croppers' song they also carry the more threatening hatchets and guns. Harrison also adds the more dramatic cannon-fire, where Thompson records that it was heavy gunfire used against the Luddites.[67]

The politics of selection in "Rhubarbarians, I" arguably enhances the heroic mythology of Luddism and does not refer to the defeat of the Luddite attack on Rawfolds mill, nor to the subsequent assassination of Horsfall of Ottiwells. The assassination is more ethically complex than the attack on property represented in the sonnet. The assassination also occasioned some "revulsion of feeling" among Horsfall's community, but not very much.[68] Each of the struggles Harrison honors, the Luddites, the Cato Street conspiracy, and the London Corresponding Society, were forcibly defeated. In "Rhubarbarians, I" and "On Not Being Milton" Harrison, a poet without a revolution, a "tribune" without an official constituency, renders his services to the artisans and working class, not as an official identified with the political or cultural establishment but as a cheering supporter, poet, remembrancer, and mythologist.

Why Harrison makes Luddism a cornerstone of his political mythology is best understood by considering the historical account to which he directs us in his opening epigraph. Thompson writes that the Luddites were among the first agitators to fight for "an alternative political economy and morality" to the unlicensed competition of capital during the Industrial Revolution:[69] "Luddism can be seen as a violent eruption of feeling against unrestrained industrial capitalism."[70] Like many other guerrilla armies, the Luddites were supported and sheltered by their communities.[71] In many historical accounts and in the popular imagination Luddism has become synonymous with primitive reaction against technological progress, unconnected to any credible political tradition. "Rhubarbarians, I" builds on Thompson's historical account to remind us of the honorable and intelligent purpose of the Luddites. Their resistance to being forced into the factories was also part of a more comprehensive and continuing fight for the subordination of profit to human need. It is for these reasons that the remembrancer poet gives the Luddites an honored place in his political mythology for the North, as does Thompson who regards the Luddites as part of "the long and tenacious revolutionary tradition of the British commoner."[72]

In the last stanza of "Rhubarbarians, I" the poet, having immortalized the Luddites in verse, ironically ponders the redundancy of his own trade. That "wiseowl" mocks the wise guy poet and scholar because poetry is no more useful to a military action than a grammar drill:

It wasn't poetry though. Nay, wiseowl Leeds

pro rege et lege schools, nobody needs

your drills and chanting to parrot right

the *tusky-tusky* of the pikes that night.[73]

"*Pro rege et lege*" ["for king and law"] is the motto of Leeds schools and of the city, while the owl is the emblem of the schools and the city.[74] Harrison's view, suggested in the sonnet, that education and language are not always enough to dethrone the *status quo* aligns him with Nedd Ludd, General of the Army of Redressers. After every petition to Parliament to protect their livelihoods failed, the Luddites' General wrote: "We petition no more—that won't do—fighting must."[75] The sonnet's simultaneous exercising of, and regret at the limitations of, the power of language in political struggles partially sets the tone for "Rhubarbarians, II."

The limitations of the poet's power to control reception, and the futility of verse consumed by the bourgeois reader and theatre set, are unhappily contemplated in "Rhubarbarians, II." By contrast, "Rhubarbarians, I" derives confidence from its affinity with the mythology, folk-lore and grassroots struggle of the Luddites. In "Rhubarbarians, II" the modern day rhubarbarbian poet Harrison is presented as a radically isolated and compromised figure. He successfully occupies the theatre stage while the fashionable "MET-set," flocking to see his verse plays, become the mob muttering "rhubarb."[76] The sonnet likens Harrison's performance to the skilled Northern stand-up comic George Formby's, though it is high cultural forms that the poet-as-entertainer gives a honed Leeds character to: "Rhubarb arias, duets, quartets / soar to precision from our common tongue."[77] He gives a high cultural voice to "Uz." But the poet who would be a guerrilla fighter like *Frelimo* or the Luddites finds himself, in the absence of insurrection in his historical time and place, "busking" a bourgeois mob, as he does in "Turns." He feels it heavily as his "*hanba* (shame)."

The significance of the Luddites' lost struggle against being forced
into the factories, mills, and mines for Harrison's other sonnets about
the North is given particular historical clarity in "Working." Set several
decades after the Luddite period of activity from 1812–1816, "Working" is
about child labour in the Northern mines during the Industrial Revolution.
Dedicated to Patience Kershaw, an adolescent girl who was a "hurryer" in
the coal mines, the sonnet is informed by testimony Patience gave to the
Children's Employment Commission of 1842.[78] Patience explained that "the
bald place upon my head is made by thrusting the [coal-filled] corves"
with her head.[79] "Working" imagines the young girl's circumstances: "I
stare into the fire. Your skinned skull shines. / I close my eyes. That makes
a dark like mines."[80] The coal-pits are an emblem of historical silences,
but "Working" also makes this illiterate girl's words and work a metaphor
for Harrison's working: "*th'art nobbut summat as wants raking up.*"[81] The
"*art*" of the poet is to rake up the scraps of history, people like Patience,
and break the silence about their hardship: "Wherever hardship held its
tongue the job / 's breaking the silence of the worked-out-gob."[82] The
sonnet that immediately follows "Working," "Cremation," is also about a
"lifetime down below" in the Northern mines but is set a century later and
depicts a miner slowly dying of "black lung," pneumoconiosis, or another
incurable lung disease common amongst miners.[83] In "Cremation," as
in "Working," there is no sign of the Northern artisan's and working-
class' traditions of resistance championed in "On Not Being Milton" and
"Rhubarbarians, I." Victimization in the mines and historical silences are
also a theme of the next sonnet to be discussed, "National Trust," but
the context is Cornwall and the subjugation of the miners is presented
as a matter of class and colonial power.

IV

"National Trust" is an exemplary sonnet of that preoccupation in *The
School of Eloquence* with economic and linguistic dispossession in the
regions. "National Trust" contemplates the extinction of the Cornish

language and the remnants of its poetry, the annexation of Cornwall, and the dispossession of the Cornish tin-miners. The title punningly raises the historical occlusion of the Cornish nation, a matter returned to in the last lines of the sonnet. In the tenth century Cornwall became "the first part of the Celtic periphery to be incorporated within the English state."[84] Toward the end of the fifteenth century English replaced Cornish as the majority language in Cornwall,[85] and by the end of the eighteenth century the traditional Celtic vernacular of Cornwall was extinct.[86] An irony conveyed in "National Trust" is that the appropriation of the Cornish nation by Britain was not a matter of trust or goodwill but "the beginning of a thousand years of political and cultural subordination."[87] The abuse of trust is a charge extended to the British "gentlemen" and the anglicized elite who owned the Cornish tin-mines, and the "scholars" who have constructed and perpetuated the orthodoxy that Cornwall was never anything other than an organic part of England.[88] Economic colonization by capital and the extinction of the language that might have carried the Cornish account of the colonization of their country are obfuscated by euphemistic notions of national unity and "trust."

The sonnet momentarily recovers the Cornish tin-miners and their language from the "bottomless pits" and black holes in official histories.[89] In "National Trust" the police do unscrupulous deals with capital, and the mine-owners publicly regarded as "stout upholders of our law and order" "borrowed a convict hush-hush from his warder." They torture the convict in a macabre game, flaying and dangling him down a pit, and leaving him mute. The incident becomes a parable for what the sonnet presents as the mine-owners' defeat of the Cornish miners and the extinction of their language: "those gentlemen who silenced the men's oath / and killed the language that they swore it in."[90] The ironic use of the term "gentlemen" for the mine-owners is equalled by contempt for the scholars who remained silent about the suppression of the Cornish tin-miners and the colonization of their country. As Luke Spencer observes, "National Trust" is concerned with the *trahison de clercs*, as well as the economic and linguistic dispossession of the miners.[91] Harrison recommends dangling down a pit scholars who discredit their trade by being "dumb":

> O gentlemen, a better way to plumb
>
> the depths of Britain's dangling a scholar,
>
> say, here at the booming shaft at Towanroath,[92]

"National Trust" is preoccupied with the political role of language in resisting or occluding historical injustices. Harrison has elsewhere observed, with evident reference to "National Trust," "that certain languages, like Cornish, have been made extinct: the language of the powerful ruling class always kills off the language of the class beneath it."[93]

  In the sonnet the suppression of the language by the ruling class "gentlemen" is presented as a strategy in the economic and political suppression of a people:

> The dumb go down in history and disappear
>
> and not one gentleman 's been brought to book:
>
> *Mes den hep tavas a-gollas y dyr*
>
> (Cornish)—
>
> "the tongueless man gets his land took."[94]

Harrison fleetingly restores the Cornish language by quoting and then translating the line "*Mes den hep tavas a-gollas y dyr*," from the "one genuine survival in Cornish" of an englyn, a Celtic poetic form that is particularly difficult to translate.[95] There are two other surviving versions of this englyn, and in them the line translated in "National Trust" is alternately translated as "But he that had no tongue, lost his land," and "but a man without a tongue shall lose his land."[96] In "National

Trust" economic and linguistic colonization are presented as mutually reinforcing processes. The job of the bard and remembrancer is to make history tell the truth about the defeat of the Cornish people, who "raged against the dying of their own particular light," fighting with great tenacity,[97] and the crimes British gentlemen and the anglicized elite were not "booked" for by the police, nor by scholars in the history books.

In "National Trust" the use of the Cornish language, which more than anything else demonstrated the distinct cultural identity of the Cornish, is a subversion of the now dominant "four nations" history, wherein the English, Irish, Welsh, and Scottish are recognized as separate peoples. "Four nations" history was a progressive revision of "British" history because it challenged the dominant view of Britain as an organic and homogeneous nation-state,[98] but it sometimes downplayed other instances of oppression and expressions of difference.[99] "Four nations" history recognized that Britain was an archipelago containing distinct nations: the English, Irish, Welsh, and Scottish—but Cornwall is rarely mentioned. "National Trust" reminds us that the Cornish lost their land, their language, and the recognition that they ever existed.[100] Writing during a period of defeat for the Northern working-class, Harrison remembers the subjugation of the Cornish and the death of their language, and implicitly asks how far the Southern English ruling-class colonization of his native North will go.

"National Trust" also deploys historical remembrance for a contemporary polemical purpose. The use of the Cornish language in "National Trust" demonstrates that the language and the distinct cultural identity it carries are not altogether lost. There is a significant minority within Cornwall seeking autonomy from Britain, and to be recognized as a national minority within the European community. It has petitioned for an independent assembly, and called for recognition of traditional Cornish Stannary Law. The Cornish language has recently been recognized by the British government as an indigenous language of the United Kingdom. The sonnet on the page seems to suggest that the recognition of the Cornish nation, people, and language is a question of correcting the historical record. However, the passionate addressing in the sonnet of grievous historical injustices, the extinction of the Cornish nation, people, and language, is echoed in and lends cultural weaponry to contemporary calls for cultural recognition and political autonomy.

The final sonnet I wish to discuss as evidence of the concern with territorial and linguistic dispossession in the United Kingdom in *The School of Eloquence* is "t' Ark."[101] Harrison lived in Wales in 1973–1974 as the Gregynog Arts Fellow at the University of Wales, and "t' Ark" seems to be a product of this period. It is the only sonnet in what later became the "Art & Extinction" sequence to appear in *From "The School of Eloquence" and Other Poems* (1978). "t' Ark" brings together his concern with forms of extinction and imperialism in a Welsh context, and with reference to Africa, Papua, Cornwall, and Northern England. This neglected sonnet can be more fully explained by disclosing its engagement with the Welsh poetic tradition, and placing it in the historical and contemporary contexts of Welsh cultural and political nationalism. The sonnet is also concerned with the imperial erasure of native cultures from Europe to Africa.

Harrison's sympathy with an alternative nationalism in Wales and other regions of the United Kingdom is clear in an undated letter from the 1970s. He was attending a Miners' Strike in Wales, probably the 1974 Miners' Strike which was in progress when he was there. He wrote: "In Wales it was good: someone asked can you think of a decent poet worth reading who lives in London? Surrounded by nationalists Scottish, Welsh and Northern, London seemed like an appendix that was withering away."[102] In 1974 questions about the revival of the Welsh language and political devolution were major issues in Wales. The rise of Welsh cultural and political nationalism was importantly a consequence of several major twentieth-century events, one of which was the flooding of the ancient Welsh village of Capel Celyn in 1965 to provide a water reservoir for Liverpool.[103] Capel Celyn was the home of one of the last entirely Welsh-speaking villages. The flooding was "seen in terms of a colonization of Welsh land but also, and inextricably linked, an attack on the Welsh language."[104] This appropriation of Welsh water and land by an act of Parliament in London led to an upsurge in Welsh nationalism and the formation of *Cymdeithas yr Iaith Gymraeg* [Welsh Language Society].[105] "t'Ark" seems to allude to the historic flooding of Capel Celyn and to draw upon its place in Welsh political mythology.

The title begins the sonnet's use of the biblical mythology of the Great Deluge to illuminate the shared terrors of distinct histories that washed away colonized peoples and their languages, and may specifically recall the flooding of a Welsh-speaking village by the imperial power in the region:

> Not only dodo, oryx and great auk
>
> waddled on their tod to t'monster ark,
>
> but "leg", "night", "origin" in crushed people's talk,
>
> tongues of fire last witnessed mouthing: *dark!* [106]

The sonnet uses the divine genocide as a metaphor to dramatize man-made genocides and prophesy ecological disasters: "dark." The last word of the sonnet is *cynghanedd*, a Welsh word that refers to Welsh poetry in strict meter, and which may be "the oldest surviving poetic tradition in Europe."[107] In the sonnet the Ark that survived the Deluge is also a symbol of enduring poetic forms that carry the languages and stories of threatened or extinct peoples.

Contemplating the extinction of languages, poetry, peoples, and species Harrison, true to form, turns to a poetic tradition which has survived for centuries, and to translation as a method of preserving poetry and languages: "(or mourn in Latin their imminent death, / then translate these poems into *cyghanedd*.)"[108] The final couplet is an example of the use in "t' Ark" of "the epigrammatic concentration which is a feature of so much Welsh poetry."[109] *Cynghanedd* is characterised by "the harmony, the interlocking, by alliteration, assonance, and rhyme, all through the lines."[110] "t' Ark" uses the Meredithian sonnet form but integrates some of the poetic features of *cynghanedd*, such as alliteration, assonance, rhyme, and a dense sequence of metaphors.[111] The Welsh writer Emyr Humphreys argues that the continuation of the Welsh poetic tradition from the sixth century to the present day has "contrived to be a major factor in the maintenance, stability and continuity of the Welsh identity and the fragile concept of Welsh nationhood."[112] "t' Ark" similarly suggests the importance of poetic traditions for the survival of eroded or threatened cultural identities and nations.

"t' Ark" draws on a Modernist conception of cultural survival, under conditions of great and often destructive historical change, that Raymond Williams called a "dynamics of mobility,"[113] where remnants of extinct languages survive as traces in other languages:

> Now when the future couldn't be much darker,
>
> there being fewer epithets for sun,
>
> and Cornish and the Togoland *Restsprache*
>
> name both the animals and hunter's gun,[114]

Restsprache is not in the German dictionary but "*sprache*" means language, and "*rest*" means a variety of things including remains, remnants, and also the balance of things. The sonnet suggests that the remnants of their language are what is left of extinct cultures. Harrison's neologism, *restsprache*, also imitates the way the requirements of *cynghanedd* often compelled its poet to coin new words.[115] The unfamiliar term *restsprache* invites the reader to consider the linguistic consequences of imperialism, which involve destruction but also, in the struggle to survive, creative adaptation and cultural hybridity. The conception of cultural survival in the sonnet is not the backward looking mythologizing of an idealized and timeless past, like that propagated by the cultural Right, from F.R. Leavis to T.S. Eliot to the Welsh nationalist leader and poet Saunders Lewis.[116]

Instead the sonnet suggests a forward looking, hopeful conception of continuity amidst tragedy, in which languages decimated by imperial powers can survive by changing shape, a theme of Welsh literature that reflects historical processes.[117]

Harrison certainly seems to have regarded the Welsh as a colonised people. In "t' Ark" the situation of Wales is linked to Cornwall, and in turn to the now extinct Togoland. The comparison of Cornwall's fate to Togoland's is consistent with the lament for the erasure of Cornwall from the map, and the suppression of the Cornish language in "National Trust." In "t' Ark" Togoland symbolizes national dismemberment through imperial cartography. After a series of carve-ups by imperial powers, Togoland ceased to exist. Finally divided into a French and a British mandate, in 1957 British Togoland became part of the independent state of Ghana, while French Togoland became the independent Republic of Togo in 1960. Togoland no longer exists but fragments of it survived in altered forms. The sonnet's allusions to Togoland, Cornwall, and a Welsh-speaking village render visible the imperial erasures of places, communities, and languages. The use of the word "reserve" in the opening line of "t'Ark" seems to pun upon a reserve or reservoir of water: "Silence and poetry have their own reserves." "t' Ark" contemplates the chances of linguistic survival in violent, genocidal, and sometimes apocalyptic historical circumstances: "tongues of fire last witnessed mouthing: *dark!*" It suggests that a humanist poetry which is committed to history and human beings can offer limited refuge to the remnants of the languages of destroyed peoples.

"t' Ark" is also the only sonnet in the "Art & Extinction" sequence that uses the Northern dialect, with "t'" replacing R.P.'s "the." An implicit comparison is made in the sonnet between the linguistic and political situation in Northern England and in Wales, and similarly "National Trust" suggests that the extinction of Cornish serves as an historical warning for Harrison's North. "t' Ark" is a poetic vessel carrying threatened or extinct indigenous languages, from Togoland to Leeds to Capel Celyn.

The flooding of the ancient Welsh-speaking village of Capel Celyn was authorized by an Act of Parliament in London despite eight years of political opposition to the project in Wales. The event suggested that self government was the only way that the Welsh could control their destiny and protect their culture. The British Labour Party had, for most of the twentieth century, rejected Welsh nationalism. It viewed devolution as undermining the British nation and the unity of the British working class, a position also on display in the debates surrounding the 2015 Scottish independence referendum. The stance was part of why Williams thought that the British Left had to move away from centralised politics, and rethink its attitude to nationalism. Williams's advocacy of alternative nationalisms and political autonomy for regions like Wales and Northern England is consonant with the presentation in Harrison's sonnets of the regions as places where political power is far removed from the local people, and where languages and communities are dissolving.[118]

"t' Ark" offers a poetic mythology of imperial dispossession and regeneration. It uses the Meredithian sonnet form but instead of sixteen lines composed of four quatrains, there are eighteen lines in "t' Ark." Where the Meredithian sonnet has one hanging couplet, "t' Ark" has two. The last couplet is: "(or mourn in Latin their imminent death, / then translate these poems into *cynghanedd.*)"[119] In this final couplet Harrison, on the one hand, translates a dead language, Latin, into a dead language, Welsh. The "dead" status of these languages is emphasized by the rhyme on "death" / "*cynghanedd.*" Paradoxically though, the act of translation keeps these "dead" languages alive. The sonnet's reference to the biblical tongues of fire, symbols of a universal language, also evokes the powers of language and translation. The ideas in "t' Ark" about linguistic and cultural survival through resourcefulness and creativity suggest that "powers of a certain kind—hope, fidelity, eloquence—are repeatedly distilled from defeat."[120] The form of the sonnet also reflects its thematic preoccupations. The last couplet is a tail in the tail of the sonnet. Wittily, in a sonnet about death and resistance, the tail in the tail is fighting back.

Notes

1. Claude Rawson, "Family Voices," *Times Literary Supplement* (4 January 1985), 10; Robert Sheppard, *The Poetry of Saying: British Poetry and its Discontents 1950-2000* (Liverpool: Liverpool University Press, 2005), 131. Tom Leonard, "On Reclaiming the Local," in *Reports from the Present: Selected Works 1982–94* (London: Cape, 1995), 38.
2. Morrison, "The Filial Art," 55.
3. "Interview," 231.
4. "Marked with D," *CP*, 168.
5. Note on the dust jacket of *From "The School of Eloquence" and Other Poems* (London: Rex Collings, 1978).
6. Acknowledgements page, *From "The School of Eloquence"* (1978).
7. "Interview," 228.
8. "Interview," 231-232.
9. "Tony Harrison in conversation with Michael Alexander," *Talking Verse: Interviews with Poets*, ed. Robert Crawford, Henry Hart, David Kinloch and Richard Price (Verse: St Andrews and Williamsburg, 1995), 82-91, 83-84.
10. "Tony Harrison in interview with John Tusa," BBC Radio 3 (March 2008).
11. Ezra Pound *Hugh Selwyn Mauberley, Selected Poems 1908-59* (London: Faber and Faber, 1975), ll. 90-1, 101.
12. "All Out," review of *The Penguin Book of Socialist Verse*, London Magazine, new series, vol. 10, no. 12 (March 1971), 87-91, 90.
13. "Interview," 237.
14. E.P. Thompson, *The Making of the English Working Class* (London: Penguin, 1991 [1963]), 191.
15. *Harrison: Poets and People*, Channel 4.
16. "Interview with Bailey," Radio 3.
17. "Rhubarbarians, II," *CP*, 124.
18. *Harrison: Poets and People*, Channel 4.
19. John Stuart Mill, "Thoughts on Poetry and its Varieties," in *Dissertations and Discussions: Political, Philosophical and Historical*, 2nd ed., vol. 1 (London: Longmans, 1867), 63-94, 71.
20. I am adapting what Terry Eagleton has said of Milton, Blake, and Yeats, which even more precisely applies to Harrison. See Terry Eagleton, "The God that Failed," in *Re-Membering Milton: Essays on the Texts and Tra-*

ditions, ed. Mary Nyquist and Margaret W. Ferguson (London and New York : Methuen, 1987), 342–349, 342. See also Emyr Humphreys, *The Taliesin Tradition: A Quest for the Welsh Identity* (London: Black Raven Press, 1984), 227–228.

21. Karl Marx, *The Eighteenth Brumaire of Louis Bonaparte* (Oxford: Oxford University Press, 2000), 329. Also quoted in Eagleton, "The God that Failed," 344.
22. See also Eagleton, "The God that Failed," 343.
23. "Interview," 236.
24. David Norbrook, *Writing the English Republic: Poetry, Rhetoric and Politics 1627–1660* (Cambridge: Cambridge University Press, 1999), 7.
25. See T.W. Harrison, "English Virgil: *The Aeneid* in XVIII Century," *Philologica Pragensia,* X (1967), 1–11 and 80–91. Norbrook attributes this reference to Oliver Taplin. See Norbrook, *Writing the English Republic,* 7.
26. Dustin Griffin, *Regaining Paradise: Milton and the Eighteenth Century* (Cambridge and New York: Cambridge University Press, 1986).
27. T.S. Eliot. It is used as an epigraph in Hill, *Milton and the English Revolution.*
28. Norbrook, *Writing the English Republic,* 129.
29. "A Celebratory Ode on the Abdication of King Charles III," *CP,* 321, 323.
30. Thompson, *Working Class,* 24.
31. John Milton, *Areopagitica ,* in *Complete Prose Works of John Milton,* vol. 2, 1643–48, ed. Ernest Sirluck (New Haven and London: Yale University Press and Oxford University Press, 1953), 485–570.
32. Norbrook, *Writing the English Republic,* 129.
33. Sharon Achinstein, *Milton and the Revolutionary Reader* (Princeton: Princeton University Press, 1994), 59.
34. Milton, *Areopagitica,* 554.
35. Thompson, *Working Class,* 211.
36. "Beating the Retreat," *London Magazine,* new series, vol. 10, no. 8 (November 1970), 91–96, 91–92.
37. "Interview," 245.
38. Milton, *Areopagitica,* 485.
39. Norbrook, *Writing the English Republic,* 127.
40. Norbrook, *Writing the English Republic,* 131.
41. "Hypatia," *CP,* epigram 67, 95.
42. John Toland, *Hypatia: or, the History of a Most Beautiful, Most Vertuous, Most Learned, and Every Way Accomplish'd Lady; Who was Torn to*

Pieces by the Clergy of Alexandria (London: M. Cooper, W. Reeve and C.A. Sympson, 1753)

43. "Preface" to *Pallas: Poems*, in *Bloodaxe 1*, 133–135, 134.
44. "Hypatia," *CP*, 95.
45. *CP*, 122; and Thomas Gray, *Elegy Written in a Country Churchyard, The Complete Poems of Thomas Gray: English, Latin and Greek*, ed. H.W. Starr and J.R. Hendrickson (Oxford: Clarendon Press, 1966), 37–43, l. 59, 39.
46. Gray, *Elegy*, ll. 49–50, 39.
47. Gray, *Elegy*, l. 55, 39.
48. Thompson, *Working Class*, 787.
49. *CP*, 122.
50. *Harrison: Poets and People*, Channel 4.
51. Thompson, *Working Class*, 770–771, 768, 762.
52. "Interview," 232.
53. See also Smith, *The Politics of Language, 1791–1819*; and Tony Crowley, *Standard English and the Politics of Language* (Urbana: University of Illinois Press, 1989).
54. *CP*, 122.
55. "Rhubarbarians, I," *CP*, 123.
56. "Conversation," 39.
57. *CP*, 123.
58. Thompson, *Working Class*, 612.
59. Thompson, *Working Class*, 612.
60. *CP*, 123.
61. Sidney Oldall Addy, *A Glossary of Words used in the Neighborhood of Sheffield*, vol. 1 (London: Trubner, 1888), 126. See also George Walker, *The Costume of Yorkshire*, 2nd ed. (Sussex: Caliban Books, 1978[1814]), Plate XII.
62. Thompson, *Working Class*, 540.
63. *CP*, 123.
64. Thompson, *Working Class*, 611.
65. *CP*, 123.
66. Thompson, *Working Class*, 614.
67. Thompson, *Working Class*, 612.
68. Thompson, *Working Class*, 624.
69. Thompson, *Working Class*, 603.
70. Thompson, *Working Class*, 601.
71. Thompson, *Working Class*, 615–616.

72. E.P. Thompson, "Revolution," in *Out of Apathy*, ed. E.P. Thompson et al (London: New Left Books, Stevens and Sons, 1960), 287–308, 308.
73. *CP*, 123.
74. *Permanently Bard*, 146.
75. Thompson, *Working Class*, 579
76. "Rhubarbarians, II," *CP*, 124.
77. *CP*, 124.
78. Patience Kershaw, testimony to the *Children's Employment Commission of 1842*, quoted in Thompson, *Working Class*, 369–370.
79. Kershaw, quoted in Thompson, *Working Class*, 369–370.
80. "Working," *CP*, 135.
81. *CP*, 135.
82. *CP*, 135.
83. "Cremation," *CP*, 136.
84. Mark Stoyle, "The Dissidence of Despair: Rebellion and Identity in Early Modern Cornwall," *Journal of British Studies*, vol. 38, no. 4 (Oct., 1999), 423–444, 424.
85. Stoyle, "Dissidence of Despair," 435.
86. Peter Berresford Ellis, *The Cornish Language and its Literature* (London and Boston: Routledge, 1974), 124.
87. Stoyle, "Dissidence of Despair," 424.
88. Stoyle, "Dissidence of Despair," 424.
89. "National Trust," *CP*, 131. See also *Permanently Bard*, 145.
90. *CP*, 131.
91. *Poetry TH*, 73.
92. *CP*, 131.
93. "Interview," 234.
94. *CP*, 131.
95. Ellis, *The Cornish Language*, 103–104. Also quoted in *TH Holocaust*, 273–274.
96. Ellis, *The Cornish Language*, 103.
97. Stoyle, "Dissidence of Despair," 444.
98. An early and influential example of "four nations" history is Hugh Kearney's *The British Isles: A History of Four Nations* (Cambridge: Cambridge University Press, 1989).
99. Murray G.H. Pittock, *Celtic Identity and the British Image* (Manchester and New York: Manchester University Press, 1999), 98–99.
100. For more recent historical scholarship arguing that Cornwall has an independent history and retains a distinct, evolving cultural identity

see, for example, Philip Payton, *Cornwall* (Fowey: Alexander Associates, 1996). The book includes a recollection by Robert Louis Stevenson of meeting emigrant Cornish tin-miners in America in 1879 and his perception that they were "more foreign in my eyes" than "a red Indian." See Payton, *Cornwall*, 323.

101. "t' Ark," *CP*, 211.
102. Letter to Alan Ross (undated).
103. Owain Llŷr ap Gareth, *Welshing on Postcolonialism: Complicity and Resistance in the Construction of Welsh Identities* (Unpublished PhD thesis, University of Wales, Aberystwyth University, 2009), 135.
104. Gareth, *Welshing on Postcolonialism*, 135.
105. Dave Ward, "Liverpool Says Sorry for Flooding Welsh Valley," *The Guardian* (13 October 2005).
106. *CP*, 211.
107. Raymond Williams, "Community," in *Who Speaks for Wales: Nation, Culture, Identity*, ed. Daniel Williams (Cardiff: University of Wales Press, 2003), 27–33, 27.
108. *CP*, 211.
109. Gweneth Lilly, "The Welsh Influence in the Poetry of Gerard Manley Hopkins," *Modern Language Review*, vol. 38, no. 3 (July 1943), 192–205, 192.
110. Rolfe Humphries, *Green Armor on Green Ground: Poems in the Twenty-Four Official Welsh Meters* (New York: Charles Scribner's Sons, 1956), xv.
111. Williams, "Community," 28.
112. Emyr Humphreys, *The Taliesin Tradition: A Quest for the Welsh Identity* (London: Black Raven Press, 1984), 2. Quoted in Williams, "Community," 28.
113. Williams, "Community," 28.
114. *CP*, 211.
115. Lilly, "Welsh Influence," 192.
116. Williams, "Community," 29. See also Richard Griffiths, "Another Form of Fascism: The Cultural Impact of the French 'Radical Right' in Britain," in *The Culture of Fascism: Visions of the Far Right in Britain*, ed. Julie V. Gottlieb, Thomas P. Linehan (London and New York: I.B. Tauris, 2004), 162–181, 175–180.
117. Williams, "Community," 30.
118. Raymond Williams, "Decentralism and the Politics of Place," in *Resources of Hope: Culture, Democracy, Socialism*, ed. Robin Gale (Lon-

don: Verso, 1989), 238–245; and "The Practice of Possibility," in *Resources of Hope*, 314–322, 318.

119. *CP*, 211.
120. Williams, "Community," 30.

CHAPTER 8

THE RIMBAUD OF LEEDS: *V.*

After exploring Africa, the United Kingdom, and Ireland, Harrison wrote
v., which is set in Leeds in 1984 when it was also written, and it was
first published in the *London Review of Books* on the 24 January 1985.[1] A
highly personal and political cultural intervention, *v.* continues Harrison's
trademark occupation of the heartland of the canonical British literary
tradition on behalf of dispossessed peoples of the North, and his entwined
class, anti-colonial, republican, and humanist poetic. It is also in *v.* that
Harrison most directly voices his elective affinity with Rimbaud, here
particularly as a regional poet from the lower classes and a "hoodlum
poet," practising a poetics of classical vandalism.

The chapter begins with an examination of *v.*'s engagement with the
historical and political conditions of its production in 1980s England.
Important "left" readings of *v.* criticized it as a liberal evasion of the
political. This chapter contests these readings quite directly, and sees
this work as in fact highly political. It presents a revisionist reading
of *v.* in the polemical contexts of its composition and reception, and
draws upon Harrison's working notebook for *v.* and draft versions of the
poem for the first time. I then seek to illuminate Harrison's identification
with Rimbaud, and to consider Rimbaud's and Harrison's ideas about

work in relation to the nineteenth-century Marxist political writer Paul Lafargue's parodic text *The Right to Be Lazy*. The chapter also examines *v.*'s attentive relationship to its literary model of difference, Thomas Gray's *Elegy Written in a Country Churchyard*. It observes the poem's valorization of labour, and Harrison's reworking of Gray's poem to make his own points, including his distinct presentation of the poet as a working man, and his disruption of a Whig political and literary tradition of resignation to injustice that Gray's *Elegy* represents. This chapter and book conclude with a coda that considers the epitaph to *v.*, the verse that Harrison the artisan intends to have chiselled upon his tombstone in a Leeds graveyard, the fighting epitaph of the Rimbaud of Leeds.

I

v. tells the story of Harrison's memorable visit to a graveyard on Beeston Hill, Leeds, to tend the family plot. He finds that the tombstones of his parents and of the working men, who are identified on the obelisks by their name and trade, have been horribly vandalized. The poet is confronted by an unemployed young skinhead who explains, in essence, that his desecration of the graves is not an attack upon the dead but upon the injustice that men of earlier generations had lifelong trades when he has no work at all: "*Ah'll tell yer then what really riles a bloke. / It's reading on their graves the jobs they did—*" (*CP*, 270). The lumpenproletarian "kid" is a Leeds United supporter, and represents a generational and regional underclass of the terminally unemployed. He says that "*Death after life on t'dole won't seem as 'ard!*" (*CP*, 270). The encounter between poet and skinhead takes place against the background of the historic 1984 miners' strike against pit closures in the North (*CP*, 266). The skinhead's degradation signifies the political victimization of the North, by the policies of the Thatcher Government in the South.

During the dialogical Bahktinian battle waged in the graveyard between the dramatic persona "Tony Harrison" and the skinhead, in the middle section of the poem, we are told the skinhead is his alter ego: "He aerosolled his name. And it was mine" (*CP*, 273). The war of words between the two Harrison personae dramatizes a series of wider divisions and connections, signified by the polyvalent "v" sign, including the chasm between the employed and almost three million unemployed in Britain, disproportionately concentrated in the North, at the time *v.* was being written. The argument between poet and skinhead is also that between a liberal and a radical politics, and their responses to human suffering. Terry Eagleton observes that *v.*'s poet is more pained by division than oppression and that this is "roughly the divide between the liberal and the radical."[2] Before the appearance of his *doppelgänger*, Harrison is cast in the sole role of a bourgeois political liberal who finds conflict regrettable and turns to metaphysical rationales for a universalized human condition. The lumpenproletarian skinhead, by giving voice to the rage of "*dole-wallahs*" and "*the shit they're dumped in*" (*CP*, 270–271), points to contestable political and historical conditions of injustice and he espouses a radical politics of "*class war*" (*CP*, 273).

The poet persona in *v.* is the subject of Harrison's critical satire, as is the skinhead, and their dialogue exposes the inadequacies of the poet's liberal ideology. A significant mistake in the commentary has been the conflation of Harrison the author with the character of the liberal poet, despite the dramatic device of the *doppelgänger*. Eagleton concludes that the skinhead "stands to the left of the poet" and "needs to harangue his author a little further...."[3] Harrison's satirical exposé of the poet-persona's liberal evasion of the political is clearest when the poet makes a heavily clichéd call for unity "to Britain and to all the nations / made in the name of love for peace's sake" (*CP*, 270). The poet in *v.* represents Harrison as he might be if he discarded his working-class formation. The skinhead represents what he might have become if he had not gained an education and left Leeds. But, in essence, the skinhead is an enduring constitutive aspect of Harrison's complex identity. There are also different facets to the identities of poet and skinhead in the Janus-faced "Tony Harrison." The discordant chorale of voices, including those of the metaphysician, class warrior, inarticulate dispossessed, and skinhead thug enrich this polyphonous political epic.

It was the skinhead's "torrent of four-letter filth" that led to calls for *v.*
to be banned following the broadcasting of Richard Eyre's film version
of the poem on Channel 4 on 4 November 1987.[4] The film brought *v.* to
a mass audience but the ensuing public discussion was largely hijacked
by attacks in the right-wing press and by Tory MPs because of alleged
obscenities. The most controversial of Harrison's poems, there are two
main critical schools of thought about *v.*. One school regards *v.* as a
cultural response from a man of the left to the polemical contexts of its
composition,[5] while the second school alleges that Harrison abandons
a radical working-class critique in *v.*.[6] An explicit literary attack on
Thatcherism, particularly its war to shut down coalmines in the North,
was what some prominent left commentators hoped for from Harrison.[7]
Instead, *v.* offers a radical humanist vision of an ailing and besieged
North, and the victimization of the unemployed, and the miners' epic
battle to defend livelihoods has implicit importance in the poem. Received
criticisms of Harrison's class political commitments in *v.* either miss
what they are looking at or reject the legitimacy of the poet's choice
of subject and angle.

Harrison is not looking firstly at the working class but at a workless
underclass. He is looking at the lumpenproletariat. He is not looking
primarily at those who still have a job but at the unemployed. Harrison
is at one level in a different political debate to his critics and is looking at
a different political class. In the manuscript version of *v.* he makes clear
"my taking on the role / of being rent-a-gob for say nowt Leeds, / dignifier
of dumbness and the dole."[8] The frustration of a left critic like Ken
Worpole with Harrison's greater focus upon an unemployed skinhead
than upon the valiant miners might also be seen in the longer perspective
of the left's disengagement from the lumpenproletariat, whom Marx for
example described as "this scum, offal, refuse of all classes."[9] Distinctly,
Harrison gives the "scum", the "SHIT," those even worse off than the
miners, "a hearing!" (*CP*, 271) and is concerned with the suffering of
those who fall to the very bottom of society.

It is also the case that *v.*'s foregrounding of the unemployed skinhead is indissolubly bound up with the crisis of Northern mining communities and with the miners' strike against pit closures that soon made twenty thousand men redundant. The young skinhead serves as a metonymic and symptomatic forecast of an increasingly grim future for Leeds if the strike is lost. A sense of tragic inevitability in an emerging post-industrial landscape is symbolically suggested by the poet's imagining a community graveyard collapsing into the worked-out pit it rests upon (*CP*, 264). The skinhead tells the poet that people dumped on the dole have as much hope as coal chucked on the fire. Harrison's rhyme on "dole" / "coal" underlines, without placing analysis in the skinhead's mouth, that the decimation of the coal industry by "Coal Board MacGregor" (*CP*, 266), appointed by Thatcher to close mines deemed unprofitable, was a policy of mass unemployment:

> Aspirations, cunt! Folk on t'fucking dole
>
> 'ave got about as much scope to aspire
>
> above the shit they're dumped in, cunt, as coal
>
> aspires to be chucked on t'fucking fire (CP, 270).

The "dole" / "coal" rhyme is similarly used in Harrison's film-poem *Crossings* (2002) to liken former mining communities to cattle culled during the 2001 foot-and-mouth epidemic in the United Kingdom: "Along with culled cattle, culled kingdoms of coal, / one dumped on the bonfire, one on the dole."[10] Harrison's feature film *Prometheus* (1998) also remembers the 1984 miners' strike and valorizes the striking miners.[11] Edith Hall regards *Prometheus* as "the most important artistic reaction to the fall of the British working class as the twentieth century staggered to its close, a fall symptomatic of the international collapse of the socialist dream."[12]

Harrison's working notebook for *v.* shows that the 1984 miners' strike and the perceived vendetta waged against the miners by Thatcher were important preoccupations in the development of a verse about "Versus," the title of a draft version of the poem. A number of the newspaper headlines, photographs, and cartoons of the strike that are collected in the notebook feature the letter "V," signifying a range of meanings. A photograph of rows of police has been juxtaposed to a photograph of miners carrying placards. Harrison's socialist sympathies seem to be reflected in his annotation of this photograph of the miners, where he has placed a red circle round the V on the placard saying "Victory to the miners."[13] His support for workers' unions is also evident in another photograph in the workbook. It shows Harrison in front of a banner of the Bakers' Union, which his father belonged to, and which has been placed on the set of his 1984–1985 production of the mediaeval Yorkshire Mystery plays,[14] which were performed by guilds, the mediaeval equivalent of trade unions. As Bernard O'Donoghue notes, in the 1984–1985 production of *The Mysteries* there is an implicit commentary on the 1984 miners' strike, with the miners and other labourers devils "prejudged to damnation. Harrison is of the devil's party; but, unlike Blake's Milton, he knows it."[15]

The notebook for *v.* also contains a copy of "V for Vendetta," a newspaper headline which references the view that Thatcher manipulated the 1984 miners' strike to avenge the Conservative Heath government, which was brought down by the miners' strikes in 1972 and 1974.[16] Cartoons of wartime Prime Minister Churchill making the V for victory sign and of Thatcher making the V sign in reverse also appear in the notebook.[17] The film of *v.* shows the photographs and footage of Churchill making the V sign and, along with footage of a militarized police force beating unarmed miners with truncheons, a Churchillian Thatcher holding up two fingers backwards. This symbol of crude aggression is what we might expect from the neo-Nazi skinhead spraying V signs in the graveyard. Thatcher too is portrayed as a thuggish warrior of the hard Right.

The poem of *v.* also invites readers to see the conflict between the Thatcher Government in the South and mining communities in the North as a colonial war because it is paralleled to the war between British Northern Ireland and the free Irish Republic. In *v.* the "national news" moves seamlessly between civil unrest involving British soldiers in Ireland, British "police v. pickets at a coke-plant gate," and the war between Iran and Iraq (*CP*, 277–278). The imperial economic character of the war to close down coal production in the North is also suggested by presenting it alongside the Gulf War. The conflict is presented as "class v. class" (*CP*, 266), but also as a colonial war between North and South. *v.*'s attentiveness to the political power of language and representation in this war and more widely is signaled by its epigraph, a quotation from a newspaper interview with Arthur Scargill, then President of the National Union of Miners: "My father still reads the dictionary every day. He says your life depends on your power to master words" (Arthur Scargill, *Sunday Times*, 10 January 1982). The notebook for *v.* includes a copy of the cover of *Time* in December 1984 featuring Scargill and Thatcher on the cover. The two figures represent opposed forces in the historic clash between the industrial arm of the working class movement and the ruling class. *v.* stages a polemically acute cultural intervention against the vilification of the miners by Thatcher and most of the press during the strike.

v. contests Thatcherite rhetorical attacks on the miners, and also on the unemployed and soccer hooligans like the skinhead, groups demonized as "enemies within" the nation during the Thatcher decade (1979–1990). "The enemies within" is a key political phrase of the period *v.* examines. The poem offers an alternative account of these "enemies." The poet in *v.* says: "Half versus half, the enemies within / the heart that can't be whole till they unite" (*CP*, 274). *v.* explores "the enemies within" "Tony Harrison" but also within Thatcher's England. Thatcher used the language of war against British citizens in a widely reported description of the miners as "the enemies within": "In the Falklands we had to fight the enemy without. Here is the enemy within."[18] "The enemies within" registers the resonances between the public language of the day and the language of *v.*.

v.'s imaginative dissent from the political language and argument of the New Right includes a defence of another of Thatcher's enemies within, the

unemployed, who were rhetorically targeted as "scroungers."[19] *v*. stages
the moral adventure of having a safely middle-class liberal get beneath
the skin of one of these "scroungers," only to find a man who desperately
wants work. The skinhead contemptuously anticipates his epitaph:

> When dole-wallahs fuck off to the void
>
> what'll t'mason carve up for their jobs?
>
> The cunts who lieth 'ere wor unemployed? (CP, 271)

v. challenges the Tory imputation that the unemployed do not want work
and are lazy. Indeed in his way the skinhead is really the self-reliant
entrepreneur elsewhere celebrated by Thatcher, independently staging
"*mi work on show all over Leeds*" (*CP*, 273). Targeting the unemployed,
the miners, and also soccer hooligans was, like prosecuting the 1982
Falklands War, electorally popular for Thatcher.[20]

   v. demystifies another of Thatcher's "enemies within," the soccer
hooligans, who the Tories regarded as a "law and order issue." Regional
rivalries are long standing features of the soccer competitions and there
have always been rogue elements among the hundreds of thousands
of Leeds United supporters. *v*. registers Thatcher's demonization of the
soccer hooligans, whose presence at Leeds United's matches became
more obvious as United's successes and crowds declined in the 1980s,
and unemployment rose. One of the newspaper articles of the day that
Harrison has pasted into the notebook for *v*. is "Inside the Evil Mind of a
Soccer Hooligan."[21] *v*. emphasizes that those labelled hooligans include
poorly educated, unemployed "kids" whose largely impotent "aggro"
is caused by more than Leeds United getting "relegated": "the lads /
who spray a few odd FUCKS when they're depressed" (*CP*, 268). In a
draft version of *v*. Harrison writes that "It's hard / to imagine doling out
punishment to Leeds kids / and sparing / club-footed bard."[22] Soccer fans'
names sprayed on gravestones in Leeds are likened to "the chiselled name
of Byron" on an ancient column on Mount Parnassus. The inscriptions

of the aristocratic rebel and unruly Leeds lads invite the same question in this draft: "what is he / a mindless vandal or just having fun?" In "Polygons" (2015) Harrison writes that he has been making the pilgrimage to Byron's faded name on the ancient column for thirty years, or the three decades since he wrote *v.*. He is haunted in "Polygons" by Byron's reflections about the ruins of ancient Greece in *Childe Harold's Pilgrimage* and his vision of universal extinction in *Darkness*. In "Polygons" the great "Byron's graffito" is partially a gesture of defiance against time, intertextually enhancing the suggestion in *v.*, where Byron's namesake the Leeds tanner lies buried in Holbeck cemetery, that a universal "*cri-de-coeur* because man dies" (*CP*, 269) partially drives the vandalism of Leeds United soccer fans.[23]

Harrison is interested in the classically educated Byron's presence in Greece and his belief in political ideals of liberty that derive from the ancient Greek republic, and that are found in classical and modern Greek poetry.[24] In "The Isle of Greece," for example, Byron "dream'd that Greece might still be free," and expresses the wish for national liberty that led him back to Greece to resist Turkish rule, only to die prematurely in 1824. Through his references to Byron in a draft version and in the published version of *v.*, Harrison implicitly speaks through Byron to signal his republican rejection of a different kind of oppression in the North. When the semi-literate skinhead tells the poet "*don't speak Greek*" (*CP*, 271) his not understanding the Greek language also decodes as not being educated in Greece's and wider republican political history and principles, and denotes the confused nature of his rebellion.

A further political complexity of *v.* is that it focuses on unsympathetic subcultures associated with the Leeds working class. The skinhead is linked to the extreme right political organization, the National Front. The poem registers the infiltration of the Leeds United fan base and the terraces by the National Front, as do newspaper articles pasted in the notebook for *v.*, such as "United Must Ban Fascists."[25] The National Front's presence at soccer grounds and distributing of propaganda is also shown in the photographs that accompany the text in the second Bloodaxe edition of *v.*.[26] The poet in *v.* observes "a swastika with NF (National Front)'s / sprayed on a grave" and that "another hand / has added, in a reddish colour, CUNTS" (*CP*, 266). An NF skinhead has put a swastika on a tomb. A communist (writing in a reddish colour) has responded by calling the NF "cunts," and also defacing the tombstone. The graffiti has a misogynistic application but primarily signals that the "Left v. Right" division (*CP*, 266) pervades all strata of society.

The offence or challenge of *v.* derives from Harrison's imaginative identification with a neo-Nazi skinhead. In draft versions of *v.* the character that became the skinhead was originally called a "punk," which Harrison has crossed out and replaced with "skin." The change emphasizes his sense of sharing the same skin or identifying with the vandal who emerges as his *doppelgänger*, and his interest in interrogating the presence of skinheads in Leeds. The racism of the NF is on show in the local graveyard, where the graffiti includes "Yid's" and "Niggers" (*CP*, 269), and is deplored by the poet. However, *v.*'s poet sympathetically interprets the NF's vandalizing of a giant sign in the city as a protest against the monopolization of public space by capital and by the cultural establishment, including "Tony Harrison" with "my name" "in Broadway lights," and asks "why can't skinheads with spraycans do the same?" (*CP*, 269). Harrison is sympathetic to the act rather than the content of the skinheads' vandalism, which is linked to his own poetic vandalism.

The republican Harrison enjoys the NF's inadvertent jibe at monarchy and capital. The NF nicked the missing letters of the giant sign but it is Harrison who gets the meaning out of the remaining sign:

> Some, where kids use aerosols, use giant signs
>
> to let the people know who's forged their fetters
>
> like PRI CE O WALES above West Yorkshire mines

(no prizes for who nicked the missing letters!) (*CP*, 268)

v. registers the greater visibility of the NF in 1980s England. It also refers to the German Krupp dynasty, industrialists who opened an arms factory in Auschwitz: "Letters of transparent tubes and gas / in Düsseldorf are blue and flash out KRUPP" (*CP*, 269). The Krupps and the skinheads are punningly and typographically linked in *v.*. Like KRUPP, the skinhead's obscenities such as 'SHIT' are capitalized. Another common English slang word for "shit" or faeces is "crap," which sounds very similar to the German "KRUPP." The near rhyme on "gas" / "KRUPP" also requires the German pronunciation. The Krupps and the skinhead are both viewed as Nazi "SHIT." In *v.* Harrison does not present his most recognizable political identity as "laureate of the left." But he remains "squarely on the side of Old Left decencies."[27]

In *v.* the word "UNITED" refers to a fascist politics, as well as to the soccer team that represents Leeds. "United" also links the fascism of the NF to the Thatcher regime, which politically appropriated the racism of the extreme right. The poet's witnessing of the crude racist graffiti in the graveyard also exhibits the obscenity of Tory rhetoric. When the poet calls for the skinhead's "UNITED" to "apply to higher things, and to the nation" (*CP*, 268) *v.* again reflects the political language of the day. Stuart Hall argues that Thatcher's rhetoric of national unity was important to her ideological campaign to establish a consensus based on the exploitation of racial divisions and the denial of class.[28] Thatcher strove to define the English as a unified people with common interests, while Harrison has consistently presented the English as a class-divided people, as "Them & [uz]." The Tory rhetoric of unity replaced "them" vs "us" with "we," and "deployed the discourses of 'nation' and 'people' against 'class' and 'unions'."[29] *v.* depicts the conflict between the N.U.M. and the State as an urgent example of "the unending violence of US and THEM" (*CP*, 266).

In *v.* it is still "class v. class, as bitter as before" and *v.* shares with the quatrain poem "Y" (1992) an identification of Thatcherism with the discursive occlusion of class. The epigraph for "Y" is a quotation of Thatcher: "I'm good with curtains."[30] Harrison, a passenger in Y (economy) class seating on an airplane, sees a curtain discretely drawn between economy and business class and observes that "as on earth, so in the sky." The divide between economy and business class seating is used in the poem as a metaphor and instance of class division. The epigraph punningly implies the "Iron Lady"'s manipulation of a stereotypical femininity, and also disrupts the ideological curtain or illusion of a unified nation, and so does *v.*.

That *v.* sign also points to the divide between the post-war Keynesian welfare state and the period of its undermining, which began under a Labour government in 1975 and escalated under Thatcher.[31] *v.* makes a humanist defence of the welfare state by witnessing the human cost of its dismantling, including the ending of the State's commitment to full employment. The skinhead's unemployment and bare literacy, and the impoverishment of pensioners like Harrison's dad create a grim impression of the rotting welfare state in the 1970s and 1980s. Those canned beans his dad "fancied" reflect the loneliness of the elderly widower, who has no need to buy "whole lambs for family freezers" (*CP*, 276), but they also suggest poverty. *v.* is not a liberal evasion of the political as interpreted by Worpole and Eagleton. It is a deeply personal poem but also a public "state of the nation" poem.

II

The author Tony Harrison is not either of the dramatic personae that share his name in *v.*. Harrison's distance from both poet and skinhead is evident, for example, in the satirical treatment of the characters, such as the use of heavily clichéd language in articulating the poet-persona's liberal politics. But a critical complexity of the poem is that there are also points at which the author's own sympathies and identifications are reflected in different facets of the two "Harrison" characters, who are in part imaginative projections of aspects of Harrison's complex identity. Harrison has referred in an interview to, for example, the skinhead's vandalism in *v.* as signaling "that act of vandalism that I would like to commit on English literature."[32]

In the case of the identification with Rimbaud, *v.* does reflect the author Harrison's affinity with Rimbaud and his "classical vandalism." It is in *v.* that Harrison explicitly identifies with Rimbaud. He defines himself, and Rimbaud, as a divided union of high cultural poet and dispossessed vandal. The poet-persona reveals that half of his identity is a poet and the other half is the skinhead who "aerosolled his name. And it was mine" (*CP*, 273). The skinhead and poet are united in "Harrison." He also declares that "the skinhead and poet united fucking Rimbaud" (*CP*, 271).

v. not only paraphrases but enacts Rimbaud's famous poetic dictum that "*Je est un autre*" ["I is someone else"].[33] Adapting Rimbaud's phrase, Harrison the law-abiding poet metamorphizes into the skinhead thug: "the *autre* that *je est* is fucking you" (*CP*, 271). The union of poet and skinhead in Harrison is manifest in that gradual merging of their idioms as the poet begins to speak the language of the cultural elite and of the street:

> "You piss-artist skinhead cunt, you wouldn't know
>
> and it doesn't fucking matter if you do,
>
> the skinhead and poet united fucking Rimbaud
>
> but the *autre* that *je est* is fucking you." (*CP*, 271)

"I is someone else" has been variously interpreted but is often understood to mean the series of identities a poet imaginatively enters in poetry. Harrison's identification with the skinhead, however, is not only an imaginative exercise. In *v.* he wanted to "take on my own instinct to vandalize my own art."[34] The Rimbaudian poet is the hoodlum speaking the language of assault in rhyming quatrains.

v. imagines Tony Harrison as a lumpenproletarian skinhead and a canonical nineteenth-century French poet. *v.*'s poet expects that a half-savage, unemployed skinhead in Leeds "wouldn't know" Rimbaud. But he evokes Rimbaud as a poet the skinhead *could* identify with. Rimbaud was born into the lower classes in the Ardennes region of France and, when he lived in Paris and London, was usually unemployed. He was regarded by most of the literati as a half-civilized "little peasant" and "a brutish little vagrant."[35] In his life, Rimbaud became someone else many times. He famously lived many lives including those of a poet, factory worker, languages tutor, sailor, a gun-runner, a Communard, and a vagabond.[36] In *The Eighteenth Brumaire* Marx observed the poor of Paris roughly twenty years before Rimbaud was begging on the city's streets. The chronic unemployed and petty criminals like the skinhead, the depraved poor, beggars, gypsies, vagabonds, and literati like Rimbaud are listed amongst the spectacle of the lumpenproletariat.[37] *v.* suggests there are shades of Rimbaud discernible in the *dole-wallah* skinhead, whose obscene eloquence suggests a Rimbaudian lineage, and in the poet Harrison. *v.* boldly reclaims Rimbaud for what it suggests is his true constituency, and Harrison's: not the bourgeoisie, or the cultural elite who appropriated Rimbaud after his death, but "outsider" regional rebels like the skinhead and Harrison.

Like the young Harrison's Leeds accent, Rimbaud's provincial Northern accent "was thick and distinctive, with emphatic working-class vowels."[38] Rimbaud's roots were a mixture of "urban and rural, bourgeois and peasant."[39] His use of regional accents and rhymes, and low diction and subjects in his poetry are attempts to solve a problem that is also fundamental to Harrison's poetic project: "if literature is a bourgeois institution, how can it be used to convey an anti-bourgeois ideology?"[40] Harrison responds to this question, and to the skinhead's charge that the bourgeois poet can no longer represent "*the class yer were born into*" (*CP*, 273), by having the lumpenproletarian express his alienation from poetry in a poem: "*A book, yer stupid cunt, 's not worth a fuck!*" (*CP*, 271).

The poet-as-skinhead is, like Rimbaud, a classical vandal defacing high cultural forms with regional idioms, aggressive slang, shocking subjects, and unacceptable sentiments. Harrison, like Rimbaud, mastered classical forms and the rhythms and prosody of their respective native tongues. Rimbaud's earliest verse was composed in perfect Latin.[41] His earliest poetry in French was written in alexandrine verse and rhyming couplets, but "while observing the classical mould Rimbaud perversely fills it with the most unseemly content."[42] Robb observes that some of Rimbaud's subsequent poetry is criticized for "incorrect rhymes" which are perfectly harmonious when pronounced with what Verlaine called Rimbaud's "*parisiano-ardennais*" accent.[43] Similarly, Harrison has been criticized for incorrect rhymes that instead require a Leeds pronunciation.[44] Harrison's and Rimbaud's poetry also shares the inclusion of non-aesthetic elements and disturbing experience. Rimbaud brought revolution and pack rape into verse such as "*Qu'est-ce pour nous*" ["What Are They To Us"] and "*Le coeur volé*" ["The Stolen Heart"]. Rimbaud and Verlaine co-authored "*Sonnet du trou du cul*" ["Sonnet to an Arsehole"] and contributed to the ribald communal scrapbook *The Album Zutique*. Violent emotions and masturbation feature prominently in Rimbaud's early verse. In *Loiners* in particular Harrison also uses traditional verse forms to convey explicitly sexual and violent experiences, including masturbation, sodomy, rape, and genocide. In like manner *v.* strikingly transgresses bourgeois aesthetic and political boundaries in its use of obscenities, which appear in capital letters to resemble graffiti and to create the visual appearance that the high cultural form has been vandalized by the poet-as-skinhead: "SHIT"; "PISS"; "CUNT"; "FUCK"; "YID"; "NIGGER."

v. is Harrison's most explicit and sustained appropriation of neoclassical verse for language and subjects shocking to the sensibility of the assumed bourgeois reader, and this is part of why it is in *v.* that Rimbaud appears in the guise of the classical vandal. In *v.* the poet recalls being called a "damned vandal" as a boy because he sprayed a soprano with a fire-hose, a symbolic sexual assault against her art and its "prick-tease of the soul" (*CP*, 272). *v.* shows that Harrison's instinct is still to vandalize the traditional transcendent art that the soprano represents. Rimbaud "trampled the flower-beds of French poetry with an expert boot,"[45] and Harrison-as-skinhead vandal has taken his aerosol to English poetry. Even as late in Rimbaud's trajectory towards a revolutionary aesthetic as *A Season in Hell* his contradictory mixture of the old fashioned and the revolutionary resonates with Harrison's poetry. In *v.* he adopts the traditionally reconciling form of the elegy but has the skinhead within rebel against it. However, by contrast with Rimbaud's seeking a new form, Harrison's sustaining of classical forms appears deeply conservative. But his radical political-poetic project is to take over the traditional forms of the British literary tradition on behalf of the Northern working class and subaltern voices, the project dramatized as a people's occupation of "your lousy leasehold Poetry" in "Them & [uz], II."[46] Unlike Rimbaud, Harrison does not reject classical forms but instead occupies them on behalf of the excluded, especially "uz."

Rimbaud's early subversion of traditional verse forms is comparable to Harrison's poetics but in the last stage of his poetic life Rimbaud wrote prose poems. Rimbaud took breaking the rules of French prosody as far as he could before "doing away with it all altogether."[47] One received view is that the prose poem genre originated in nineteenth-century France with Aloysius Bertrand.[48] Other poets of the period were also breaking the rules of French prosody, and some such as Stéphane Mallarmé wrote prose poems. Baudelaire, an important influence upon Rimbaud, developed the prose poem but it remained for him "a kind of sideline, an experiment," whereas for Rimbaud the prose poem was "the only form of expression that remained after the rejection of the conformities imposed by the meter and rhyme of the French poetic language."[49]

A fundamental difference between Rimbaud and Harrison is that the iambic pentameter remains essential to all Harrison's work, whereas Rimbaud with his prose poems and other works aimed to destroy the alexandrine, the formal line of much French poetry, from as early as 1869 with "The Sleeper in the Valley." Similarly in England at the start of the twentieth century Ezra Pound and others aimed to break the pentameter line of English verse. Rimbaud, like Pound, sought a new form where Harrison clearly works within received traditional forms, including elegiac and heroic couplets, lyric stanzas, epodic stanzas, terza rima, and sonnets. Rimbaud's movement towards free verse and the largely new form of prose poetry anticipated the future movement of poetry at large whereas Harrison is in formal terms a very conservative, even anachronistic poet. The breakdown of regular versification has been a major development in twentieth-century European poetry, and this is an aspect of Rimbaud's great significance for later poets.[50] By contrast, it remains to be seen to what extent Harrison's poetry will significantly influence subsequent poets, and he is a singular presence to date.

The connection forged in *v.* between Rimbaud and the skinhead implicitly observes an historical contrast and irony in the ostracization of Thatcher's "scrounger," the skinhead desperate for work, and of nineteenth-century vagabonds like Rimbaud, who were often provincial youth who refused menial work and fled to the city.[51] Vagabonds were defined under the French penal code of 1810 as those without a home and without a trade or profession.[52] In contrast to the skinhead, who laments that he will "*croak / doing t'same nowt ah do now as a kid*"(*CP*, 270), it was not unemployment but alienated labour that Rimbaud regarded as worse than death. In a letter Rimbaud declares his rejection of work: "*Travailler maintenant, jamais, jamais; je suis en grève.*" ["Work now?—never, never, I am on strike."][53]

Rimbaud describes his idleness and freedom in *A Season in Hell*: "*Sans me servir pour vivre même de mon corps, et plus oisif que le crapaud, j'ai vécu partout.*" ["Without making use of my body in any way, and lazier than a toad, I have lived everywhere."][54] Kristen Ross argues that before Rimbaud gave up poetry he rejected employment in favour not of bourgeois leisure but "laziness," which in this context means the refusal to turn the body into a tool or to surrender mobility.[55] Ross discusses the politics of Rimbaud's refusal of employment partly through a reading of *A Season in* Hell, and argues that it has a double in the field of political theory, *The Right to be Lazy* by the nineteenth-century French Marxist political writer Paul Lafargue.[56] *The Right to be Lazy* parodies *The Right to Work*, the document that elevated work "to the status of a revolutionary principle."[57] Lafargue observed the wretchedness of the industrial proletariat and regarded factory work as "the end of all that makes life worth living."[58] *The Right to be Lazy* advocates that workers abandon "the miseries of compulsory work."[59] Lafargue's comic concluding appeal to "Laziness, mother of the arts and noble virtues"[60] is ostensibly antithetical to Harrison's personal need for poetry "to be hard work."[61] Harrison may though well sympathize with Lafargue's more serious arguments that if the hours of labour were reduced, and if the economy and wealth distribution were more sanely organized, the common people could enjoy the pleasures of life reserved for the affluent.[62]

v. deploys a polemically acute plea against forced unemployment but Harrison's distance from the miners' strike in *v.* may manifest an ironic sadness that it is an exploitative and dangerous industry that the working class are placed in the position of fighting for. He likens the mines to Hell in the 1984–1985 production of *The Mysteries,* where the only light in Hell comes from the miners' pit-helmets. In *v.* the likening of the unemployed to coal dumped on the fire suggests that the dole queue replaces the mines as another form of victimization of the Northern working class. By contrast, the nineteenth-century artisans, whose graves the poet meditates upon in the opening stanzas and who share the names of great Romantic poets, are depicted in *v.* as having an autonomous, dignified, and organic relationship to their work and community in a pre-industrial era. In *v.* and more widely in his poetry it is the artisans, rather than the working class, with whom the autonomous wordsmith Harrison identifies his poetic craft.

III

v. is a late twentieth-century urban elegy, and a radical revising, updating, and "vandalizing" of the aesthetics and politics of its literary model of difference, Thomas Gray's *Elegy Written in a Country Churchyard* (1751). *v.* and the *Elegy* might be regarded as elegies if we define the genre as "a poem of mourning occasioned by a specific death,"[63] as they mourn, respectively, the anticipated and imaginary deaths of their poet-narrators. Also, the initial occasion of *v.* is Harrison tending the graves of his parents, and Gray's residual grief for Richard West is important to the *Elegy*.[64] It is the public dimension of these elegies and the amplification in *v.* "of pre-existent tendencies in elegy toward what might be termed national critique" that I am concerned with here.[65] In an eighteenth-century literary manner Harrison speaks through Gray to articulate their shared republicanism, and both elegies honour the "artless" and lament illiteracy and poverty. However, *v.* adopts Gray's canonical *Elegy* as its poetic vehicle to transgress a Whig and liberal literary tradition of political resignation to injustice and to the silence of the poor.

Gray's *Elegy* is part of "the persisting tradition of mournful alienation in English writing about the dispossessed...That tradition sees victims sympathetically, but does not speak in their voice."[66] Gray's gentleman poet speaks the language of the eighteenth-century educated class to describe the lives of "the rude Forefathers" buried in the churchyard of a rural labouring community.[67] Gray's poet, "mindful of the unhonour'd Dead / Dost in these lines their artless tale relate."[68] Less reverently, and in a combative, contemporary street vernacular, *v.*'s bourgeois poet tells the skinhead that he is writing the poem "to give ungrateful cunts like you a hearing!" (*CP*, 271). In Gray's *Elegy* the language and worldview of the poet are also placed in the mouth of the unlettered Swain. In *v.* too the unlettered skinhead speaks, but not the language or perspective of the poet. Although the skinhead is the poet's alter-ego, he is imaginatively endowed with a distinct voice and vision, through the device of the dramatic dialogue. In this sense, *v.* lets the illiterate skinhead speak for himself, whereas in Gray's *Elegy* the gentleman poet represents the inarticulate, and this is the major aesthetic and political difference between the poems.

The *Elegy* reflects Gray's Whig political persuasions, but there are ambiguities in his ultimately conservative portrayal of the peasantry. His famous *Elegy* was a popular poem which expresses compassion for the "chill Penury" and illiteracy of the rural poor. To lament injustice inevitably implies the desirability of change, but this does not lead Gray to advocate wealth redistribution, nor to admit any alternatives to injustice. Instead, Gray's *Elegy* naturalizes the social order by locating it within the cycles of nature. *v.*'s poet comparably laments injustice only to minimize the social by locating it alongside vast millennial and geological cycles. Gray's and Harrison's poets have, respectively, religious and metaphysical frameworks which here encourage fatalism and occlude questions of political agency. *v.*'s poet suggests that the human condition is essentially unalterable and that man's tragedy is to be the ground eternal metaphysical divisions "are fought out on" (*CP*, 266). William Empson observed that Gray's *Elegy* was "an odd case of poetry with latent political ideas" but that its ultimate acceptance of injustice was disappointing to many readers.[69] The attentive intertextual relationship between the *Elegy* and *v.* suggests that Harrison's intention is to rhetorically expose essentially the same liberal evasion of the political, as exhibited by the poets in both poems, not to endorse it. The *Elegy's* politics of resignation are echoed by *v.*'s poet, two centuries later, but its limitations are exposed by the inclusion of the skinhead's voice and by Harrison's larger vision in *v.*.

v.'s bourgeois liberal poet is partly modelled on Gray's gentleman Whig poet, while the poor, uneducated Swain is a partial model of antithesis for the skinhead. The poets in both elegies are solitary observers isolated from their humble communities of origin by their education. Gray's poet is visibly wracked by an internal conversation: "Mutt'ring his wayward fancies he wou'd rove."[70] When *v.*'s skinhead is revealed as the poet's

alter-ego it is evident that Harrison is another lone "mutt'ring" poet.
The idea of the *doppelganger* in *v.* draws upon Gray's *Elegy*. Towards
the end of the *Elegy* the poet-narrator addresses "thee" as the author of
"these lines," as if another person had written the poem in an identical
voice. Because Gray's poet is alone, it is as if his alter-ego had written
the poem. Because Gray's poet is of "humble birth" it seems that the
unlettered Swain is his alter ego, and therefore also the author of the
poem. But, again, the key point is that Gray's poem only has one voice
and one vision and it is not that of the poor, but of an educated Whig poet
who laments but accepts the unjust fate of the poor. *v.* gives the poet-
persona's alter-ego a distinct voice and vision, that of an impoverished
skinhead violently protesting against his dispossession.

The politics and aesthetics of giving the skinhead a distinct voice in
v. is also clarified by the punning parallels and contrasts between the
belligerent skinhead and Gray's amiable Swain. The Hoary-headed Swain,
a grey-haired old servant, silently and affectionately observed Gray's
poet from a distance. "Harrison" is berated by a bald young skinhead. The
Swain laments the poet's death. The skinhead wants to "*boot yer fucking
balls to Kingdom Come*" (*CP*, 271). A peasant in the *Elegy* is "this pleasing
anxious being e'er resign'd."[71] The cursing skinhead is not resigned to
his fate but enraged by it. Like Gray's *Elegy*, *v.* ends with the epitaph of
the poet. The imagined conversation in the *Elegy* between the Swain and
the kindred Spirit is paralleled in *v.* by the poet-as-skinhead addressing
the "poetry supporter" in his epitaph, which includes the idiom of the
skinhead: "SHIT." The epitaph in the *Elegy* asks the kindred Spirit to
enquire no further into the nature of the dead poet. In *v.* the epitaph tells
the "poetry supporter" how "to understand" where Harrison's poetry
comes from. The *Elegy* and its epitaph reflect Gray's Christianity while
v. and its epitaph exhibit Harrison's atheism. The poet in *v.* is not silently
resting his head in "*the bosom of his Father and his God*,"[72] like Gray's poet.
In *v.* the epitaph, which will be returned to at the end of this discussion,
is that of the poet-as-skinhead. The skinhead is, in one way, another of

Harrison's graceless Palladian figures who will not go down quietly, and
v. gives him a stage upon which to roar his wrath.

The politics of *v.*'s form involves bringing lumpenproletarian and
working-class Leeds content and idiom into the iambic pentameter in
alternately rhymed quatrains adopted from Gray's *Elegy. v.* metrically
distinguishes itself from its model by introducing irregularities into the
iambic pentameter, which are comparatively minor during the poet's
monologue. But when the civilized poet starts using the skinhead's savage
idiom, "the verse-forms really have to flail around to hold together,
and their ironic awareness of this, magnificent in *v*, is part of their
meaning."[73] As Rowland observes, "the aesthetics of the elegy suit the
steady rhythms of the poet's philosophizing," and not the anti-literary
invective of the skinhead.[74]

Harrison's and Gray's elegies are concerned with silences but only *v.*'s
skinhead disrupts the literary censorship of the uneducated class. *v.*, like
"On Not Being Milton," is preoccupied with the *Elegy*'s famous phrase
"some mute, inglorious Milton," those whose potential was denied by
illiteracy and hard labour.[75] The *Elegy*'s stanza beginning "full many a
gem of purest ray serene" also seems to say that there are bright inspired
geniuses among the poor but they are unseen.[76] In "On Not Being Milton"
the honourable artisan and Cato Street conspirator Richard Tidd has one
line. In *v.* the skinhead has half the dialogue in the middle section of the
poem. The poet of Gray's *Elegy* reasons that although the illiterate will
never have great achievements their lack of power means that they will
also never cause great harm, or "wade through slaughter to a throne."[77]
v.'s concern with a skinhead and his political organization, the National
Front, presents some grim political potentialities of the downtrodden.
"On Not Being Milton" implicitly asks what the mute Miltons might say
if Literature let them speak, and *v.* provides one disturbing answer.

Gray's and Harrison's elegies honour, in different ways, those who
have led lives of hardship rather than privilege and this reflects their
shared republicanism. Gray is part of the English republican literary

lineage in which Harrison locates himself. The republican contempt for poets who court power expressed in the *Elegy* is part of its attraction for Harrison. The *Elegy* evokes the corrupt obsequiousness of poets who "heap the shrine of Luxury and Pride / With incense kindled at the Muse's flame."[78] In "Laureate's Block" (1999) Harrison explicitly identifies with Gray's rejection of the poet-laureateship because he was not prepared to be "*rat-catcher to his Majesty.*"[79] Gray's *Elegy* refers to heroes of the seventeenth-century English republican revolution, Milton, Hampden, and ambivalently to Cromwell. *v.* identifies the monarchy with an oppressive status quo (*CP*, 268). Modelling *v.* on an eighteenth-century elegy that does not valorize kings but working men also adds historical depth to *v.*'s sense of the loss of identity and pride experienced by unemployed men in 1980s England, in the masculinist discourse the elegies share.

The poet in the *Elegy*, however, is not a working man but a gentleman, and Gray's rejection of professional writers is evident in the poem. *v.*'s presentation of the poet as a working man involves a settling of accounts with Gray, who identified with a historically specific form of literary production, that of the literary landed gentry (although Gray had no estate and became a gentleman of letters with chambers at Cambridge University).[80] In *v.* the poet refers to the graves of Wordsworth and Byron in the local cemetery and notes "that's two peers already, of a sort" (*CP*, 264). We are then told that Wordsworth was the local man who built church organs and Byron was the Leeds tanner, not the famous poets. *v.* humorously conveys that there were no literary models for a poet of working-class Leeds. The point is also though that artisans like Wordsworth the organ builder are Harrison's models for the poet not as a gentleman or a recipient of patronage, but as an artisan.

The poet William Wordsworth is also important in *v.*. The third stanza alludes to Wordsworth's lyric "I Wandered Lonely as a Cloud," in which the narrator walking in nature saw "a host, of golden daffodils."[81] *v.* refers to the flowers and also adapts the rhyme on "hill's" / "daffodils" (*CP*,

264), from the first stanza of "I Wandered Lonely as a Cloud."[82] In Leeds daffodils are not recognized as symbols in high cultural poetry but are the flowers "by which dad dignified the family plot" (*CP*, 264). The allusions to "I Wandered Lonely as a Cloud" also signal *v.*'s break with what Harrison regarded as the persistence of the popular belief that poetry is synonymous with nature,[83] despite some prominent twentieth-century poetry about the city by T.S. Eliot, W.H. Auden, Philip Larkin, and other poets. There is grim humour in the implicit contrast between the idyllic pastoral landscape Wordsworth's poem recalls, and *v.*'s scene of urban desolation. Wordsworth recollects in tranquility "what wealth the show to me had brought" and his heart "dances with the daffodils."[84] In a political and urban poem like *v.*, the ironic allusions to "I Wandered Lonely as a Cloud" suggest Harrison's distance from the evasion of the political through a retreat into nature and personal feelings, as found in the later Wordsworth and the conservative strand of Romanticism.

The Wordsworth of the *Lyrical Ballads* adapted "the language of conversation in the middle and lower classes of society" to create "poetic pleasure" for the bourgeois reader.[85] *v.* uses the speech of the lumpenproletariat to confront readers with unpleasant social realities. *v.* also alludes to Wordsworth as an elegist. The line "will Earth run out of her 'diurnal courses'" (*CP*, 279) quotes from Wordsworth's "A slumber did my spirit seal."[86] Like Wordsworth and Gray, Harrison is an elegist preserving a cultural memory of the dead and of a declining way of life, including that of his parents and the Northern working-class in an emerging post-industrial era, but without idealization. Harrison tries to explain rather than condone, for example, the white working-class xenophobia associated in *v.*, and in the "Next Door" sonnets, with his parents' generation and depicted in the character of "Mr Harrison." In *v.* the poet's father is a frail and isolated widower disorientated by the increasingly multicultural landscape of Leeds, and he feels "fear / of foreign food and faces" (CP, 276). Comparably, *v.* abhors but tries to understand the violent racism of the skinhead who has defaced the gravestones.

v. also speaks through Wordsworth's "Upon Epitaphs" and Gray's *Elegy* to suggest that the memorialization of the dead reflects the character of a civilization. In Wordsworth's first essay from "Upon Epitaphs" the purpose of an epitaph is "to guard the remains of the deceased from irreverent approach or from savage violation: and, secondly, to preserve their memory."[87] Similarly, in Gray's *Elegy* gravestones are frail memorials which serve "these bones from insult to protect,"[88] and to prevent "dumb Forgetfulness."[89] Harrison's dad preserves the memory of his parents by tending their graves each week although he has not read Wordsworth. Harrison has spent the "odd ten minutes" tending his parents' graves and is of a generation that has "gone away / for work or fuller lives, like me from Leeds" (*CP*, 267). The skinhead has savagely violated the graves. Wordsworth also quotes Camden's view that only savage nations and barbarous peoples neglect their dead,[90] and this idea is intertextually adapted in *v.*. The violation and neglect of the graves in *v.* is a sign of a savage nation where the weakest amongst the living are also abused and neglected, and may become savagely vengeful like the skinhead.

How Harrison defines his poetic and political identity in *v.* is disclosed by whether he will neglect the ailing place and people he came from and "go, / with not one glance behind, away from Leeds" (*CP*, 275). This line directly refers to Gray's *Elegy*, whose poet wonders if a dying peasant "cast one longing ling'ring look behind?"[91] *v.* is a dramatic examination of whether Harrison's connection to his background, symbolized by the skinhead within him, and his attendant class political loyalties survive. *v.* also contains an ironic allusion to Milton's *Paradise Lost*. Adam and Eve are forced to leave paradise without looking behind.[92] Leeds is not paradise. Asserting that the skinhead in him dies in the graveyard (*CP*, 274), the poet resolves to return to his wife and the materially and culturally richer life he has built far away from "*fucking Leeds!*" (*CP*, 270).

Byrne argues that *v.* ultimately "comes down comfortably" on the ideological "right" and that in it Harrison concedes "that familial (and thus, perhaps, class) affiliations are replaced by romantic and sexual ones."[93]

Byrne contends that when the skinhead cries "wanker!" to the poet's affirmation of love it entices readers to finally side with the "tolerant liberal aspect" of the poem,[94] and critics have generally regarded the "home to my woman" section of *v.* as affirming a liberal retreat from the political. His relationship to the skinhead and soprano do symbolize his relationships to their respective social classes in *v.*. In the poem "Harrison" listens to the opera *Lulu* with his wife (a character in *v.* implicitly linked to the author's then wife, the soprano Teresa Stratas, who also came from a working-class background, and whose performances include starring in a production of *Lulu*). In *v.* the marriage implicitly symbolizes the poet's union with high culture and the bourgeoisie. However, the idealization of marriage in *v.* is heavily ironized, including by having the boy footballers hum *Here Comes the Bride*, which the poet knows is from *Lohengrin*, a tragic opera about doomed love.

 v.'s celebration of love is weighed against the animosity of the wedding "match," of "man v. wife" (*CP*, 266), and the division and impermanence it understands as the human condition. The poet says "I doubt" that time or adversity will erode the love that unites him with his bride, which is associated in *v.* with age-old geographical strata (*CP*, 277). Their love is likened to coal and fire, and "we burn" refers to the lovers as well as the flames which, however, become smoke "escaping insubstantial up the flue" (*CP*, 277). There is a rhyme on "flue" and "you," and "your name" is rhymed with "brief flame." The "united" of his marriage remains a question that "a man of doubt at life's mid-way"[95] addresses to the beloved, and to the reader: "And now it's your decision: does it stay?" (*CP*, 278). But the underlying relationship to his second skin, his alter-ego, is ontological: "the skinhead's UNITED underwrites the poet, / the measures carved below the ones above." This line shifts the focus from "the ones we choose to love" to the place and early experiences that shaped a fundamental and permanent part of Harrison's complex identity. The poet's inescapable union is not with the beautiful soprano but the skinhead and the wider community of underdogs he represents: "uz."

It is the "ghosts from all Leeds matches humming" that the poet remembers when he hears the *Bridal Chorus* and embraces his bride. From the moment he asserts the death of the skinhead within him and begins his journey away from Leeds, images and sounds of the boy footballers and metonymically their team, Leeds United, occupy his imagination. It is not only soccer hooligans but the local boys, their families, and Harrison's dad who are Leeds United supporters. In a manuscript version of *v.*, his elderly father is "a lifetime's staunch Leeds United supporter."[96] Harold "had a season ticket for the stand / but the hooligans were getting out of hand." Mr Harrison's season ticket is for the stands, where peaceful Leeds United supporters usually sit, while the terraces were where "it's not football anymore its open war!"[97] In *v.* references to Leeds United's losing streak in the 1980s symbolize the declining fortunes of the place and people the team represented. A signification of "Leeds United" is akin to "uz" and, with an ambivalent love, Harrison is still on their side.

Coda

v. ends with the planned epitaph of "Tony Harrison," a famous poet whom supporters will honour, to be inscribed upon his tombstone in the Holbeck cemetery, Leeds. In the verse epigraph that introduces *Loiners*, a white rose, a symbol of the poet's native Leeds culture, "*grew out of his nose.*" The epitaph that concludes *v.* tells us that his hybrid cosmopolitan poetry will always have deep roots in Leeds ground. The poem has provoked considerable controversy about Harrison's personal and political identity but, buried in the family plot, he has not left Leeds with "not one glance behind." Instead, he tells the poetry supporter to "*look behind*" to Leeds if they want to understand him and his poetry. The epitaph is his account to posterity of who he is:

> Beneath your feet's a poet, then a pit.
>
> Poetry supporter, if you're here to find

how poems can grow from (beat you to it!) SHIT

find the beef, the beer, the bread, then look behind. (CP, 279)

The epitaph anticipates the assumed bourgeois poetry supporters'
incredulity that high cultural poetry could grow from "SHIT," from
working-class Leeds. The epitaph to *v.* reformulates the question posed
in "Heredity," the verse epigraph that introduces *The School of Eloquence.*
In "Heredity" the sneering, condescending bourgeois is fathoming the
"*mystery!*" of a poet from working-class Leeds: "*Wherever did you get your
talent from?*"[98] "Heredity" presents the poet's compensatory eloquence
as the legacy of his tongue-tied uncles' struggle to speak. In *v.* the source
of Harrison's poetry is still firstly filial and, implicitly, the ghosts of Joe
and Harry are with him in the family plot.

The poetry supporter wanting to understand Harrison's work should
also look to the community of artisans and other working men he will be
buried alongside. The epitaph of the "Yorkshire poet who came to read
the metre"[99] will be "chiselled" on the tombstone of the poet as artisan.
The poetry supporter should then "*look behind*" to Elland Road, home
of Leeds United, and to Leeds Grammar and the conflicting formative
influences upon Harrison. The phrase "poetry supporter" connects them
to the Leeds United supporters in *v.*, as does their swearing. The epitaph
wryly points out that poetry supporters curse too when their hopes are
dashed, or when confronted with their perceived social inferiors: "SHIT."
The epitaph mocks the hypocrisy and class prejudice of the genteel poetry
reader, including a scatological reminder of our literal and metaphorical
"shit."[100] The epitaph of an ambivalent poet, it also makes a gesture of
fraternity to his readers by pointing to what unites us across cultural
and political divisions, including the capacity to hate and to mourn, our
embodiment and our mortality.

In *v.* Harrison's connection to his Northern roots hinges on the
endurance of the skinhead within him. Critically, the epitaph's aggressive

slang, the idiom of the skinhead, signals that his skin is with him to the grave. In his readings of *v.* Harrison also adopts the "yob" skinhead voice when he reads the words "(beat you to it!)." The bracketed words, along with "SHIT," are the only words in the epitaph not italicized, typographically signaling that they belong to a second speaker, although "SHIT" is pronounced in the cultivated poet's voice, in a complexly choreographed, dialogical dance of signification. "Tony" the skinhead is not separable from "Tony" the poet and, united as one, they create an iconoclastic poetics of classical vandalism. There will be one man buried in that grave, but Harrison's epitaph witnesses his dual identity as a high cultural poet and the great outsider.

v. is Harrison's most confrontational transgression of the aesthetic and political boundaries of Poetry, which he consistently presents as a bourgeois institution, because *v.* gives a polyvalent voice to the suffering and inchoate rage of an illiterate, impoverished, terminally unemployed, lumpenproletarian neo-Nazi thug. Harrison's epitaph bears no traces of the resignation or reconciliation traditionally found in epitaphs and elegies, and instead declares the unwavering aesthetic and political battle he intends to wage even from the grave. *v.* charts new and familiar territory in Harrison's humanist poetics of inclusion, his continuous effort to open the doors of Poetry: "*Fling our doors wide! all, all, not one, but all!*"[101]

* * *

The political meanings of Tony Harrison's imaginative works and the political character of the poet, the importance of Milton, and of history for understanding the poetry, and the haunting presence of Rimbaud in the poems have been the primary concerns of this study. The poet's political convictions are essentially unchanging across the decades, from *Loiners* to the present day. He is a cultural hero of the left but has no public party-political allegiances and is critical of established political parties in Britain. He seems influenced by certain political theorists, notably by Marx and also by Raymond Williams's particular emphasis upon the relationship between class and place, but Harrison is a creative thinker and an iconoclast skeptical of orthodoxies. A cosmopolitan Leeds poet, his ideological commitments are consistent in the different historical and literary contexts that the poems take as their subjects. The dialectical interplay between the class, anti-colonial, republican, and humanist aspects of the poetry, and his literary elective affinities, are essential for understanding the aesthetics and the politics of the Rimbaud of Leeds.

NOTES

1. *v.*, *London Review of Books*, vol. 7, no. 1 (24 January 1985), 12–13. *v.* was also published in a variorum edition by Bloodaxe Books in 1985 (second edition 1989), and Richard Eyre's film of *v.* was first broadcast by Channel 4 on 4 November 1987. All references to *v.* in this chapter are from the *CP* and will be given in brackets after the text.
2. Terry Eagleton, "Antagonisms: Tony Harrison's *v.*," in *Bloodaxe 1*, 348–350, 350.
3. Eagleton, "Antagonisms," 349–350.
4. For a record of the media and political reaction to the poem and film see *v.: New Edition* (Newcastle-upon-Tyne: Bloodaxe Books, 1989).
5. See for example Douglas Dunn, "Abrasive Encounters," in *Bloodaxe 1*, ed. Astley, 346–347, 346; John Lucas, "Speaking For England," in *Bloodaxe 1*, 351–361, 351–353; and Neil Corcoran, *English Poetry since 1940* (London and New York: Longman, 1993), 162.
6. See for example David Kennedy, "'Past Never Found': Class, Dissent and the Contexts of Tony Harrison's *v.*," *English*, vol. 58, no. 221 (2009), 162–181; *TH Holocaust*, 283; Sandie Byrne, "On Not Being Milton, Marvell, or Gray," in *TH: Loiner*, 57–83, 80–82.
7. See for example Woodcock "'Internal Colonialism'", 59 and 62; and Ken Worpole, 'Scholarship Boy: The Poetry of Tony Harrison', in *Bloodaxe 1*, 61–74, 73.
8. *Poems 1984: v.*, Tony Harrison's Notebooks, 59.
9. Karl Marx, *The Eighteenth Brumaire of Louis Bonaparte*, ed. C.P. Dutt (New York: International Publishers, 1975), 75.
10. *Crossings*, *CP*, 399–414, 405.
11. *Prometheus* (London: Faber and Faber, 1998), 7.
12. Edith Hall, "Tony Harrison's *Prometheus*: A View from the Left," *Arion*, vol. 10, no. 1 (2002), 129–140, 129.
13. *v.: Notebook*, 101.
14. *v.: Notebook*, 233.
15. Bernard O'Donoghue, "*The Mysteries*: T.W.'s Revenge," in *Bloodaxe 1*, 316–323, 323.
16. *Daily Mirror*, 8 August 1984. See also *v.: Notebook*, 136.
17. *v.: Notebook*, 138, 139.

18. Margaret Thatcher, Address to the 1922 Committee in the House of Commons (19 July 1984), reported in "Thatcher makes Falklands Link," *The Times* (20 July 1984).

19. Ian Gough, "Thatcherism and the Welfare State," in *The Politics of Thatcherism*, ed. Stuart Hall and Martin Jacques (London: Lawrence and Wishart, 1983), 148–168, 155–156.

20. Steve Redhead, *Subculture to Clubcultures: An Introduction to Popular Cultural Studies* (Cambridge: Blackwell, 1997), 17.

21. *v.*: Notebook, 207.

22. *v.*: Notebook, 52.

23. *v.*: Notebook, 52. See also "Polygons," *London Review of Books*, 17.

24. See Jerome McGann, *Byron and Romanticism*, ed. James Soderholm (Cambridge: Cambridge University Press, 2002; and Kiriakoula Solomou, "The Influence of Greek Poetry on Byron," *The Byron Journal*, volume 10, 1982, 4–19.

25. *Evening Chronicle*, 18 September, 1984; and *v.*: Notebook, 207.

26. *v.*: *New Edition with Press articles* (Newcastle-upon-Tyne: Bloodaxe Books, 1989 [1985]).

27. Dunn, "Abrasive Encounters," *Bloodaxe 1*, 347.

28. Stuart Hall, "The Great Moving Right Show," in *Politics of Thatcherism*, 19–39, 27.

29. Hall, "Moving Right," 27.

30. "Y," *CP*, 286.

31. Gough, "Thatcherism and the Welfare State," *Politics of Thatcherism*, 148–168.

32. *Exploring v.*, BBC Radio 4, 18 February 2013.

33. Letter to Georges Izambard (13 May 1871), the famous *Lettre du Voyant* ["The Prophet's Letter"], *RCWSL*, 370–371.

34. Maya Jaggi, "Beats of the Heart," *The Guardian* (Saturday 31 March 2007).

35. Robb, *Rimbaud*, 117 and 442.

36. Enid Starkie, *Arthur Rimbaud in Abyssinia* (Oxford: Clarendon Press, 1937), 112–113; Kristin Ross, *The Emergence of Social Space: Rimbaud and the Paris Commune* (Minneapolis: University of Minnesota Press, 1988), 56–57.

37. Marx, *The Eighteenth Brumaire*, 75.

38. Robb, *Rimbaud*, 57 and 119. Robb does not refer to Harrison.

39. Robb, *Rimbaud*, 95.

40. Robb, *Rimbaud*, 162.

41. Robb, *Rimbaud*, 27–28.

42. LeRoy C. Breunig, "Why France?," in *The Prose Poem in France*, ed. Mary Ann Caws and Hermine Riffatere (New York: Columbia University Press, 1983), 3–20, 7–8.

43. Robb, *Rimbaud*, 162.

44. For a discussion of the mixed critical responses to Harrison's metrical "irregularities" see, for example, Lucas, "Speaking For England?," 359–360; Morrison, "Filial Art," 57.

45. Robb, *Rimbaud*, 442.

46. *CP*, 134.

47. Breunig, "Why France?," 9.

48. Marvin N. Richards, "Famous Readers of an Infamous Book: The Fortunes of *Gaspard de la Nuit*," *The French Review*, vol. 69, no. 4 (1996), 543–555, 543–546. See also David Lehmann, "The Prose Poem: An Alternative to Verse," *The American Poetry Review*, vol. 32, no. 2 (2003), 45–49, 46.

49. Breunig, "Why France?," 3–4.

50. Breunig, "Why France?," 11.

51. Ross, *The Emergence of Social Space*, 56.

52. Ross, *The Emergence of Social* Space, 58.

53. Letter to Georges Izambard (13 May 1871), *RCWSL*, 370–371.

54. *RCWSL*, 266 67.

55. Ross, *The Emergence of Social Space*, 59–60.

56. Paul Lafargue, "The Right to Be Lazy," in *Selected Marxist Writings of Paul Lafargue*, ed. Richard Broadhead, trans. Charles Kerr (Berkeley: Center for Socialist History, 1984), 425–484.

57. Ross, *Emergence of Social Space*, 60.

58. Lafargue, *Right to Be Lazy*, 444.

59. Lafargue, *Right to Be Lazy*, 438.

60. Lafargue, *Right to Be Lazy*, 479.

61. "Inkwell," 33.

62. Lafargue, *Right to Be Lazy*, 470–472.

63. Peter M. Sacks, *The English Elegy: Studies in the Genre from Spenser to Yeats* (Baltimore and London: Johns Hopkins University Press, 1985), 133.

64. Sacks, *English Elegy*, 133.

65. Kennedy, "'Past Never Found'," 164.

66. Rylance, "'On Not Being Milton'," 117–118.

67. Thomas Gray, *Elegy Written in a Country Churchyard*, *The Complete Poems of Thomas Gray: English, Latin and Greek*, ed. H.W. Starr and J.R. Hendrickson (Oxford: Clarendon Press, 1966), l. 16, 38.

68. Gray, *Elegy*, ll. 93–94, 41.
69. William Empson, *Some Versions of Pastoral* (London: Chatto and Windus, 1935, [1950]), 11–12.
70. Gray, *Elegy*, l. 106, 42.
71. Gray, *Elegy*, l. 86, 41.
72. Gray, *Elegy*, l. 128, 43.
73. Eagleton, "Antagonisms," 349.
74. *TH Holocaust*, 284.
75. Gray, *Elegy*, l. 59, 39.
76. Gray, *Elegy*, ll. 53–56, 39.
77. Gray, *Elegy*, l. 67, 40.
78. Gray, *Elegy*, ll. 71–72, 40.
79. "Laureate's Block," *CP*, 330.
80. Suvir Kaul, *Thomas Gray and Literary Authority: Ideology and Poetics in Eighteenth-Century England* (Delhi: Oxford University Press, 1992), 9–12, 26.
81. William Wordsworth, "I Wandered Lonely as a Cloud," *The Poetical Works of William Wordsworth*, ed. E. De Selincourt (Oxford: Clarendon Press, 1944), l. 4, 216.
82. Wordsworth, "I Wandered Lonely as a Cloud," ll. 2 and 4, 216.
83. "Conversation," 41.
84. Wordsworth, "I Wandered Lonely as a Cloud," ll. 18 and 24, 216.
85. William Wordsworth, Advertisement to *Lyrical Ballads* (1798), in *Wordsworth's Literary Criticism*, ed. Nowell C. Smith (Bristol: Bristol Classical Press, 1980 [1905]), 1–3, 1.
86. William Wordsworth, "A slumber did my spirit seal," *Lyrical Ballads, and Other Poems, 1797–1800*, ed. James Butler and Karen Green (Ithaca and London: Cornell University Press, 1992), l. 7, 164.
87. William Wordsworth, "Essays Upon Epitaphs" (1), in *Wordsworth's Literary Criticism*, ed. Smith, 79–98, 79.
88. Gray, *Elegy*, l. 77, 40.
89. Gray, *Elegy*, l. 85, 40.
90. Wordsworth, "Upon Epitaphs," 79.
91. Gray, *Elegy*, l. 88, 41.
92. John Milton, *Paradise Lost, The Poems of John Milton*, ed. John Carey and Alastair Fowler (Harlow: Longman, 1968), Book XII, ll. 641–650, 1059–1060.
93. Byrne, "On Not Being Milton, Marvell, or Gray," 82.
94. Byrne, "On Not Being Milton, Marvell, or Gray," 82.

95. "A Kumquat for John Keats," *CP*, 221.

96. *v.*: Notebook, 187.

97. *v.*: Notebook, 49.

98. "Heredity," *CP*, 121.

99. "Preface," *The Mysteries* (London: Faber and Faber, 1985), 6.

100. See also Edith Hall, "Classics, Class, and Cloaca: Harrison's Humane Coprology," *Arion*, vol. 15, no. 2 (2007), 111–136.

101. "Wordlists, III," *CP*, 129.

SELECT BIBLIOGRAPHY

TONY HARRISON'S WORKS

Published Books and Pamphlets

Earthworks. Leeds: Northern House, 1964.

With James Simmons, *Aikin Mata.* Ibadan: Oxford University Press, 1966.

Newcastle is Peru. Newcastle-upon-Tyne: Eagle Press, 1969.

The Loiners. London: London Magazine Editions, 1970.

Translations in Peter Jay, ed. *The Greek Anthology.* London: Allen Lane, 1973.

The Misanthrope. London: Rex Collings, 1973.

Newcastle is Peru, 2nd ed. with introductory essay by Tony Harrison Newcastle-upon-Tyne: Northern House, 1974.

Phaedra Brittanica. London: Rex Collings, 1975.

Palladas: Poems. London: Anvil Press, 1975.

Phaedra Brittanica, 3rd ed., with introductory essay by Tony Harrison. London: Rex Collings, 1976.

Ten Poems from "The School of Eloquence." London: Rex Collings Christmas Book, 1976.

Bow Down. London: Rex Collings, 1977.

From "The School of Eloquence" and Other Poems. London: Rex Collings, 1978.

With Philip Sharpe, *Looking Up.* Malvern: Migrant Press, 1979.

Continuous: Fifty Sonnets from "The School of Eloquence." London: Rex Collings, 1981.

A Kumquat for John Keats. Newcastle-upon-Tyne: Bloodaxe Books, 1981.

The Oresteia. London: Rex Collings, 1981.

U.S. Martial. Newcastle-upon-Tyne: Bloodaxe Books, 1981.

Selected Poems. London: Penguin Books, 1984.

Dramatic Verse 1973–1985. Newcastle-upon-Tyne: Bloodaxe Books, 1985.

The Fire-Gap. Newcastle-upon-Tyne: Bloodaxe Books, 1985.

The Mysteries. London: Faber and Faber, 1985.

v.. Newcastle-upon-Tyne: Bloodaxe Books, 1985.

Theatre Works 1973–1985. London: Penguin Books, 1986.

Anno 42. Scargill Press [private press]), 1987.

Selected Poems, 2nd ed. London: Penguin Books, 1987.

Ten Sonnets from "The School of Eloquence." London: Anvil Press, 1987.

v.: New Edition with Press articles. Newcastle-upon-Tyne: Bloodaxe Books, 1989.

The Trackers of Oxyrhynchus. London: Faber and Faber, 1990.

v. and Other Poems. New York: Farrar Straus Girroux, 1990.

A Cold Coming. Newcastle-upon-Tyne: Bloodaxe Books, 1991.

The Common Chorus: A Version of Aristophanes' Lysistrata. London: Faber and Faber, 1992.

The Gaze of the Gorgon. Newcastle-upon-Tyne: Bloodaxe Books, 1992.

Square Rounds. London: Faber and Faber, 1992.

Black Daisies for the Bride. London: Faber and Faber, 1993.

Poetry or Bust. Saltaire, Bradford: Salts Mills, 1993.

Permanently Bard: Selected Poetry, ed. and with annotations by Carol Rutter. Newcastle-upon-Tyne: Bloodaxe Books, 1995.

The Shadow of Hiroshima and other film poems. London: Faber and Faber, 1995.

Plays 3: Poetry or Bust, The Kaisers of Carnuntum, and The Labourers of Herakles. London: Faber and Faber, 1996.

The Prince's Play [Le Roi s'amuse]. London: Faber and Faber, 1996.

Prometheus. London: Faber and Faber, 1998.

Laureate's Block and Other Occasional Poems. Harmondsworth: Penguin, 2000.

Hecuba. London: Faber and Faber, 2005.

Under the Clock. London: Penguin, 2005.

Collected Film Poetry: Arctic Paradise, The Big H, Loving Memory, The Blasphemer's

Banquet, The Gaze of the Gorgon, Black Daisies for the Bride, A Maybe Day in Kazakhstan, Prometheus, Metamorpheus, Crossings. London: Faber and Faber, 2007.

Collected Poems. London: Viking, 2007.

FRAM. London: Faber and Faber, 2008.

Poems Published in Periodicals

"When Shall I Tune my 'Doric Reed?," *Poetry and Audience,* vol. 4, no. 11 (25 January 1957)

"When the Bough Breaks," *Poetry and Audience,* vol. 4, no 15 (22 February 1957), 5.

"Plato Might Have Said," *Poetry and Audience,* vol. 4, no. 22 (22 May 1957), 4–5.

"Prologue," *Critical Quarterly,* vol. 28, no. 3 (Autumn 1986), 69–70.

"PM am," *London Review of Books,* vol. 25, no. 10 (22 May 2003), 33.

"October 2006," *London Review of Books,* vol. 28, no. 21 (21 November 2006), 10.

"Diary," *London Review of Books,* vol. 31, no. 3 (17 February 2009), 21.

"Piazza Sannazaro," *London Review of Books,* vol. 32, no. 20 (21 October 2010), 27.

"Cornet and Cartridge," *London Review of Books,* vol. 33, no. 4 (17 February 2011), 19.

"Black Sea Aphrodite," *London Review of Books,* vol. 35, no. 22 (21 November 2013), 22.

"Polygons," *London Review of Books*, vol. 37, no. 4 (19 February 2015), 16–17.

Prose

"Preface," in *Aikin Mata.* Ibadan: Oxford University Press, 1966. Reprinted in *Bloodaxe 1*, 84–87.

"English Virgil: *The Aeneid* in XVIII Century," *Philologica Pragensia*, X (1967) 1–11 and 80–91.

"Dryden's *Aeneid*," in *Dryden's Mind and Art*, ed. Bruce King, Edinburgh: Oliver and Boyd, 1969, 143–67.

"Shango the Shaky Fairy," *London Magazine*, new series, vol. 10, no. 6 (April 1970) reprinted in *Bloodaxe 1*, 88–103.

"New Worlds for Old," *London Magazine*, new series, vol. 10, no. 6 (September 1970), 81–85.

"Beating the Retreat," *London Magazine*, new series, vol.10, no. 8 (November 1970), 91–96.

"All Out," *London Magazine*, new series, vol. 10, no. 12 (March 1971), 87–91.

"The Inkwell of Dr Agrippa," in *Corgi Modern Poets in Focus: 4*, ed. Jeremy Robson. London: Corgi, 1971. Reprinted with this title in *Bloodaxe 1*, 32–35.

"Black and White and Red All Over: The Fiction of Empire," *London Magazine*, new series, vol. 12, no. 3 (September 1972), 90–103.

"Preface," in *The Misanthrope*. London: Rex Collings, 1973. Longer version reprinted in *Bloodaxe 1*, 138–153.

"Introduction," in *Newcastle is Peru*, 2nd ed. Newcastle-upon-Tyne: Northern House, 1974, unnumbered.

"Preface," in *Palladas: Poems*. London: Anvil Press, 1975. Reprinted in *Bloodaxe 1*, 133–137.

"Preface," in *Phaedra Brittanica*, 3rd ed. London: Rex Collings, 1976. Reprinted in *Bloodaxe 1*, 174–191.

"Author's Statement," in *Tony* Harrison. Contemporary Writers Series. London: Booktrust, 1987. Reprinted in *Bloodaxe 1*, 9.

"Facing up to the Muses," Presidential Address to the Classical Association, April 1988. Reprinted in *Bloodaxe 1*, 429–454.

"Fire & Poetry," in *Prometheus*, London: Faber and Faber, 1998, vii–xxix.

"The Tears and the Trumpets," *Arion: A Journal of Humanities and the Classics*, third series, vol. 9, no. 2 (2001), 1–22.

"Egil & Eagle-Bark," *Arion*, vol. 9, no. 3 (2002), 81–113.

"Flicks and This Fleeting Life," in *Collected Film Poetry*, London: Faber and Faber, 2007, vii–xxx.

"The Poetic Gaze," *The Guardian* (24 October 2009).

Manuscript Sources

"Newcastle is Peru" Mss. Misc., the Robinson Library, Newcastle-upon-Tyne [dated 1968]

Northern Arts Ms. Collection Vol. 6, "Tony Harrison," The Literary and Philosophical Society, Newcastle-upon-Tyne.

Notebook: Poems 1984: v., uncatalogued, Special Collections, Brotherton Library, University of Leeds.

Tony Harrison's Papers and Correspondence

23 letters to Jon Silkin / *Stand* editors (4 December 1962–8 August 1980), in BC MS 20c Stand/3 / HAR–11, Special Collections, Brotherton Library, University of Leeds.

Tony Harrison papers relating to *Loiners*, 73 uncatalogued and unnumbered items (including 33 letters to Alan Ross between 28 January 1967–8 December 1973), Special Collections, Brotherton Library, University of Leeds.

18 letters to Alan Ross (7 Mar 1972–14 Dec 1980), the Alan Ross Collection, in BC MS 20c London Magazine, Special Collections, Brotherton Library, University of Leeds.

4 letters to Vivienne Lewis (11 October 1972–2 May 1974), in BC MS 20c London Magazine, Special Collections, Brotherton Library, University of Leeds.

13 letters from Tony Harrison to Jeffrey Wainwright (24 October 1973– 31 October 1984), in BC Ms 20c Wainwright.

Papers relating to radio programs on Harrison by Rodney Pybus, including 2 letters from Harrison to Pybus (31 August–28 October 1977; 4 October 1978), in BC MS 20c Pybus/4/4.

1 letter to Jon Silkin (29 September 1980), in BC MS 20c Silkin / 8 / HAR-4, Special Collections, Brotherton Library, University of Leeds.

Interviews and Poetry Readings

"Tony Harrison in interview with John Haffenden" (1983), in *Bloodaxe 1*, 227–246.

Tony Harrison: Poets and People, a Freeway Films Production for Channel 4 (1984).

Them & [uz]: A Portrait of Tony Harrison, *Arena*, BBC TV (15 April 1985).

"Tony Harrison in conversation with Richard Hoggart" (1986) in *Bloodaxe 1*, 36–45.

"Tony Harrison in interview with Paul Bailey," *Third Ear*, Radio 3 (23 February 1988).

"Tony Harrison in interview with Clive Wilmer," in *Poets Talking: The "Poet of the Month"*.

Interviews from BBC Radio 3, ed. Clive Wilmer (Manchester: Carcanet, 1994), 97–103.

"Tony Harrison in conversation with Michael Alexander," in *Talking Verse: Interviews With Poets*, ed. Robert Crawford et al (St Andrews and Williamsburg: Verse, 1995), 82–91.

"Tony Harrison in interview with Melvyn Bragg," *The South Bank Show*, London Weekend Television (28 March 1999).

"Tony Harrison in interview with John Tusa," BBC Radio 3 (March 2008).

Other Primary Sources

Achebe, Chinua. *Things Fall Apart.* Oxford: Heinemann Educational, 1996 [1964].

Auden, W. H. *Collected Shorter Poems 1927–1957.* London: Faber and Faber, 1969 [1966].

———, and Louis MacNeice. *Letters From Iceland.* London: Faber and Faber, 1967 [1937].

———. verse text for *Nightmail* (1936), in *We Live in Two Worlds: The GPO Film Unit Collection,* vol. 2, British Film Institute.

Baudelaire, Charles. *Flowers of Evil.* Trans. James McGowan. Oxford: Oxford University Press, 1993 [1857].

Benjamin, Walter. *Illuminations,* ed. and Introduction Hannah Arendt, trans. Harry Zohn. New York: Schocken, 1969.

Betjeman, John. *Summoned by Bells.* London: J. Murray, 1960.

Blake, William. *The Complete Poetry and Prose of William Blake.* Ed. David V. Erdman. Berkley: University of California Press, 1982 [1965].

Bronte, Emily. *Wuthering Heights.* Ed. William M. Sale, New York: Norton, 1972 [1963].

Browne, Thomas. *Religio Medici.* Ed. Jean-Jacques Denonain. Cambridge: Cambridge University Press, 1953.

Burroughs, Edgar Rice. *Tarzan of the Apes.* Ed. Jason Haslam. Oxford: Oxford University Press, 2010 [1914].

Byron, George. *Byron: Selected Poetry and Prose.* Ed. Donald A. Low. London: New York: Routledge, 1995.

Césaire, Aimé. *Aimé Césaire: The Collected Poetry.* Trans. Clayton Eshleman and Annette Smith. Berkeley: University of California Press, 1983.

Cicero, Marcus Tullius. *The Poems of Cicero.* New York: Garland, 1978.

Cleveland, John. In *Minor Poets of the Caroline Period.* Vol. 3. Ed. George Saintsbury. Oxford: Oxford University Press, 1921.

Conrad, Joseph. *The Collected Letters of Joseph Conrad.* Vol. 2. Ed. Laurence Davies and Gene M. Moore. Cambridge: Cambridge University Press, 2005.

———. *Heart of Darkness: Background and Criticisms.* Ed. Leonard F. Dean. New Jersey: Prentice Hall, 1960.

Dryden, John. *Virgil's Aeneid.* London: Routledge, 1884.

Dunn, Douglas. *Selected Poems 1964–1983.* London: Faber and Faber, 1986.

Fracastorius, Heironymus. *Syphilis: Or, A Poetical History of the French Disease.* Trans. N.Tate. London: J. Tonson, 1686.

Gide, André. *Corydon.* New York: Octagon Books, 1977 [1950].

———. *If it Die: An Autobiography.* Trans. Dorothy Bussy. New York: Vintage Books, 2001 [1935].

———. *The Immoralist,* trans. by Dorothy Bussy (New York: Alfred. A Knopf, 1948 [1930]).

Gray, Thomas. *The Complete Poems of Thomas Gray: English, Latin and Greek.* Ed. H.W. Starr and J.R. Hendrickson. Oxford: Clarendon Press, 1966.

Heaney, Seamus. *New Selected Poems 1966–1987.* London: Faber and Faber, 1990.

Hoffman-Donner, Heinrich. *Struwwelpeter, or, Merry Rhymes and Funny Pictures.* London: Blackie, 1900.

Hopkins, Gerard Manly. *The Poetical Works of Gerard Manley Hopkins.* Ed. Norman H. MacKenzie. Oxford: Clarendon Press, 1990.

Hugo, Victor. *Les Misérables.* Trans. Lee Fahnestock and Norman MacAfee. New York: Signet, 1987.

———. *Notre-Dame de Paris.* Trans. Alban Krailsheimer. Oxford and New York: Oxford University Press, 1999 [1993].

Ibsen, Henrik. *Ghosts; A Public Enemy; When We Dead Awake.* Trans. Peter Watts. Harmondsworth: Penguin Books, 1964.

———. *Letters of Henrik Ibsen.* Trans. John Nilson Laurvik and Mary Morison. New York: Fox, Duffield and Co, 1905.

Joyce, James. *Dubliners: An Illustrated Edition with Annotations.* Ed. John Wyse Jackson and Bernard McGinley. New York: St Martin's Press, 1995.

———. *Stephen Hero: Part of the First Draft of "A Portrait of the Artist as a Young Man."* Ed. T. Spencer. Rev. ed. London: Jonathon Cape, 1969.

———. *Ulysses.* Ed. Hans Walter Gabler, Wolfhard Steppe, and Claus Melchior. New York: Garland, 1984.

Juvenal. *Satyrae.* Basingstoke: Macmillan, 1979.

Khayyam, Omar. *Rubaiyyat of Omar Khayyam.* Trans. Edward Fitzgerald. London: Bernard Quaritate, 1859.

Kipling, Rudyard. *Rudyard Kipling: Complete Verse.* New York: Anchor Press, 1989 [1889].

MacNeice, Louis. *Modern Poetry: A Personal Essay.* Oxford: Clarendon Press, 1968 [1938].

———. *Selected Poems.* Ed. Michael Longley. London: Faber and Faber, 1988.

Marvell, Andrew. *The Poems of Andrew Marvell.* Ed. Nigel Smith. Harlow: Pearson Longman, 2003.

Masefield, John. *The Collected Poems of John Masefield.* London: William Heinemann, 1923.

Meredith, George. *Modern Love.* London: Rupert Hart Davis, 1948.

Milton, John. *Complete Prose Works of John Milton.* Vol. 2, 1643–1648. Ed. Ernest Sirluck. New Haven and London: Yale University Press and Oxford University Press, 1953.

———. *The Poems of John Milton.* Ed. John Carey and Alastair Fowler. London and Harlow: Longman, 1968.

Moore, Marianne. *The Complete Poems.* London: Faber and Faber, 1968.

Neruda, Pablo. *Canto General: 50th Anniversary Edition.* Trans Jack Schmitt. Berkley and Los Angeles: University of California Press, 2000 [1991].

Olsen, Tillie. *Silences.* New York: Delacorte Press, 1978 [1965].

Orwell, George. *The Road to Wigan Pier.* London: Victor Gollancz, 1937.

Pound, Ezra. *The ABC of Reading.* London: Faber and Faber, 1968.

———. *The Cantos of Ezra Pound.* London: Faber and Faber, 1975.

———. *Selected Poems 1908–1959.* London: Faber and Faber, 1975.

Raleigh, Walter. *Sir Walter Raleigh: Selected Writings.* Ed. Gerald Hammond. Manchester: Carcanet, 1984.

Rimbaud, Arthur. Arthur Rimbaud: Selected Poems and Letters. *Trans. and ed. Jeremy Harding and John Sturrock. London: Penguin Books, 2004.*

———. *I Promise to be Good: The Letters of Arthur Rimbaud.* Trans. and ed.Wyatt Mason. New York: Modern Library, 2004.

———. *Rimbaud: Complete Works, Selected Letters.* Trans. and notes Wallace Fowlie. Rev. ed. Seth Whidden. Chicago: University of Chicago Press, 2005 [1966].

Shelley, Percy Bysshe. *Percy Bysshe Shelley: Selected Poetry and Prose.* Ed. K.N. Cameron. New York: Holt, Rinehart and Winston, 1951.

Shelley, Percy Bysshe. *Shelley's Prose, or The Trumpet of a Prophecy.* Ed. D.L. Clark. New York: New Amsterdam Books, 1988 [1955].

Stewart-Young, JM. [O Dazi Oka]. *The Seductive Coast: Poems Lyrical and Seductive from*

———. *Western Africa.* London: Ousley, 1909.

Tacitus, Cornelius. *Agricola, Germania, Dialogus.* Trans. William Peterson and Maurice Hutton. Cambridge, Massachusetts: Harvard University Press, 1970 [1914].

Thoreau, Henry. *Walden and Other Writings of Henry David Thoreau.* Ed. Brooks Atkinson New York: Modern Library, 1937.

Toland, John. *Hypatia: or, the History of a Most Beautiful, Most Vertuous, Most Learned, and Every Way Accomplish'd Lady; Who was Torn to Pieces by the Clergy of Alexandria.* London: M. Cooper; W. Reeve; and C.A. Sympson, 1753.

Verlaine, Paul. *Paul Verlaine: Selected Poems.* Trans. Martin Sorrell. Oxford: Oxford University Press, 1999.

Virgil. Publius Maro. *The Aeneid.* Trans. Robert Fagles. London: Penguin, 2006.

Williams, Raymond. *Loyalties.* London: Hogarth Press, 1985.

Wordsworth, William. *The Poetical Works of William Wordsworth.* Ed. E. De Selincourt. Oxford: Clarendon Press, 1944.

———. *Lyrical Ballads, and Other Poems, 1797–1800.* Ed. James Butler and Karen Green. Ithaca and London: Cornell University Press, 1992.

———. *The Prelude: The Four Texts, 1798–1799.* Ed. Jonathon Wordsworth. London: Penguin, 1995.

———. *Wordsworth's Literary Criticism.* Ed. Nowell C. Smith. Bristol: Bristol Classical Press, 1980 [1905].

Yeats, W.B.. *The Collected Poems.* London: MacMillan, 1950.

Critical Studies on Tony Harrison

Astley, Neil, ed. *Bloodaxe Critical Anthologies 1: Tony Harrison* (Newcastle-upon-Tyne: Bloodaxe Books, 1991.

Barker, Jonathon. "Peru, Leeds, Florida, and Keats." In *Bloodaxe 1*, 46–53.

Berkan-Birz, Carole. "Public or Private Nation: Poetic Form and National Consciousness in the Poetry of Tony Harrison and Geoffrey Hill." In *Intimate Exposure: Essays on the Public-Private Divide in English Poetry Since 1950.* Ed. Emily Taylor Merriman and Adrian Grafe. London: McFarland & Co., 2010, 174–190.

Bragg, Melvyn. "*v.* by Tony Harrison, *or* Production No 73095, LWT Arts." In *Tony Harrison: Loiner.* Ed. Sandie Byrne. Oxford: Clarendon Press, 1997, 49–56.

Burton, Rosemary. "Tony Harrison: An Introduction." In *Bloodaxe 1*, 14–31.

Byrne, Sandie. *H, v. & O: The Poetry of Tony Harrison.* Manchester: Manchester University Press, 1998.

———. Ed. *Tony Harrison: Loiner.* Oxford: Clarendon Press, 1997.

———. "On Not Being Milton, Marvell, or Gray." In *Tony Harrison: Loiner*, 57–83.

———. "Introduction: Tony Harrison's Public Poetry." In *Tony Harrison: Loiner*, 1–27.

Chillington-Rutter, Carol. "The Poet and the Geldshark: War and the Theatre of Tony Harrison." In *Acts of War: The Representation of Military Conflict on the British Stage and Television since 1945*. Ed. Tony Howard and John Stokes. Aldershot: Scolar Press, 1996, 145–163.

Cluysenaar, Anne. "New Poetry," *Stand*, vol. 12, no 1 (1970), 73–74.

Crucefix, Martyn. "The Drunken Porter Does Poetry: Metre and Voice in the Poems of Tony Harrison." In *Tony Harrison: Loiner*, 161–170.

Deane, Patrick. *At Home in Time: Forms of Neo-Augustanism in Modern English Poetry*. London: McGill-Queen's University Press, 1994.

Dunn, Douglas. "Abrasive Encounters." In Bloodaxe 1, 346–347.

———. "Acute Accent." In *Bloodaxe 1*, 212–215.

———. "Formal Strategies in Tony Harrison's Poetry." In *Bloodaxe 1*, 129–132.

———. "The Grudge," *Stand*, vol. 16, no. 4 (1975), 4–6.

———. "'Importantly Live': Tony Harrison's Lyricism." In *Bloodaxe 1*, 254–257.

Eagleton, Terry. "Antagonisms: Tony Harrison's v.." In *Bloodaxe 1*, 348–350.

———. "Metre v Madness," *Poetry Review*, vol. 82, no. 4 (winter 1992/3), 53–54.

Eyre, Richard. "Such Men are Dangerous." In *Bloodaxe 1*, 362–366.

———. "Tony Harrison the Playwright." In *Tony Harrison: Loiner*, 43–48.

Forbes, Peter. "The Bald Eagles of Canaveral." In Bloodaxe 1, 486–495.

———. "In the Canon's Mouth: Tony Harrison and Twentieth-Century Poetry." In *Tony Harrison: Loiner*, 189–199.

Garner, Brent. "Tony Harrison: 'The School of Eloquence', *Transactions of the Yorkshire Dialect Society*, 17: 87 (1988), 24–31.

Graham, Desmond. 'The Best Poet of 1961', in *Tony Harrison: Loiner*, 29–41.

Grant, Damien. "Poetry Versus History: Voices Off." In *Bloodaxe 1*, 104–113.

Hall, Edith. "Classics, Class, and Cloaca: Harrison's Humane Coprology," *Arion*, vol. 15,

no. 2 (2007), 111–136.

———. "Tony Harrison's Prometheus: A View from the Left," *Arion*, vol. 10, no. 1 (2002), 129–140.

Hargreaves, Raymond. "Tony Harrison and the Poetry of Leeds." In *Poetry in the British*

———. *Isles: Non-Metropolitan Perspectives.* Ed. HansWerner Ludwig and Lotar Fietz. Cardiff: University of Wales Press, 1995, 231–252.

Hélie, Claire. "Private Voice and Public Discourse: A Poetics of Northern Dialect." In *Intimate Exposure: Essays on the Public-Private Divide in English Poetry Since 1950.* Ed. Emily Taylor Merriman and Adrian Grafe. London: McFarland & Co., 2010, 160–173.

Huk, Romana "Poetry of the Committed Individual: Jon Silkin, Tony Harrison, Geoffrey Hill, and the Poets of Post-war Leeds." In *Contemporary British Poetry: Essays in Theory and Criticism*, ed. James Acheson and Romana Huk. New York: State University of New York Press, 1996), 175–219.

———. "Postmodern Classics: the Verse Drama of Tony Harrison." In *British and Irish Drama Since 1960.* Ed. James Acheson. New York: St Martin's Press, 1993, 202–226.

———. "Tony Harrison, The Loiners and the 'Leeds Renaissance'." In *Bloodaxe 1*, 75–83.

Jenkins, Lee M. "On Not Being Tony Harrison: Tradition and the Individual Talent of David Dabydeen," *Ariel: A Review of International English Literature*, vol. 32, no. 2 (2001), 69–88.

Kelleher, Joe. *Tony Harrison.* Plymouth: Northcote House, 1996.

Kennedy, David. "Ideas of Community and Nation in the Poetry of the "Middle Generation": Douglas Dunn, Tony Harrison and Seamus Heaney." Unpublished PhD thesis, University of Sheffield, 1999.

———. *New Relations: The Refashioning of British Poetry1980–1984*. Bridgend: Seren, 1996.

———. "'Past Never Found': Class, Dissent and the Contexts of Tony Harrison's v.," *English*, vol. 58, no. 221 (Spring 2009), 162–181.

———. "What does the fairy DO?': The Staging of Antithetical Masculine Styles in the Poetry of Tony Harrison and Douglas Dunn," *Textual Practice*, no. 14, vol. 1 (2000), 115–136.

Larkin, Philip. "Under a common flag," *Observer* (14 November 1982), 23.

Levi, Peter. "Pagan Idioms: Palladas." In *Bloodaxe 1*, 136–137.

———. "Tony Harrison's Dramatic Verse." In *Bloodaxe 1*, 158–166.

Lucas, John. "Speaking For England?" In *Bloodaxe 1*, 351–361.

Marshall, Cécile. "'Inwardness' and the 'Quest for a Public Poetry' in the Works of Tony Harrison." In *Intimate Exposure: Essays on the Public-Private Divide in English Poetry Since 1950*. Ed. Emily Taylor Merriman and Adrian Grafe. London: McFarland & Co., 2010, 147–159.

McGuirk, Kevin. "'All Wi' Doin': Tony Harrison, Linton Kwesi Johnson, and the Cultural Work of Lyric in Post-War Britain." In *New Definitions of Lyric: Theory, Technology and Culture*. Ed. Mark Jeffreys. New York and London: Garland Publishing, 1998, 49–75.

Merten, Kai. "Scholastic Performances: Seamus Heaney and Tony Harrison (Back) at School," *Critical Survey*, vol. 14, no. 2 (2002), 101–112.

Morrison, Blake. "The Filial Art." In *Bloodaxe 1*, 54–60.

———. "Labouring: Continuous." In *Bloodaxe 1*, 216–220.

Mortimer, Anthony. Ed., *Poetry and Audience 1953–1960*. Leeds: University of Leeds, 1961.

Murray, Oswyn. "Tony Harrison: Poetry and the Theatre." In *Bloodaxe 1*, 262–274.

Nicholson, Colin. *Fivefathers: Interviews with late Twentieth Century Scottish Poets*. Tirril: Humanities–Ebook, 2007.

———. "'Reciprocal Recognitions': Race, Class and Subjectivity in Tony Harrison's The Loiners," *Race & Class*, vol. 51, no. 4 (2010), 59–78.

———. "Towards an 'Other Sense' of Identity: Political Subjectivity in Margaret Atwood's Poetry." In *Identity Issues: Literary and Linguistic Landscapes*. Ed. Vesna Lopičić and Biljana Mišić Ilić. Newcastle-upon-Tyne: Cambridge Scholars Publishing, 2010, 71 –94.

O'Brien, Sean. "Tony Harrison: Showing the Working." In *The Deregulated. Muse: Essays on Contemporary British and Irish Poetry*. Newcastle-upon-Tyne: Bloodaxe Books, 1998, 51–64.

O'Donoghue, Bernard. "The Mysteries: T.W.'s Revenge." In *Bloodaxe 1*, 316–323.

Peach, Linden. "Them and Uz: Tony Harrison's Eloquence." In *Ancestral Lines: Culture & Identity in the Work of Six Contemporary Poets*. Bridgend: Seren, 1993, 111–133.

Porter, Peter. "In the Bosom of Family," *London Magazine*, vol. 10, no. 5 (1970), 72–78.

Poster, Jem. "Open to Experience: Structure and Exploration in Tony Harrison's Poetry." In *Tony Harrison: Loiner*, 85–91.

Rawson, Claude, "Family Voices," *Times Literary Supplement*, 4 January 1985, 10.

Roberts, Neil. "Poetic Subjects: Tony Harrison and Peter Reading." In *British Poetry from the 1950s to the 1990s: Politics and Art*. Ed. Gary Day and Brian Docherty. Basingstoke: Macmillan Press, 1997, 48–62.

Rowland, Antony. *Holocaust Poetry: Awkward Poetics in the Work of Sylvia Plath, Geoffrey Hill, Tony Harrison and Ted Hughes*. Edinburgh: Edinburgh University Press, 2005.

———. *Tony Harrison and the Holocaust*. Liverpool: Liverpool University Press, 2001.

Rusbridger, Alan. "Tony Harrison and the Guardian." In *Tony Harrison: Loiner*, ed. Byrne, 133–136.

Rylance, Rick. "Doomsongs: Tony Harrison and War." In *Tony Harrison: Loiner*, 137–160.

———. "On Not Being Milton." In *Bloodaxe 1*, 114–128.

Silver, Jonathon. "Poetry or Bust: Tony Harrison and Salt Mills." In *Tony Harrison: Loiner*, 185–187.

Smalley, Rebecca. "The Role of Memory in the Poetry of Douglas Dunn and Tony Harrison with Specific Reference to Elegy." Unpublished PhD thesis, University of Durham, 1991.

Spencer, Luke. *The Poetry of Tony Harrison.* Hemel Hempstead: Harvester Wheatsheaf, 1994.

Taplin, Oliver. "The Chorus of Mams." In *Tony Harrison: Loiner*, 171–184.

Thompson, N.S.. "Book Ends: Public and Private in Tony Harrison's Poetry." In *Tony Harrison: Loiner*, 115–132.

Wainwright, Jeffrey. "Something to Believe In." In *Bloodaxe 1*, 407–415.

Whitehead, Anne. "Tony Harrison, the Gulf War and the Poetry of Protest," *Textual Practice* vol. 19, no. 2 (2005), 349–372.

Widdowson, H.G.. "Person to Person: Relationships in the Poetry of Tony Harrison." In *Twentieth Century Poetry: From Text to Context.* Ed. Peter Verdonk. London: Routledge, 1993.

Woodcock, Bruce. "Classical vandalism: Tony Harrison's invective," *Critical Quarterly*, vol. 32, no. 2 (1990), 50–65.

–––. "'Internal colonialism': Is Tony Harrison a Post-Colonial poet?" *New Literatures Review*, no. 35 (1998), 76–94.

Worpole, Ken. "Scholarship Boy: The Poetry of Tony Harrison." In *Bloodaxe 1*, 61–74.

Young, Alan. "Weeds and White Roses: The Poetry of Tony Harrison." In *Bloodaxe 1*, 167–173.

Bibliographies
Kaiser, John R., Ed. *Tony Harrison: A Bibliography 1957–1987.* London: Mansell Publishing, 1987.

Other Secondary Sources

Achebe, Chinua. "An Image of Africa: Racism in Conrad's Heart of Darkness." In *Heart of Darkness*. Ed. Robert Kimbrough. 3rd ed. New York: Norton, 1988, 251–261.

———. *Morning Yet On Creation Day:* Essays. London: Heinemann Educational, 1975.

Acheson, James. Ed., *British and Irish Drama Since 1960*. London: Macmillan, 1993.

Achinstein, Sharon. *Milton and the Revolutionary Reader*. Princeton: Princeton University Press, 1994.

Addy, Sidney Oldall. *A Glossary of Words Used in the Neighborhood of Sheffield*. Vol. 1, London: Trubner, 1888.

Adorno, Theodor. *Minima Moralia: Reflections from Damaged. Life*. Trans. E.F.N. Jephcott. London: New Left Books, 1974.

Anderson, Ewan. *International Boundaries: A Geopolitical Atlas*. New York: Routledge, 2003.

Anderson, Frank Maloy. Ed., *The Constitution and Other Select Documents Illustrative of the History of France, 1789–1907*. New York: Russell and Russell, 1908.

Arendt, Hannah. *The Origins of Totalitarianism*. New York: Harcourt, Brace and Company, 1951.

Armitage, Simon, and Crawford, Robert. Eds., *The Penguin Book of Poetry from Britain*

and Ireland Since 1945. London: Viking, 1998.

Barthes, Roland. *Mythologies*. Trans. Annette Lavers. London: Vintage, 2000.

Boubacar Barry. *Senegambia and the Atlantic Slave Trade* (Cambridge: Cambridge University Press, 1998.

Behrman, Lucy. "The Political Significance of the Wolof Adherence to Muslim Brotherhoods in the Nineteenth Century." *African Historical Studies*, vol. 1, no. 1 (1968), 60–78.

Bello, Ahmadu. *My Life*. London: Cambridge University Press, 1962.

Bernstein, Basil. *Class, Codes and Control: Theoretical Studies Towards a Sociology of Language.* London and New York: Routledge, 2003 [1971].

Berresford Ellis, P. *The Cornish Language and its Literature.* London and Boston: Routledge, 1974.

Bhabha, Homi K. *The Location of Culture.* London: Routledge, 2005 [1994].

Blanning, T. C. W.. *The French Revolutionary Wars, 1787–1802.* London and New York Arnold, 1996.

Bradbury, Malcolm. *The Modern World: Ten Great Writers.* London: Secker & Warburg, 1988.

Bradshaw, Brendan and Morrill, John. Eds. *The British Problem, 1534–1707: State Formation in the Atlantic Archipelago.* London: St. Martin's Press, 1996.

Brantlinger, Patrick. *Rule of Darkness: British Literature and Imperialism, 1830–1914.* Ithaca: Cornell University Press, 1988.

Breunig, LeRoy C.. "Why France?" In *The Prose Poem in France: Theory and Practice.* Ed. Mary Ann Caws and Hermine Riffatere. New York: Columbia University Press, 1983, 3–20.

Brombert, Victor. *Victor Hugo and the Visionary Novel.* Cambridge, Massachusetts: Harvard University Press, 1984.

Broom, Sarah. *Contemporary British and Irish Poetry: An Introduction.* Basingstoke and New York: Palgrave Macmillan, 2006.

Bush, Barbara. *Imperialism, Race and Resistance: Africa and Britain, 1919–1945.* London: Routledge, 1999.

Carey, John. *The Intellectuals and the Masses: Pride and Prejudice Among the Literary Intelligentsia 1880–1939.* London: Faber and Faber, 1992.

Carroll, Robert and Prickett, Stephen. Ed., *The Bible: Authorized. King James Version,* Oxford and New York: Oxford University Press, 1997.

Césaire, Aimé, "Interview with Aimé Césaire," in Aimé Césaire, *Discourse on Colonialism.* Trans. Joan Pinkham. New York: Monthly Review Press, 1972, 65–79.

———. "The Liberating Power of Words: An Interview with the Poet Aimé Césaire," *Journal of Pan African Studies*, vol. 2, no. 4 (June 2008), 1–11.

Champlin, John Denison. "The Discoverer of the Philippines," *Bulletin of the American Geographical Society*, vol. 43, no. 8 (1911), 587–597.

Cheng, Vincent. *Joyce, Race and Empire*. Cambridge and New York: Cambridge University Press, 1995.

Cheyfitz, Eric. *The Poetics of Imperialism: Translation and Colonization from The Tempest to Tarzan*. New York: Oxford University Press, 1991.

Corcoran, Neil. *English Poetry since 1940*. London and New York: Longman, 1993.

Cowan, Ruth Schwartz. *Sir Francis Galton and the Study of Heredity in the Nineteenth Century*. New York: Garland, 1985.

Crawford, Robert. *Devolving English Literature*. Oxford: Clarendon Press, 1992.

Crowley, Tony. *Standard English and the Politics of Language*. Urbana: University of

Illinois Press, 1989.

Curtin, Philip. *Economic Change in Pre-colonial Africa: Senegambia in the Era of the Slave

Trade*. Madison: University of Wisconsin Press, 1975.

Daudet, Alphonse. *In The Land of Pain*. Trans. Julian Barnes. London: Jonathan Cape, 2002.

Davidson, Peter. *The Idea of North*. London: Reaktion Books, 2005.

Diamond, Larry. "Class, Ethnicity, and the Democratic State: Nigeria, 1950–1966," *Comparative Studies in Society and History*, vol. 25, no. 3 (1983), 457–489.

Dibua, J.I.. "Citizenship and Resource Control in Nigeria: The Case of Minority Communities in the Niger Delta," *Africa Spectrum*, vol. 40, no. 1 (2005), 5–28.

Diop, Samba. "The Wolof Epic: From Spoken Word to Written Text', *Research in African Literatures*, vol. 37, no. 3 (2006), 120–132.

Dodd, Philip. "Lowryscapes: Recent Writings About the North," *Critical Quarterly*, vol. 32, no. 2 (Summer 1990), 17–28.

Dudley, B. J. *Parties and Politics in Northern Nigeria.* London: Frank Cass and Co.,1968.

Eagleton, Terry. *Exiles and Emigres: Studies in Modern Literature.* London: Chatto & Windus, 1970.

———. "The God that Failed." In *Re-Membering Milton: Essays on the Texts and Traditions.* Ed. Mary Nyquist and Margaret W. Ferguson. London and New York: Methuen, 1987, 342–349.

———. *Heathcliff and the Great Hunger: Studies in Irish Culture.* London: Verso, 1995.

———, ed. *Raymond Williams: Critical Perspectives.* Cambridge: Polity Press, 1989.

———. *Walter Benjamin, or Towards a Revolutionary Criticism.* London: New Left Books, 1981.

Easthope, Antony. *Poetry as Discourse.* London: Methuen, 1983.

Ellis, Alexander J.. *On Early English Pronunciation: With Especial Reference to Shakespere and Chaucer, Containing an Investigation of the Correspondence of Writing with Speech in England from the Anglo-Saxon Period to the Present Day.* Vol.1. London: E.E.T.S., 1869–1936.

Empson, William. *Some Versions of Pastoral.* London: Chatto and Windus, 1935, [1950].

Engels, Friedrich. *The Origin of the Family, Private Property and the State.* Trans. E. Untermann. Chicago: C.H Kerr, 1902.

Fanon, Frantz. *Black Skin, White Masks.* Trans. Charles Lam Markmann. New York: Grove Press, 1967 [1952].

———.*The Wretched of the Earth.* Trans. Constance Farrington. Harmondsworth: Penguin, 1965 [1961].

Fraser, Robert. *West African Poetry: A Critical History.* Cambridge: Cambridge University Press, 1986.

French, John. *The Art of Distillation Or, A Treatise of the Choicest Spagyrical Preparations Performed. Way of Distillation, Being Partly Taken Out of the Most Select Chemical Authors of the Diverse languages and Partly Out of the Author's Manual Experience together with, The Description of the Chiefest Furnaces and Vessels Used. Ancient and Modern Chemists also A Discourse on Diverse Spagyrical Experiments and Curiosities, and of the Anatomy of Gold and Silver, with The Chiefest Preparations and Curiosities Thereof, and Virtues of Them All.* London: Printed by Richard Cotes, 1651.

Furlong, Patrick J. "Azikiwe and the National Church of Nigeria and the Cameroons: A

———. Case Study of the Political Use of Religion in African Nationalism," *African Affairs*, vol. 91, no. 364 (1992), 433–452.

Galton, Francis, *Essays in Eugenics.* London: Eugenics Education Society, 1909.

———. *Hereditary Genius: An Inquiry Its Laws and Consequences.* 2nd ed. London: MacMillan, 1892.

———. "Hereditary Talent and Character," *The Occidental Quarterly*, vol. 2, no.3 (August 2002 [1865]), 45–68.

———. *Narrative of an Explorer in Tropical South Africa.* London: John Murray, 1853.

Gareth, Owain Llŷr ap. *Welshing on Postcolonialism: Complicity and Resistance in the Construction of Welsh Identities.* Unpublished PhD thesis, University of Wales Aberystwyth University, 2009.

Genette, Gerard. *Paratexts: Thresholds of Interpretation.* Trans. Jane E. Lewin. Cambridge: Cambridge University Press, 1997.

Genova, Ann. "Nigeria's Biafran War: State, Oil Companies, and Confusion', *XIV International Economic History Congress*, Helsinki, 2006.

Gikandi, Simon. "Chinua Achebe and the Invention of African Literature." In Chinua Achebe, *Things Fall Apart.* Oxford: Heinemann Educational, 1996 [1994], ix–xxvii.

Gimson, A.C.. "The RP Accent." In *Language in the British Isles.* Ed. Peter Trudgill. Cambridge: Cambridge University Press, 1984, 45–54.

Gökyiğit, Emel Aileen. "The Reception of Francis Galton's 'Hereditary Genius' in the

Victorian Periodical Press', *Journal of the History of Biology*, vol. 27, no. 2 (Summer, 1994), 215–240.

Gray, J.M.. *History of the Gambia*. Cambridge: Cambridge University Press, 1940.

Greene, Roland. *Unrequited. Conquests: Love and Empire in the Colonial Americas*. Chicago: University of Chicago Press, 1999.

Griffin, Dustin. *Regaining Paradise: Milton and the Eighteenth Century*. Cambridge and New York: Cambridge University Press, 1986.

Griffiths, Richard. "Another Form of Fascism: The Cultural Impact of the French 'Radical Right' in Britain." In *The Culture of Fascism: Visions of the Far Right in Britain*. Ed. Julie V. Gottlieb, Thomas P. Linehan. London and New York: I.B. Tauris, 2004, 162–181.

Hackett, Cecil, *Arthur Rimbaud: A Critical Introduction*. Cambridge: Cambridge University Press, 1981.

Hall, Edith. *Introducing the Ancient Greeks: From Bronze Age Seafarers to Navigators of the Western Mind*. New York, London: W.W. Norton & Company, 2014.

Hall, Stuart, and Jacques, Martin. Eds. *The Politics of Thatcherism*. London: Lawrence and Wishart, 1983.

Hardy, John and Nicholas Brown. "Shelley's 'Dome of Many-Coloured Glass," *Sydney Studies*, 103–106.

Hassan, Salah D. "Inaugural Issues: The Cultural Politics of the Early *Présence Africaine*, 1947–55," *Research in African Literatures*, vol. 30, no. 2 (1999), 194–221.

Higgins, Ian. "Dryden and Swift." In *John Dryden (1631-1700): His Politics, His Plays, and His Poets*. Delaware: University of Delaware Press, 2004, 217-234.

———. *Jonathan Swift*. Northcote House: Devon: Northcote House, 2004.

———. "Jonathan Swift's political confession." In *Politics and Literature in the Age of Swift: English and Irish Perspectives*. Ed. Claude Rawson. Cambridge: Cambridge University Press, 2010, 3-30.

———. *Swift's Politics: A Study in Disaffection.* Cambridge: Cambridge University Press, 2006 [1994].

Hill, Christopher. *Milton and the English Revolution.* London: Faber and Faber, 1977.

———. *The Experience of Defeat: Milton and Some Contemporaries.* London: Faber and Faber, 1984.

Hiro, Dilip. *Black British, White British.* London: Eyre Spottiswoode, 1971.

Hofman, Heinz. "*Adveniat tandem Typhis qui detegat orbes*: Columbus in Neo-Latin Epic Poetry." In *The Classical Tradition and the Americas.* Ed. Wolfgang Haase and Meyer Reinhold. Vol. 1, pt. 1. Berlin and New York: W de Gruyter, 1994.

Hoggart, Richard. *The Uses of Literacy: Aspects of Working-Class Life, With Special Reference to Publications and Entertainments.* London: Chatto & Windus, 1957.

Hughes, Arnold, and Perfect, David. Eds. *Historical Dictionary of the Gambia.* Lanham: Rowman & Littlefield, 2008.

Humphreys, Emyr. *The Taliesin Tradition: A Quest for the Welsh Identity.* London: Black Raven Press, 1984.

Humphries, Rolfe. *Green Armor on Green Ground: Poems in the Twenty-Four Official Welsh Meters.* New York: Charles Scribner's Sons, 1956.

Hunt, Lynn. Ed. *The French Revolution and Human Rights: A Brief Documentary History.* Boston: Bedford Books of St Martin's Press, 1996.

Hynes, Samuel. *The Auden Generation: Literature and Politics in the 1930s.* London: Bodley Head, 1976.

Irele, Abiola. "*Négritude* or Black Cultural Nationalism," *Journal of Modern African Studies,* vol. 3, no. 3 (1965), 321–348.

Isichei, Elizabeth Allo. *A History of African Societies to 1870.* Cambridge: Cambridge University Press, 1997.

Jones, Daniel. *The Cambridge English Pronouncing Dictionary.* Ed. Peter Roach, James Hartman and Jane Setter. Cambridge: Cambridge University Press, 2006 [1909].

Kahaner, Larry. *AK–47: The Weapon That Changed the Face of the War.* New Jersey: John Wiley & Sons, 2007.

Kaul, Suvir. *Thomas Gray and Literary Authority: Ideology and Poetics in Eighteenth Century England.* Delhi: Oxford University Press, 1992.

Kearney, Hugh. *The British Isles: A History of Four Nations.* Cambridge and New York: Cambridge University Press, 1989.

Kelman, James. *Some Recent Attacks: Essays Cultural and Political.* Stirling: AK Press, 1992.

Kenner, Hugh. *Dublin's Joyce.* London: Chatto and Windus, 1955.

Killick, Rachel. *Victor Hugo: Notre-Dame de Paris.* Glasgow: University of Glasgow French and German Publications, 1994.

Kirk, John. "Class, Community and 'Structures of Feeling." In Working-Class Writing from the 1980's," *Literature and History*, vol. 8, no. 2 (1999), 44–63.

Kirke-Greene, A.H.M.. "His Eternity, His Eccentricity, or His Exemplarity? A Further Contribution to the Study of H.E. the African Head of State," *African Affairs*, vol. 90 (1991), 163–187.

Klein, Martin A.. "Social and Economic Factors in the Muslim Revolution in Senegambia," *Journal of African History*, vol. 13, no. 3 (1972), 419–441.

Korieh Chima J. and Nwokeji, G. Ugo. Eds., *Religion, History and Politics in Nigeria: Essays in Honor of Ogbu U. Kalu.* Maryland: University Press of America, 2005.

Lackey, Michael. "The Moral Conditions for Genocide in Joseph Conrad's *Heart of Darkness*," *College Literature*, vol. 32, no. 1 (winter 2005), 20–41.

Lafargue, Paul. *The Right to Be Lazy.* In *Selected Marxist Writings of Paul Lafargue.* Ed. Richard Broadhead, trans. Charles Kerr. Berkeley: Center for Socialist History, 1984, 425–284.

Lang, George. "Ghana and Nigeria." In *European-Language Writing in Sub–Saharan Africa.* Vol. 1. Ed. Albert S. Gérard. Budapest: Akadémiai Kiadó, 1986, 108–115.

Lehmann, David. "The Prose Poem: An Alternative to Verse," *The American Poetry Review*, vol. 32, no. 2 (2003), 45–9, 46.

Leonard, Tom. *Reports from the Present: Selected Works 1982–94*. London: Cape, 1995.

Lilly, Gweneth. "The Welsh Influence in the Poetry of Gerard Manley Hopkins," *Modern Language Review*, vol. 38, no. 3 (July 1943), 192–205.

Lindqvist, Sven. *Exterminate All the* Brutes. Trans. Joan Tate. New York: New Press, 1996.

Machel, Samora. *Establishing People's Power to Serve the Masses*. Toronto: Toronto Committee for the Liberation of Southern Africa, 1976.

———. *Mozambique: Revolution or Reaction? Two Speeches*. California: LSM Information Center, 1975.

Macherey, Pierre. *A Theory of Literary Production*. Trans. Geoffrey Wall. London, Boston: Routledge and Kegan, 1978.

Maquet, Jacques. *Africanity: The Cultural Unity of Black Africa*. Trans. Joan R. Rayfield. New York: Oxford University Press, 1972.

Marx, Karl. *The Eighteenth Brumaire of Louis Bonaparte*. Oxford: Oxford University Press, 2000.

McGann, Jerome. *Byron and Romanticism*. Ed. James Soderholm, Cambridge: Cambridge University Press, 2002.

Mercer, John. "The Canary Islanders in Western Mediterranean Politics'," *African Affairs*, vol. 78, no. 311 (1979), 159–176.

Miles, William F. S.. "Partitioned. Royalty: The Evolution of Hausa Chiefs in Nigeria and Niger," *Journal of Modern African Studies*, vol. 25, no. 2 (1987), 233–258.

Mill, John Stuart. "Thoughts on Poetry and its Varieties." In *Dissertations and Discussions: Political, Philosophical and Historical*. Vol. 1. London: Longmans, 1867, 63–94.

Miller, Christopher L. *Blank Darkness: Africanist Discourse in French*. Chicago: University of Chicago Press, 1985.

———. "Unfinished. Business: Colonialism in Sub-Saharan Africa and the Ideals of the French Revolution." In *The Global Ramifications of the French Revolution.* Eds. Joseph Klaits and Michael H. Haltzel. Cambridge, New York: Cambridge University Press, 1994, 105–126.

Minahan, James. *Encyclopaedia of Stateless Nations: Ethnic and National Groups Around the World.* Westport: Greenwood Press, 2002.

Momoh, Abubakar. "Popular Struggles in Nigeria 1960–1982," *African Journal of Political Science,* vol. 1, no. 2 (1996), 154–175.

Morrison, Blake and Motion, Andrew. Eds., *The Penguin Book of Contemporary British Poetry.* Harmondsworth: Penguin, 1982.

Munslow, Barry. *Mozambique: The Revolution and its Origins.* New York: Longman, 1983.

Neserius, Philip George. "Ibsen's Political and Social Ideas," *The American Political Science Review,* vol. 19, no. 1 (1925), 25–37.

Newell, Stephanie. *The Forger's Tale: The Search for Odeziaku.* Athens: Ohio University

Press, 2006.

Nicholl, Charles. *Somebody Else: Arthur Rimbaud in Africa 1880–91.* London: Jonathon Cape, 1997.

Noble, David Cook. "Sickness, Starvation, and Death in Early Hispaniola," *Journal of Interdisciplinary History,* vol. 32, no. 3 (winter 2002), 349–386.

——— with George W. Lovell. Eds., *Secret Judgements of God: Old World Disease in Colonial Spanish America.* Norman: University of Oklahoma Press, 1992.

Nolan, Emer. *James Joyce and Nationalism.* London: Routledge, 1995.

Norbrook, David. "*Areopagitica,* Censorship, and the Early Modern Public Sphere." In *The Administration of Aesthetics: Censorship, Political Criticism, and the Public Sphere.* Ed. Richard Burt. Minneapolis: University of Minnesota Press, 1994, 3–33.

———. *Writing the English Republic: Poetry, Rhetoric and Politics 1627–1660.* Cambridge: Cambridge University Press, 1999.

Nyquist, Mary, and Ferguson, Margaret W. Eds., *Re-Membering Milton: Essays on the Texts and Tradition.* London, New York: Methuen, 1987.

Oliveira, Ricardo Soares de. *Oil and Politics in the Gulf of Guinea.* New York: Columbia University Press, 2007.

Oloruntimehin, B. Olatunji. "Resistance Movements in the Tukulor Empire," *Cahier d'Études Africaines,* vol. 8, *Cahier* 29 (1968), 123–143.

Onimode, Bade. "Imperialism and Multinational Corporations: A Case Study of Nigeria," *Journal of Black Studies,* vol. 9, no. 2 (1978), 207–232.

Oyowe, A. "The Canary Islands Sing out for Freedom," *New African* (May 1978), 45–46.

Palmer-Fernandez, Gabriel. *Encyclopaedia of Religion and War.* New York and London: Routledge, 2004.

Panter-Brick, S.K.. Ed., *Nigerian Politics and Military Rule: Prelude to the Civil War* London: Athlone Press, 1970.

Park, Mungo. *Travels in the Interior Districts of* Africa. Appendix and Illustrations by Major James Rennell. London: W Bulmer & Co, 1799.

Parras, John. "Poetic Prose and Imperialism: The Ideology of Form in Joseph Conrad's *Heart of Darkness,*" Nebula, vol. 3, no. 1 (2006), 85–102.

Payton, Philip. *Cornwall.* Fowey: Alexander Associates, 1996.

Pittock, Murray G.H.. *Celtic Identity and the British Image.* Manchester and New York: Manchester University Press, 1999.

———. *Inventing and Resisting Britain: Cultural Identities in Britain and Ireland, 1685–1789.* Basingstoke, New York: MacMillan Press and St Martin's Press, 1997.

Porter, Bernard. *The Lion's Share: A Short History of British Imperialism 1850–2004.* London: Pearson Longman, 2004.

Rabasa, José. *Writing Violence on the Northern Frontier: the Historiography of Sixteenth-Century New Mexico and Florida and the Legacy of Conquest.* Durham: Duke University Press, 2000.

Raglan, Lord. "Canute and the Waves," *Man,* vol. 60 (1960), 7–8.

Ramazani, Jahan. *The Poetry of Mourning: the Modern Elegy from Hardy to Heaney*. Chicago: University of Chicago Press, 1994.

Rawson, Claude. "Family Voices," *Times Literary Supplement*, 4 January 1985, 10. *God, Gulliver and Genocide: Barbarism and the European Imagination, 1492–1945*. Oxford: Oxford University Press, 2001.

Recorde, Robert. *The Grounde of Artes*. New York: Da Capo Press, 1969 [1542].

Redhead, Steve. *Subculture to Clubcultures: An Introduction to Popular Cultural Studies*. Cambridge: Blackwell Publishers, 1997.

Reed, Michael C.. "Gabon: a Neo-Colonial Enclave of Enduring French Interest," *Journal of Modern African Studies*, vol. 25, no. 2 (1987), 283–320.

Rhodes, Enid H.. "Arthur Rimbaud: The Aesthetics of Intoxication." In *Intoxication and Literature*. Ed. Enid Rhodes Peschel. Yale French Studies. Yale: Yale University Press, 1974.

———. "Under the Spell of Africa: Poems and Letters of Arthur Rimbaud inspired by the Dark Continent," *The French Review*, no. 2, Studies in Nineteenth-Century French Literature (winter 1971), 20–28.

Richards, Marvin N.. "Famous Readers of an Infamous Book: The Fortunes of *Gaspard de la Nuit*," *The French Review*, vol. 69, no. 4 (1996), 543–555.

Robb, Graham. *Rimbaud*. London: Picador, 2000.

———. *Victor Hugo: A Biography*. New York, London: W.W. Norton and Company, 1997.

Robinson, David. "France as a Muslim Power in West Africa," *Africa Today*, vol. 46, no. 3 (1999), 105–127.

———. "French 'Islamic' Policy and Practice in Late Nineteenth-Century Senegal," *Journal of African History*, vol. 29, no. 3 (1988), 415–435.

———. *The Holy War of Umar Tal: The Western Sudan in the Mid-Nineteenth Century*. Oxford: Clarendon Press, 1985.

Ross, Kristin, *The Emergence of Social Space: Rimbaud and the Paris Commune*. Minneapolis: University of Minnesota Press, 1988.

―――. *May '68 And Its Afterlives*. London: University of Chicago Press, 2002.

―――. "Rimbaud and Spatial History," *New Formations*, no. 5 (Summer 1988), 53–68.

Sacks, Peter M. *The English Elegy: Studies in the Genre from Spenser to Yeats*. Baltimore, London: Johns Hopkins University Press, 1985.

Said, Edward. *Culture and Imperialism*. London: Chatto & Windus, 1993.

Sartre, Jean Paul. "Black Orpheus," trans. John MacCombie, *The Massachusetts Review*, vol. 6, no. 1 (autumn 1964-winter 1965) 13–52.

―――. "Preface." In Frantz Fanon. *The Wretched. of the Earth*. Trans. Constance Farrington. Harmondsworth: Penguin, 1963[1983].

―――. *What is Literature?* Trans. B. Frechtman. London: Methuen, 1967 [1948].

Searing, James F. *West African Slavery and Atlantic Commerce: The Senegal River Valley, 1700–1860*. Cambridge: Cambridge University Press, 1993.

Searle, Chris. "The Mobilization of Words: Poetry and Resistance in Mozambique." In *Marxism and African literature*. Ed. Georg M Gugelberge. Trenton, NJ: Africa World Press, 1985, 150–164.

Senghor, Léopold. "What is '*Négritude*'?" In *The Idea of Race*. Ed. Robert Bernasconi and Tommy Lee Lot. Indianapolis and Cambridge: Hackett Publishing, 2000.

Sheppard, Robert. *The Poetry of Saying: British Poetry and its Discontents 1950–2000*. Liverpool: Liverpool University Press, 2005.

Smith, Olivia. *The Politics of Language 1791–1819*. Oxford: Oxford University Press, 1984.

Snell, K.D.M. "The Regional Novel: Themes for Interdisciplinary Research." In *The Regional Novel in Britain and Ireland, 1800–1990*. Ed. K.D.M. Snell. New York: Cambridge University Press, 1998.

Soyinka, Wole. *Conversations with Wole Soyinka*. Ed. Biodun Jeyifo. Jackson: University Press of Missouri, 2001.

Solomou, Kiriakoula. "The Influence of Greek Poetry on Byron," *The Byron Journal*, vol. 10, 1982, 4–19.

Sprinchorn, Evert. "Syphilis in Ibsen's Ghosts," *Ibsen Studies*, vol. 4, no. 2 (2004), 191–204.

Stallybrass, Peter. "Marx and Heterogeneity: Thinking the Lumpenproletariat," *Representations*, no. 31 (Summer 1990), 69–95.

Starkie, Enid. *Arthur Rimbaud*. London: Hamish Hamilton, 1947 [1938].

Arthur Rimbaud in Abyssinia. Oxford: Clarendon press, 1937.

———. "On the Trail of Arthur Rimbaud," *The Modern Language Review*, vol. 38, no. 3 (1943), 206–216.

Stern, Hans Heinrich. *Fundamental Concepts of Language Teaching*. Oxford, New York: New York University Press, 1983.

Still, Judith. "Not Really Prostitution: The Political Economy of Sexual Tourism in Gide's *Si Le Grain Ne Meurt*," *French Studies*, vol. 54, no. 1 (2000), 17–34.

Stoyle, Mark. "The Dissidence of Despair: Rebellion and Identity in Early Modern Cornwall." In *Journal of British Studies*, vol. 38, no. 4 (1999), 423–444.

Taylor, A.J.P.. *Essays in English History*. London: Hamilton, 1976.

Taylor, Stan. *The National Front in English Politics*. London: Holmes & Meier, 1982.

Thatcher, Margaret. Address to the 1922 Committee in the House of Commons, 19 July 1984, reported in "Thatcher makes Falklands Link," *The Times* (20 July 1984).

Thompson, E.P.. *The Making of the English Working Class*. London: Penguin,1991 [1963].

———. "Revolution." In *Out of Apathy*. Ed. E.P. Thompson et al. London: New Left Books,1960, 287–308.

Thwaite, Anthony. *Poetry Today: A Critical Guide to British Poetry 1960–1984*. London and New York: Longman, 1985.

Touray, Omar A.. *The Gambia and the World: A History of the Foreign Policy of Africa's Smallest State, 1965–1995*. Hamburg: Institute of African Affairs, 2000.

Uche, Chibuike. "Oil, British Interests and the Nigerian Civil War," *Journal of African History*, vol. 49, no. 1 (2008), 111–135.

Wales, Katie. "North and South: An English Linguistic Divide?," *English Today* 61, vol. 16, no. 1 (2000), 4–15.

———. *Northern English: A Social and Cultural History*. Cambridge: Cambridge University Press, 2006.

Walker, George. *The Costume of Yorkshire*. Sussex: Caliban Books, 1978[1814].

Ward, Dave, "Liverpool Says Sorry for Flooding Welsh Valley," *The Guardian* (13 October 2005).

Watt, Ian. *Conrad in the Nineteenth Century*. London: Chatto & Windus, 1980.

Weiler, Hans. Ed., *Education and Politics in Nigeria*. Freiburg: Verlag Rombach, 1964.

Wildgen, Kathryn E.. "Romance and Myth in *Notre-Dame de Paris*," *The French Review*, vol. 49, no. 3 (1976), 319–327.

Williams, Raymond. *Keywords: A Vocabulary of Culture and Society*. New York: Oxford University Press, 1976 [1983]).

———. *Resources of Hope: Culture, Democracy, Socialism*. Ed. Robin Gale. London: Verso, 1989.

———. *Who Speaks for Wales: Nation, Culture, Identity*. Ed. Daniel Williams. Cardiff: University of Wales Press, 2003.

About the Author

Christine Regan's academic background is in literary studies, and she holds a PhD from the The Australian National University. In addition to *The Rimbaud of Leeds: The Political Character of Tony Harrison's Poetry*, Dr. Regan's work has been published in journals including *English*, *Études Britanniques Contemporaines*, and *Textual Practice*. Dr. Regan is a visiting fellow at The Australian National University.

INDEX

CPSIA information can be obtained at www.ICGtesting.com
Printed in the USA
BVOW03*2021160316

440625BV00001B/1/P

9 781604 979275